EASY ASTROLOGY GUIDE

This book is designed for "activist" astrology—the use of astrology as a tool to improve your life. Astrology reveals your strengths, weaknesses, talents, and opportunities. Understanding astrology means understanding yourself—increasing your abilities and talents, maximizing your strengths, minimizing your liabilities, and taking full advantage of optimum timing and opportunities.

If you are ready to be happy, ready to make the most of your potentials, ready to appreciate yourself and further develop your talents—this book is for you.

EASY ASTROLOGY GUIDE

How to Read Your Horoscope

Maritha Pottenger

International Standard Book Number 0-935127-49-6

Published by ACS Publications
5521 Ruffin Road
San Diego, California 92123-1314

Printed in the United States of America

First Printing March 1996

Dedication

To Marc, with Love

Acknowledgments

Many, many people contribute to the birth of a book. I would like to acknowledge a few on this page. My thanks go to:

Dr. Zipporah Dobyns—beloved mother, major teacher, and the person who above all others has taught me to trust the Goodness of life.

Astrological colleagues whose insights, compassion, understanding, suggestions, and/or wisdom have contributed to my growth as an astrologer—Stephen Arroyo, Bernie Ashman, Jamie Binder, Lynne Burmyn, Donna Cunningham, Zipporah Dobyns, Steven Forrest, Francoise Gauquelin, Michel Gauquelin, Demetra George, Rob Hand, Bill Herbst, Aline Kestenberg, Peggy Larson, Jeanne Long, Marion March, Joan McEvers, Neil F. Michelsen, Jill Morris, Joan Negus, Lois Rodden, Maria Kay Simms, Batya Stark, Carol Tebbs, Bil Tierney, Deborah Tobin, Donna Van Toen, Marilyn Waram (and anyone inadvertently omitted).

Several friends have had a rough year(s) lately, but live their lives as illustrations of the indomitable human spirit, an openness to change, and the endurance of love and compassion. Thank you for inspirational examples—Pamela Crozat English, Henri Farhi, Kit Humphrey, Anna Mathews, Marc Matz, Neil F. Michelsen, Maria Kay Simms and Michaeleen Trimarchi.

A number of friends and family have been helpful—providing the support (material and emotional) which a writer needs. Although I do not list all of you, my heartfelt appreciation.

Special thanks always to everyone at Astro Communications Services for assistance, support, suggestions, and hard work in getting this book out.

To my clients—who provide the real-life teaching about how astrological principles can manifest—thanks for your openness and your sharing. Without you, this book could not have been.

Finally, my thanks to the Universe for the wonderful playground we call life.

Contents

INTRODUCTION

Astrology for People Ready to be Happy

I've seen astrology help people transform their lives
—from the displaced homemaker whose horoscope encouraged her to undertake a new (and successful!) career in art.
—from the bank manager afraid to leave her dependable job until her chart reinforced the importance of healing work in her life (and gave her "permission" to pursue psychology).
—from the failing child who just wanted to play baseball with parents who thought he should sit for hours finishing homework until they found out how essential physical activity was for him. (His grades soared when he got to play baseball regularly and do homework in chunks rather than all at one sitting.)
—from the mother who realized, through astrology, she was taking old resentments she had toward her mother out on her own young son (and stopped!).
—from the woman who had a habit of falling for married men—until she learned, with astrology, how to combat the habit, and found a nice, unmarried man (and married him).
—from the married couple who learned, through astrology, to accept each other's different financial styles, and stop tearing apart their marriage over money.

One of my central convictions after twenty years of learning and professional work with astrology is that **every** astrological placement has an up side and a down side. Part of my motivation for writing this book is to provide a truly comprehensive look (the "good" and the "bad" and how to transform perceived negatives into positives) at astrological combinations for which some authors have presented a narrow (all "good" or all "bad") viewpoint. For that reason, I have sought feedback from other astrologers before putting these interpretations in print.

If you don't already have a copy of your horoscope, take advantage of our offer (see back pages) of a **free** chart! If you're a beginner or intermediate student, you can turn immediately to the appropriate interpretations and dig in. If you're a professional, you'll wish to read mainly those sections where you desire more insights—perhaps for writing articles, for certain clients, or for personal growth. What are apt to be most significant are those placements absent from your own chart (and thus sometimes harder to understand) or so strongly configured in one's chart that objectivity may be a challenge.

Whatever your level of exposure to astrology, the pages which follow will help you to find your own personal path to happiness—to liking yourself better, utilizing your abilities more fully, accepting the eccentricities of others, and living a more complete, satisfying, **happy** life!

CHAPTER ONE
WHAT IS ASTROLOGY?

Astrology is an ancient field of study. As far back as we have recorded history, we have astrological concepts. Scratches made on reindeer horns by Neolithic hunters as much as 20,000 years ago may have corresponded to the phases of the Moon.

Humans have used the patterns of the heavens as a clock, to keep track of time, and as a compass, to find their way in space. In ancient times, Egyptians noted that the rising of the star Sirius correlated with the Nile overflowing its banks and the optimum time to plant. They planned their agricultural work around that celestial cycle. Ancient megaliths from Stonehenge to the pyramids in Egypt and Mesoamerica were used to follow the movements of celestial bodies. The ancients were particularly concerned with mapping the exact moments of the seasonal shifts (solstices and equinoxes) and with eclipses. Many of their stone circles were set up so that certain stars or the Sun or Moon would appear in a key viewing area at the instant of a solstice or other significant cycle. For years, sailors and others have used celestial bodies to navigate.

Many ancient people had a world view based on animism—the concept that all material bodies and beings possess spirit and consciousness as well. To those people, the planets were not rocks in the sky! Rather they were gods and goddesses (or at least demi-gods). Zeus (or Jupiter) was envisioned throwing his lightning bolts from Mount Olympus. Many of the themes we associate with the planets have the roots in Greek and Roman mythology—and Egyptian and Mesopotamian before that.

As Above, So Below

The beginnings of astrology are shrouded in the mists of time. It seems likely that some ancient individual, seeing how regularities on the Earth's surface matched regularities in the sky, looked for further correspondences. Perhaps literal associations were used. Some people have theorized that Mars, our "red" planet, became seen as "the god of War" because of its color—the color of bloodshed. We do not have a source, but it seems clear that a number of people started comparing celestial cycles with earthly cycles and noting meaningful correspondences. The basic, underlying rationale for astrology was—and is—"it works!" The aphorism "as above, so below" bears out in practice. Planetary patterns **do** correspond and accurately reflect cycles and patterns on Earth. That is why thousands of years of astrological tradition exist and continue to this day. Many modern astrologers came into the field as skeptics, thinking, "this does not make sense." After examining and watching the correspondences with an open mind, most people feel—"There is something real here. There are meaningful connections between the sky and Earth." (A number also believe that some of the traditions are inaccurate or outdated. It is advisable for everyone studying astrology to check the traditions against their own experience. Do not believe anything you read—including in this book—or hear, until you have tested it for yourself.)

The basic astrological learning was trial-and-error. Astrologers (who were also astronomers—there was no split until the 18th century) would note when a planet was prominent and see what events occurred, trying to assign meanings. One story (probably apocryphal) tells of an old-time astrologer seeking the meaning of the planet Uranus. (When "new" planets were discovered, astrologers had to use trial-and-error observation to figure out their significance.) This astrologer had noted that the new planet Uranus would conjunct (occupy the same area of the sky visually) the planet Mars (which tradition associates with war, bloodshed, iron tools and weapons, fire, action, speed, soldiers, athletes, etc.) in a prominent area of his personal horoscope very shortly. He waited eagerly for the time that conjunction would be exact in terms of measurement. That evening, a sudden fire broke out and burned his house to the ground. The tale claims that the astrologer stood outside his burning domicile, shouting with glee: "Uranus/Mars means sudden fire! Uranus/Mars means sudden fire!" (The life of a researcher is often hard.)

Originally astrologers served kings and the nobility. Some Popes were astrologers and astrology was taught in the great universities before the Age of Materialism began. Astrology was used to more fully understand life on Earth. The positions of the planets were initially studied to judge the state of the world, including the weather and national affairs. An ancient stone fragment which interprets a Babylonian horoscope advises the king not to have his son visit during a certain period because Mars (symbolizing bloodshed) is prominent (and violence, perhaps assassination, is presumably possible). A time when Venus (associated with beauty, pleasure and love) is prominent is seen as preferable.

Planets, Professions and Personality

In modern times (especially with the advent of computers), research has become more sophisticated than the old trial-and-error observation used by ancient astrologers. The most striking work has been done by a French and Swiss couple—Michel and Francoise Gauquelin. They found first that specific planetary placements in the horoscope correlated with certain professions with odds of thousands (and tens of thousands) to one against this occurring by chance. (The planet Mars was found in "power" sectors of the horoscopes of athletes much more often than one would predict by chance. The planet Mars was **not** found in these sectors in the horoscopes of artists—and again the correlation was much, much more than chance would predict.)

Further study by the Gauquelins correlated the character trait words (e.g., assertive, courageous, direct, shy, reserved, etc.) used in biographies of famous people with the positions of certain planets in the horoscopes. This research had correlations even **higher** than the vocational research. Clearly, the planets indicate **character** and certain types of character lead people more strongly to particular vocations than others. The character is the fundamental issue—not the vocation. People with Mars in the Gauquelin sectors areas of the horoscope were described many more times than chance would predict as "assertive, courageous, direct, rash," etc. People with Saturn in the Gauquelin sectors were described—many more times than chance would predict—as "shy, melancholic, reserved, hardworking," etc.

Why or How Does It Work?

So humans came to realize that the sky symbolizes the personality traits and tendencies of individuals. If you are unsure whether astrology **does** work, I recommend you test it out yourself! If you accept that astrology does work, the next obvious question is **why** or **how** does it work? There are three likely answers.

(1) as yet undiscovered material forces (perhaps some kind of electromagnetic resonance) whereby the planetary configurations imprint the personality of the child at the instant of birth and influence the individual as they move daily.

It is quite improbable that personality is "set" in one instant (such as the birth moment). Most psychologists agree on a complex interweaving of heredity and environment. Another reason to question the validity of "physical forces" as an explanation of astrology is that many astrological patterns which also seem to "work" have no relationship to the instant of birth, and are not concerned with daily planetary motion. For example, one system of looking ahead equates one day of life with one year of life. To examine trends in your 30th year, you look at the patterns when you were 30 days old. It is extremely unlikely that planetary configurations at a few days of age affect one years later, yet the symbolism "works," i.e., is applicable to the issues and cycles people meet in those later years.

(2) synchronicity (the Jungian concept) which says "A correlates with B, but we do not know why." This begs the question, but can be a reasonable middle ground for people who are not comfortable with other choices.

(3) a meaningful universe. This assumes that the universe is meaningful—that is, **not** a product of random chance as reductionistic science would presume. The assumption is that a Higher Power created the universe with correspondences between the heavens and Earth ("as above, so below"). We can assume a benevolent deity who provided astrology as another tool for insight for us, or we can assume a world view of the universe as mind or consciousness where all parts are interconnected and each reflects or mirrors the other.

I happen to believe in a meaningful universe and a Higher Power. It is not necessary for you, as a reader, to accept any of the above world views. They are offered as possibilities for the individual who asks the questions "why" and "how." I view looking at a horoscope as similar to looking in a mirror: we can see ourselves more clearly and easily as unique individuals. Just as the mirror does not **set** our appearance, but only **reflects** it, so do the planets not **create** our personalities, but only **reflect** them (world view #3 above—not #1).

I believe that we are born when our nature fits the world, including the planets. Our nature creates our destiny, so if we change our natures (our habitual attitudes and actions), we can change our destinies. Each of the astrological factors represents a principle which can be manifested in many different details of life. (The principle of Mars, for example, centers around assertive drive. This **can** lead to war, bloodshed, and other forms of destruction. It can also indicate leadership, pioneering spirit, the forceful athlete, etc.) As we learn to understand the principles of our own nature, we can often choose to manifest more satisfactory details.

Your Sky Map

Using astrology to describe potential personality strengths, weaknesses, talents, abilities and challenges requires a **natal** (or birth) horoscope. A natal horoscope is like a map of the sky for your instant of birth, looking from the viewpoint of your birthplace. Your moment of birth gives a "freeze frame"—an exact snapshot of the positions of all the planets. No one else has the same horoscope as you—unless they were born in the exact same place, at the exact same minute, that you were.

The next few pages of this book will introduce you to the basic tools of astrology—planets, aspects (how the planets relate to each other at a given moment), houses (divisions of space based on your birthplace) and signs (divisions of space based on the Earth's seasons). The bulk of this work will be devoted to sample interpretations of these astrological factors (e.g., planets in aspects, planets in houses, and planets in signs). Those readers who already understand the basics of astrology may skip directly to the interpretations (beginning on page 47).

Because character leads to (or creates) destiny, a horoscope can also help us to recognize certain cycles in our lives and to become aware of upcoming issues. A horoscope does **not** determine the future, but it can help us to visualize paths which lie ahead; then we can choose between them and decide how to travel them most productively. Remember that the horoscope shows the psychological (life) principles but each principle can be manifested in many different ways and it is up to us to choose more satisfying details.

A horoscope might, for example, indicate a time when our desire to take risks, to change, to innovate, to break new ground, and to rebel is in high focus. **We can choose**, however, whether to break loose and break free in destructive ways in our lives or to make new, creative changes. If we are unaware of this inner restlessness or try to deny it, we are more apt to experience disruption, sudden upsets, accidents, or nonproductive rebelliousness. If we are aware that this is a period to be more independent and innovative, we can arrange for time and space in our life to do our own thing and seek new possibilities.

A Mars/Saturn square (90 degree relationship in the sky), for another example, traditionally shows the life principle of self-will and forceful assertion (including muscles, independence, speed, wanting one's own way) confronting societal and practical limits (including authority figures and the necessity of making a living). The details which **could** manifest from those principles include:

(1) going to jail

(2) successful endurance training

(3) starting one's own business

(4) a fight with the boss

(5) a speeding ticket

(6) increased self-direction on the job

and many other alternatives. By recognizing the principles we are facing, we can create fulfilling rather than frustrating details (life events).

A Tool for Timing

A horoscope can also help to pinpoint times of likely crisis and opportunity. Just as we use a clock and a calendar to help plan our lives and activities, so can we use a horoscope to help prepare for future possibilities. Neither the clock, calendar or horoscope **makes** time or creates trends, but they all are tools for planning ahead and dealing with possibilities. Another way to describe astrology is that it does not tell us **what** will happen; it tells us **why** things are happening, in terms of our own psychological drives and the desires which are in high focus at a given moment in our lives.

The astrology which deals with cycles, patterns and future trends is the astrology of **current patterns**. Different techniques are used to examine the movement of the planets over time from their positions in the natal horoscope. These techniques include progressions, directions, transits and returns. The appendix of this volume describes some of the choices which are available to look at your horoscope over time. The companion book to this one, *Future Signs*, is a good introduction to looking ahead with astrology.

The major focus of this book, however, is understanding **natal** (birth) astrology in terms of personality dynamics and inner strengths and challenges. The interpretations which are provided are based on birth horoscopes, each drawn for a particular date, time and place on the Earth. A clear understanding of who we **are** is an essential foundation for anticipating who we can **become**, or what we might manifest in the future.

CHAPTER TWO
ASTROLOGICAL FUNDAMENTALS

This chapter will cover many astrological terms and principles. If you wish further definitions of terms, please see the glossary in the back of this book.

Planets: *Drives and Desires*

Planets are one of the four basic building blocks of astrology. When astrologers say "planets," they usually refer to the eight known planets of our solar system other than Earth, which is our platform for viewing the rest of the system. The planets include Mercury, Venus, Mars, Jupiter, Saturn, Uranus, Neptune and Pluto, plus the Sun and the Moon. We know that the Sun is actually a star and the Moon is actually a satellite of Earth, but for convenience they are included with the planets when describing the heavenly bodies as distinct from other factors in astrology such as houses and signs.

Astrologically, each of the planets represents a drive or need within you. A planet is like the verb in a sentence; it indicates where the action is. Planets comprise the most significant building block of astrology. Following is a brief description of each of the planets. Each planet has its own glyph (symbol) used to represent it in the horoscope. Glyphs follow (in parens) the name of each planet. Each planet occupies a house in the horoscope (to be defined later) and a sign in the zodiac (definitions to follow).

Just as the **Sun** (☉) is the center of our solar system, so is it the center of the horoscope. Our Sun in the solar system provides light and makes life possible. The Sun in the horoscope is a key to vitality, life force, and our central, creative urge. The Sun represents our need to shine, our desire for recognition, our self-esteem, and pride/shame issues.

Wherever our **Sun** (☉) is (occupying one of 12 houses, and one of 12 signs), we want to be admired, noticed, loved, or applauded by the world. We feel most vital and alive when expressing the themes of our Sun's house and sign. Since it is a key to vitality and zest, we naturally pour energy into the activities represented by our Sun's house and sign.

The **Moon** (☽), which shines by reflected light, is a key to our emotions, particularly our need for emotional security and safety. It symbolizes our dependency needs and our desire to nurture and care for others. It represents the people we depend on, the parent who was a nurturing figure (usually mother), and our capacity to be an assisting, helpful, caring individual. It also is a key to our home, our roots (ancestry), and our sensitivities.

Wherever the **Moon** (☽) is (by house and sign), we want to nurture or be nurtured, to make warm, emotional connections with others. Family feelings may be sought or explored and emotions are the focus. It shows our hunger for a nest, and is connected to the unconscious side of the mind and to habits.

Mercury (☿) represents our need to communicate. It is a key to the conscious side of the mind, to our verbal ability, our logic, our capacity to be objective and detached. Mercury symbolizes the reasoning mind that observes the world, gathers information, learns, teaches, and disseminates knowledge.

Wherever **Mercury** (☿) is in our horoscope (by house and sign), we are curious, interested, and want to know. We may learn and/or teach in that area. Our Mercury placements help to describe our verbal styles and the way we use our minds.

Venus (♀) represents our need to enjoy the physical world and the pleasure principle. We may seek pleasure through money, possessions, tangible beauty, or sensual gratification.

We may also seek pleasure through relationships, through sharing, through partnerships with others. Venus is a key to affection, love, our need for balance, our appreciation of beauty, and our orientation toward ease, comfort, and personal enjoyment.

Wherever **Venus** (♀) is in our horoscope (by house and sign), we want to enjoy! We seek pleasure, comfort, ease, beauty, teamwork, grace, and goodness in the areas inhabited by Venus.

Mars (♂) represents our need to assert ourselves, to defend our own rights, to identify and go after what we want in the world. Mars can be a key to healthy self-expression and personal power, but it can also represent aggression, fights, arguments, and negative forms of assertion. Mars is an indicator of our basic physical energy and health, sexual drive, anger, where we seek freedom, our desire to do things on our own, and our sense of basic identity.

Wherever **Mars** (♂) is in our horoscope (by house and sign), we want to express ourselves, be free and be active. If the personal energy symbolized by Mars is blocked, we might experience physical or interpersonal problems as a result of not defending our own needs. If we carry Martian themes too far, (assert our own rights too strongly), we may be rash, impulsive or self-centered in the areas where Mars lies. If we balance our Martian side with other drives, we can be assertive in a healthy fashion, meeting our own needs and drives in a constructive manner.

Jupiter (♃) represents our need to believe and to aspire. It indicates our ideals, what we tend to value and where we want more in life. It is also a key to where we can exaggerate or overdo, and indicates opportunities (which we may or may not take advantage of) plus the confidence to pursue our visions.

Wherever **Jupiter** (♃) is in our horoscope (by house and sign), we tend to place our faith. We are likely to seek more in that area, and may overdo. (If we see something as good, more is better.) Jupiter's placement may indicate that an individual trusts and values money, or a partner, or power, or personal creativity, or a religion, etc. Where Jupiter is a key, we may idealize and put a part of life (e.g., a marriage, a child, a job) on a pedestal. We may expect more than is possible, that a frag-

ment of life (rather than the whole process) should give us total
fulfillment, should make our life meaningful. (If, for instance,
we idealize a marital partner, we may believe that individual
gives our life meaning. If so, we are apt to be emotionally
destroyed if the individual dies or leaves. Alternately, if we
expect our profession to provide our total meaning in life, we
are likely to be chronically dissatisfied because it will never be
enough. There could always be something more.)

Our ultimate goals in life depend on our beliefs about what
is true, desirable, possible, and morally correct. Jupiter symbolizes our optimistic spirit, where we tend to look on the
bright side, have hope, and see the highest potentials.

Saturn (♄) represents our need to structure life, to test and
cope with material reality. Saturn is a key to the limits of life in
this physical world: what we can do, cannot do, and have to do.
It is also symbolic of authority figures in our lives: from the
rulemaker parent (traditionally Dad) to police officers and
presidents.

Wherever **Saturn** (♄) is in our horoscope (by house and
sign), we learn to face reality and what is possible. We often
deal with consequences (cause and effect). Saturn represents
the principle of learning through experience (sometimes the
"school of hard knocks"). Where Saturn's rules (the power of
the external world to limit us) are given too much weight,
people may feel blocked, inhibited, incapable, incompetent, or
unable to do anything. Where Saturn's rules are ignored, people
may be overly responsible, trying to carry the whole world (the
"Atlas Syndrome"). Or, individuals might push the world (or
others) until they discover certain principles (including the
laws of the land) that are bigger than they are. Individuals in
the latter case may be irresponsible (ignoring limits, rules,
duties) or even outright criminals (fighting the laws of the
land). Eventually we reap the consequences of what we have
sown. We learn to drive on the right side of the road in the U.S.
and on the left side of the road in England. To stay healthy, we
have to eat, sleep, move our bodies, etc. People who are handling the Saturn principle properly understand the rules and
live within them voluntarily. They are practical achievers who
do not attempt the impossible but do what is necessary and
possible within the structures of society and natural law.

Uranus (♅) represents our urge to go beyond Saturn, to resist limits, to change and alter. It is a key to our drive for individuality and uniqueness, our capacity to rebel; the lure of the unusual and the unknown. Uranus symbolizes our need for the freedom to be different, to explore alternatives, and to look toward the future and progress.

Wherever **Uranus** (♅) is in our horoscope (by house and sign), we need to be independent. We need to come from our own unique essence. Uranus shows where we seek space, where we can innovate and be inventive, and where we can be surprised. Uranus mirrors our urge to consider alternatives, to be open and equalitarian, and to expand knowledge which connects it to modern technology.

Neptune (♆) represents our need to merge and seek transcendence. Neptune is a key to our search for the beautiful dream. That vision may be sought through art, through healing or helping activities, or through escapist means. Neptune indicates our drive to experience Oneness, to be attuned with something Higher or ecstatic in life. We may seek transcendence through spiritual or religious paths, be "swept away" in nature worship, look to drugs for ecstasy, live in a "perfect" fantasy world, or find inspiration in philanthropy and compassionate assistance of humanity, or in artistic expressions.

Wherever **Neptune** (♆) is in our horoscope (by house and sign), we want to be inspired and must be wary of rose-colored glasses. We need to feel uplifted where our Neptune is placed, and may fool ourselves into viewing matters through a romantic haze. But Neptune can point to inadequate as well as excessive faith. Jupiter symbolizes our more conscious search for faith—a world view we can put into words, a set of moral, religious or ethical principles. With Neptune, the search for the Absolute is partly unconscious—whether we are seeking personal "salvation" or trying to "save" others. Neptune represents an intense emotional need to be inspired, swept away, united and unified with something Higher. We seek transcendent experiences in the areas connected to Neptune in our horoscope, and need to be able to do our share and then trust a Higher Power.

For those who lack the (partly unconscious) faith in a Higher Power, who think they have to do it all themselves, (the

Atlas side of Saturn), Neptune can be associated with anxiety which is simply a lack of faith. In such cases, it is important to find ways to encourage faith, whether by reading inspirational literature, associating with people who have a strong faith, or looking for times in our lives or in the lives of others when faith brought help and healing. People who are overdoing the Neptunian themes may be passive, escapist victims who expect God to balance the checkbook, provide the ideal partner, drop the "perfect" job in their laps, etc. People need enough (but not too much) of the faith and trust that Neptune symbolizes.

Pluto (♇) represents our need to relate intimately with another person and with our own psyche. Pluto, like Mars, can be a key to sexuality. It symbolizes our drive to share the world (especially sensually and financially) with another person—and learning about ourselves through interacting with someone else. Pluto also indicates our inner drive for self-understanding and self-mastery, including mastery of our emotions and of our appetites. Pluto themes have to do with depth analysis, tearing things down to open the way for something better, regeneration and transformation.

Wherever **Pluto** (♇) is in our horoscope (by house and sign), we tend to probe beneath the surface. We are apt to pick at, and painstakingly examine those areas, looking for hidden meanings and deeper layers. We may tear down and then build up, analyze carefully, and then rework and transform. Pluto also symbolizes our approach to shared resources, money, and sexuality. Pluto represents our deepest, most intense feelings and our capacity to share power, pleasure and possessions with another person. With Pluto, we may give in to others, struggle with them, run from them, but eventually we have to learn to share with them for mutual pleasure. We have to learn what is ours and what belongs to others; when we have done, said, or had enough; and how to let go.

Following are some key words for each of the planets. These are based on astrological traditions (and trial-and-error observations of people and horoscopes). Notice that each set of key words for a planet revolves around a few central, psychological drives, such as a need to shine, to do more than one has done before in life associated with the Sun; a need to nurture, protect, be emotionally attached with the Moon; a need to learn and communicate with Mercury, etc.

Sun: self-esteem, life force, vitality, creativity, risk-taking instincts, pride, star quality, fun loving spirit, inner child, drive for excitement, need for recreation, speculative side, romantic passion, need to shine.

Moon: emotions, security needs, caretaking instincts, dependency needs, drive to nurture, vulnerabilities, homing instincts, receptivity, moods, habit patterns, women (including mother).

Mercury: urge to communicate, thinking, listening/talking, capacity to learn cognitively, adaptability/flexibility, information-gathering skills, casual contacts, logic, conscious awareness, dexterity, intellectual perception.

Venus: desire for pleasure, sensuality, urge for comfort/ease, need for tangible beauty, drive for stability/predictability, sweetness, affection, relating needs, instincts for teamwork, partnership, material assets.

Mars: assertion, self-expression, independence, personal power, desires, spontaneous instincts, immediate needs, anger, sexual drive, men in general, early identity, doing one's thing, need to be first, energy level.

Jupiter: ideals and goals, beliefs, values, morality/ethics, faith, optimism, quest for the truth, philosophy/religion, drive for expanded horizons, high expectations, seeking the best/highest, expansiveness.

Saturn: reality quotient, response to and desire for authority, authority figures (usually including father), attitudes toward the orthodox and what society deems appropriate, the personal conscience and guilt, practicality, capacity to deal with limits, career drives, sense of responsibility, discipline/effort, status ambitions, urge to solidify/contract, wisdom of experience.

Uranus: individuality, freedom drives, inventiveness, originality, humanitarian instincts, equalitarian principles, detachment, pull toward the future, eccentricity, innovation, sudden changes, interest in technology, the new or "cutting edge."

Neptune: quest for Oneness/Union/transcendence, idealism, seeking of infinite love and beauty, intuition, savior/victim potentials, compassion, imagination/fantasy, mysticism, escapism, psychic openness.

Pluto: intensity, drive for self-knowledge and self-mastery, intimacy instincts, sexual needs, drive for transformation, elimination or completion urges, resentment and forgiveness, probing, complicated motives, compulsions, addictions, ability to know when "enough is enough" and how to let go, ability to share possessions, pleasures and power with an intimate other.

Houses of the Horoscope:
Habits and Habitats

Your time of birth is required in order to calculate which houses are occupied by the planets. Houses are a division of space based on the Earth's 24-hour rotation. The Earth turns completely on its axis in one 24-hour period, creating our day and night. The space around earth is divided into 12 areas called houses which are shown as pie-shaped wedges in a circular horoscope. (Think of these wedges as three-dimensional, extending out from one's birthplace into space.)

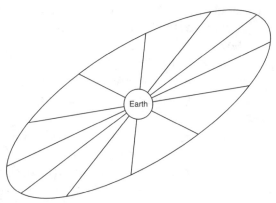

If you had looked out from your place of birth at your moment of birth, each planet would have been in one of these areas of space which are numbered from one to twelve in a counter-clockwise direction starting at the eastern horizon. Although houses are represented most commonly by 12 equally-sized wedges, they are actually of **unequal** size. One house might be only 18° wide, while another might be 45°.

When a house is more than 30° wide, an entire sign is inside that house, with no cusp of its own. Such a sign is called "intercepted" and its opposite sign will also be intercepted. In

Bruce Springsteen's chart (page 24), Virgo is intercepted in the 4th and Pisces in the 10th. When a pair of signs is intercepted, another pair must do double duty, appearing on two cusps. (That occurs in Springsteen's chart with Leo and Aquarius.) Clearly houses with intercepted signs are always larger (have more degrees in them) than houses with no interceptions.

Each sign is 30° (so 12 make up the 360° circle), but houses are of different sizes (although all 12 will total 360°).

The line which separates one house from the next is called a cusp. Certain house cusps are considered to have extra significance in astrology. Many years of observation have led to traditions as to their importance and meanings. One of the most important is the cusp of the first house which points to the eastern horizon and which is called the Ascendant in the horoscope. Planets which will soon rise above the horizon will be in the first house. If you were born around sunrise, the Sun will be near the cusp of your first house. Astrologers consider the sign on the Ascendant (the "rising sign") an important key to personal identity and action. Similarly the sign on the cusp of the tenth house (the Midheaven) is considered significant in matters of career and status. The 7th cusp (Descendant) is important in regard to relationships, while the 4th cusp (IC) reveals home and family issues. Think of the Ascendant as similar to Mars; the IC to the Moon; the Descendant to Venus; and the Midheaven to Saturn.

Cusps are the boundary lines in a horoscope (the fence posts). They show where each house begins and ends. In Bruce

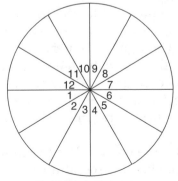

Most astrological texts portray equal-sized "apple pie" houses

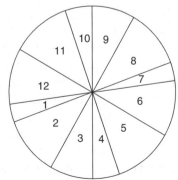

It would be more visually accurate to show houses of unequal sizes (and some astrologers do so).

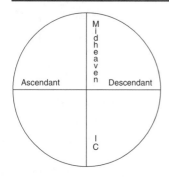

Springsteen's horoscope, for example (page 23), the Ascendant (1st house cusp) is 22 degrees Gemini 49 minutes. The cusp of the 2nd house is 13° Cancer 32′. Thus, any planets which are later in the zodiac than 22° Gemini 49′ and earlier than 13° Cancer 32′ fall in the 1st house of Bruce Springsteen's horoscope.

Houses (like planets and signs) represent inner drives and needs to experience certain areas of life. The tools of astrology represent both inner psychological desires and other people and conditions in our lives to which we are drawn to play out our inner urges. For example, the 3rd house represents our capacity to learn, our logic and objectivity, and our communication skills. The 3rd house also symbolizes the people with whom we first practice learning and communicating: brothers, sisters, neighbors and other people near-at-hand. It also represents the near-at-hand (short) trips we make to satisfy our curiosity, and the short periodicals (newspapers and magazines rather than books) which we read for the same purpose. As with each house (and planet and sign), a central thread links the various associations. For the 3rd house, the central issue is learning and communication. The people, objects and needs associated with the 3rd house all derive from the basic human drive to learn and to communicate.

No matter where they are on Earth, people born at the same moment will have their planets in the same degree of their zodiacal signs. Because the outer planets (Jupiter through Pluto) take so long to orbit the Sun, they occupy each sign of the zodiac for a rather long time. A whole generation may have Pluto in the same sign of the zodiac. But all twelve houses turn past the planets as the Earth rotates each day, and houses also shift with the individual's location on Earth. So the house a planet occupies in a horoscope is a much more personal statement than the sign it occupies.

Following is a list of keywords for the houses. Notice again that the associations of each house cluster around a central thread of related drives and the people or objects connected to those drives.

1st house: personal action, identity, self-expression, spontaneous instincts, physical body, the beginning of life, appearance, what you do instinctively and automatically.

2nd house: possessions and pleasures, sensuality, money, comfort, stability, capacity to earn a living, tangible beauty, physical security, your material base.

3rd house: communication, relatives, learning capacity, lightheartedness, short trips, transportation, media, early schooling, immediate environment, conscious mind.

4th house: home, family, emotional vulnerabilities, nurturing instincts, roots, real estate, parent who was main nurturer, heredity and ancestry, emotional needs.

5th house: procreation, creativity, onstage activities, lovers, children, romance, speculation, hobbies, recreation, risk-taking, love given and received, pride and power.

6th house: competence, efficiency, work, health, handling of details, colleagues and co-workers, tenants, service and servants, employees, routines, nutrition, hygiene.

7th house: partners and partnership, need for balance, fair play, harmony, aesthetics, especially the graphic arts and design, contracts, lawsuits, competitors, attitude toward marriage, grandparent(s), spouse.

8th house: depth investigations, shared money, resources, pleasures, and power, intimacy instincts, sexuality, debts, taxes, inheritance, hidden matters, surgery, endings, therapy.

9th house: aspirations, beliefs, values, world view (religion or philosophy), optimism, law, science, ideals, higher education, books, distant travel/cultures, grandchildren, spiritual consciousness, the judicial branch of the government.

10th house: sense of responsibility, career, authorities, and your own authority in the world, reality principle, status, employer, how the world sees you, rulemaker parent, achievements, the executive branch of the government.

11th house: drive for individuation, originality, resistance to limits, equalitarian principles, friends, networking, hopes for the future, foster and stepchildren, voluntary organizations such as clubs, the legislative branch of the government.

12th house: desire for infinite love and beauty, union, mysticism, imagination, intuition, savior/victim issues including institutions such as hospitals where victims are helped, and jails where people are prevented from victimizing people outside but often victimize fellow inmates, protective retreats (e.g., ashrams) as well as escapist withdrawals (e.g., into fantasy, illness), the unconscious mind, especially unconscious faith or fear, charity, hidden weaknesses and strengths.

The interpretations supplied (see pages 47-315) will cover some of the potentials for the house occupied by planets in your natal (birth) horoscope. If you also look over the the descriptions of the planets, and blend them with the house descriptions provided here, you may be able to identify more possibilities.

Signs of the Zodiac:
Styles and Specialties

Your "sky map" (horoscope) places planets in any of 12 signs and any of 12 houses. (There are 1440 different possible planet/house/sign combinations and the variations rise even more if you include aspects as well.) Each planet has a different meaning, depending upon the house and the sign of the zodiac which it occupies.

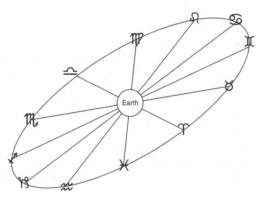

The zodiac is an imaginary circle out in space. The Earth's path around the Sun (the ecliptic) is projected against infinity and is divided into twelve equal sections.

These twelve sections of the sky are **not** the same as the constellations or groups of stars which have the same names as the zodiac signs. Constellations do not exist in neat, 30° packages. Some constellations sprawl over 45°; others are only about 18° wide. The stars in some constellations overlap, while other constellations have empty spaces between them. Some of the constellations bearing the same names as our zodiac signs

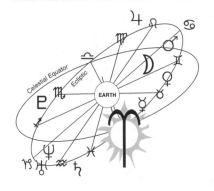

are not even located on the ecliptic; they reside above or below the plane of our Earth's orbit.

The position of the Sun at the vernal equinox (spring in the Northern Hemisphere) defines 0 degrees of the sign Aries—the beginning of the zodiac. Looking out from the Earth, we see each planet in front of a certain part of the zodiac circle and the planet is said to be "in" that sign. Around 200 AD, the seasonal zodiac which we use (also called the **tropical** zodiac) was roughly equivalent to the positions of many constellations bearing the same names. However, nothing in the universe is static. Due to the (slow) movement of the so-called "fixed" stars and the precession of the equinoxes (a slow westward motion of the equinoxes along the ecliptic), the seasonal or tropical zodiac has been diverging more and more from the constellations. They are almost one sign apart at this point. Thus, where an astrologer would define a planet as in the (tropical zodiac) sign of Aries, to an astronomer that planet would probably appear to be in the constellation of Pisces.

Some astrologers have assigned meaning to the movement of the zero Aries point (which defines our seasonal zodiac) against the backdrop of the constellations and "fixed" stars. The Song "The Age of Aquarius" made famous by the musical *Hair* refers to a future time when the zero Aries point of our seasonal zodiac will move in front of the constellation named Aquarius.

One way to envision the interweaving of planets, houses and signs is to think of the horoscope as similar to a complicated clock with two dials and many hands. The zodiac circle is the "stationary" dial. (Actually nothing in the cosmos is

Outer (house) dial rotates. Hands (planets) move. Inner (sign) dial is [relatively] stationary.

really standing still). The planets move in front of the zodiac signs, each at its own respective speed. The house dial turns past the planets and signs as the Earth rotates every day, so every day, the planets and signs "appear" to move through the houses.

Your **day of birth** determines the sign of the zodiac occupied by the Sun. That is your "Sun sign" which many popular newspaper and magazine columns abbreviate to just "your sign." The signs occupied by the other planets are determined by both your **year** of birth and your **day** of birth.

Your **time of birth** may be needed to know your Moon sign, because the Moon changes signs about every 2½ days. Also, if you were born on a day when the Sun or a planet was changing signs (near one of twelve boundary points in the zodiacal circle), you will need to know your time of birth to determine which sign that planet is in. (Remember, astrologers call the Sun and Moon "planets" for convenience, even though the Sun is a star and the Moon is a satellite of earth.)

Each planet occupies a position (a number of degrees) within a sign. Each sign is made up of 30 degrees (and 12 signs comprise the 360° circle of the zodiac). Furthermore, each degree of the zodiac has 60 minutes within it. These minutes are **not** the same as minutes of time. Zodiacal minutes are positions in space. In this chart of Bruce Springsteen (next page), for example, the positions are as follows:

Sun	00 degrees of Libra and 43 minutes or	0♎43
Moon	23 degrees of Libra and 25 minutes or	23♎25
Mercury	18 degrees of Libra and 37 minutes or	18♎37
Venus	11 degrees of Scorpio and 4 minutes or	11♏4
Mars	10 degrees of Leo and 31 minutes or	10♌31
Jupiter	22 degrees of Capricorn and 23 min. or	22♑23
Saturn	12 degrees of Virgo and 17 minutes or	12♍17
Uranus	4 degrees of Cancer and 53 minutes or	4♋53
Neptune	14 degrees of Libra and 23 minutes or	14♎23
Pluto	17 degrees of Leo and 29 minutes or	17♌29

The house cusps (boundary lines) determine in which house each of those planets falls. A planet's position in the zodiac (degree and minute of a sign) will be **after** the cusp which marks the beginning of the house that planet is in, but before the cusp of the next house. Bruce Springsteen's Saturn, for example, (at 12° Virgo 17′) is after 28♌41 (the cusp of the 4th house) and before 1♎02 (the cusp of the 5th house) so his Saturn is in the 4th house.

The signs modify the planets, like adjectives modify verbs in English. You tend to express the drive symbolized by the planet in a manner described by the sign it occupies. Here are a few traditional keywords (based on centuries of observation)

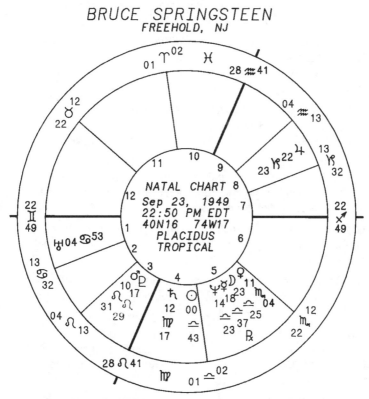

BRUCE SPRINGSTEEN
FREEHOLD, NJ

NATAL CHART
Sep 23, 1949
22:50 PM EDT
40N16 74W17
PLACIDUS
TROPICAL

Sun (☉) in Libra (♎) in 4th
Moon (☽) in Libra (♎) in 5th
Mercury (☿) in Libra (♎) in 5th
Venus (♀) in Scorpio (♏) in 5th
Mars (♂) in Leo (♌) in 3rd
Jupiter (♃) in Capricorn (♑) in 8th
Saturn (♄) in Virgo (♍) in 4th
Uranus (♅) in Cancer (♋) in 1st
Neptune (♆) in Libra (♎) in 5th
Pluto (♇) in Leo (♌) in 3rd
Ascendant in Gemini (♊)
Midheaven in Aquarius (♒)

☉ square ♅, quincunx MC
☽ conjunct ☿, square ♃, trine Asc, trine MC
☿ square ♃, conjunct ♆, sextile ♇, trine Asc
♀ square ♂, sextile ♄
♂ sextile ♆, conjunct ♇
♃ quincunx Asc
♆ sextile ♇

Aries ♈: assertive, brave, first, impetuous, energetic, self-oriented, pioneering, rash, competitive, rapid, eager, likes to be on one s own, lives in the present.

Taurus ♉: comfortable, deliberate, dependable, placid, possessive, sensual, patient, loyal, thorough, stubborn, stable, money-oriented, practical, artistic.

Gemini ♊: fluent, versatile, curious, intermittent, clever, nimble, quick-witted, adaptable, scattered, gossipy, dextrous, superficial, flexible, lighthearted, articulate.

Cancer ♋: nurturing, warm, dependent, sympathetic, protective, security-oriented, maternal, patriotic, retentive, helpful, moody, domestic, touchy (easily hurt), focused on home & family.

Leo ♌: creative, risk-taking, charismatic, fun loving, generous, exciting, dramatic, proud, self-confident, childish, ambitious, arrogant, self-conscious (fears ridicule unless self-esteem is very high), enthusiastic, magnetic.

Virgo ♍: work-oriented, painstaking, efficient, pragmatic, exacting, discreet, industrious, thorough, critical, finds flaws, pedantic, methodical, careful, detail-oriented, concerned with health/cleanliness.

Libra ♎: cooperative and/or competitive, seeing both sides and concerned with fair play which can lead to fence sitting, diplomatic, aesthetic, charming, easily deterred, refined, sociable, seeks a partner/companion, placates, equalitarian.

Scorpio ♏: penetrating, emotionally intense, resourceful, powerful, compulsive, determined, jealous, passionate, secretive, probing, suspicious, controlling, fascinated by the hidden or taboo.

Sagittarius ♐: benevolent, optimistic, extravagant, athletic, enthusiastic, idealistic, philosophical, freedom-loving, exaggerative, blunt, overindulgent, broad-minded, truth-seeking and truth-telling, just.

Capricorn ♑: responsible, formal, traditional, authoritative, career-oriented, cautious, inhibited, hardworking, scrupulous, conventional, status-seeking, economical, businesslike, thorough, conscientious, organized, ambitious.

Aquarius ♒: unique, rebellious, futuristic, independent, inventive, objective, intellectual, unpredictable, tolerant, eccentric, aloof, progressive, has a wide perspective.

Pisces ♓: compassionate, mystical, illusory, sensitive, spiritual, dreamy, artistic, passive, sacrificial, intuitive, charitable, impractical, escapist, visionary, inspirational.

for the signs. The glyph (symbol) for each sign follows its name. As with planets and houses, note that each sign has a central, connected thread of shared drives and psychological principles. The central core of Aries radiates around forceful initiative; the central core of Taurus revolves around physical pleasures and comfort; the central core of Gemini emphasizes hunger for knowledge, etc.

As you can see, each sign has a number of different possibilities. The symbols of astrology work on many levels. Everything has **more than one** meaning when you deal with the details of life. Each principle in astrology has both "up" and "down" sides—both positive and negative possibilities. An emphasis in the chart on a particular planet, house or sign simply means that the individual has to deal often with the issues associated with that planet, house or sign. They may overdo certain drives or have trouble expressing them. Astrology only mirrors our potentials. When we express the life principles which astrology reflects, we have the power to manifest either positive or painful details in our lives, and with awareness and effort, we can change from one to the other.

The interpretations supplied (see pages 47-315) make use of some of the sign positions of **your** planets (but probably not all). Nor are the potentials discussed the only ones. You could extrapolate additional possibilities by combining the key words given here for signs with the descriptions provided of the planets.

Astrological Alphabet

You can think of the astrological model of life as an alphabet. An alphabet can be printed with capital letters, small case letters, script, etc., but we recognize an "A" as the same principle as an "a." Similarly in astrology, the same twelve basic drives or "sides of life" are symbolized by the planets, the houses, and the signs.

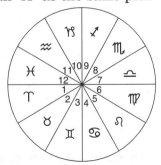

Each sign of the zodiac is associated with a house of the horoscope: the first sign (Aries) with the 1st house; the second sign (Taurus) with the 2nd house, and so on. These

**KEY PHRASES FOR HOUSE-PLANET-SIGN COMBINATIONS
by Zipporah Pottenger Dobyns, Ph.D.**

1. Free self-expression; self-will in spontaneous action; initiative, impulse, courage, pioneering spirit, vitality, skilled coordination, enthusiasm for the new, ready to fight against any limits on personal freedom. **"I do my thing."** ♂ ♈ 1st House

2. Pleasure in manipulating the physical sense world; comfort, security, contentment, love of beauty in tangible possessions; deliberate, persisting determination, slow to become angry or to forget. **"I enjoy the sense world."** ♀ ♉ 2nd House

3. Consciousness; capacity to learn and communicate; thought, language, contact with nearby equals, dexterity, curiosity, versatility, multiple interests, flexibility, cheerful, witty, flippant. **"I see, conceptualize and talk."** ☿ ♊ 3rd House

4. Memory, nurturance-dependence; absorption, protection, preservation, sensitivity, empathy, need for warmth and emotional closeness and rootedness. **"I save, protect, nourish and assimilate."** ☽ ♋ 4th House

5. Creativity and self-expression; capacity to transcend the past; joy, love, drama, need for admiration, the limelight, power; increase through children, speculation; intensifying emotions through stage, screen, etc.; pride, generosity, magnetic vitality. **"I rejoice in expansion."** ☉ ♌ 5th House

6. Service; productive work; analysis, discrimination, pragmatism, quiet efficiency, attention to detail, self-restraint, humility, interest in health and healing. **"I work competently."** ☿ ♍ 6th House

7. Partnership; cooperation or competition with equals; justice, both sides in balance; harmony, arbitration, pleasure from grace, line, form, a feeling for space and from interaction with peers; need for "equal others" to feel complete. **"I enjoy balance."** ♀ ♎ 7th House

8. Insight and self-control for regeneration; intensity, passion, no surrender to death; where we learn the boundary of self-will by accepting what comes, using what is of value, purifying or eliminating waste for optimal functioning; search for hidden knowledge. **"I penetrate, control, absorb or eliminate according to my desire."** ♇ ♏ 8th House

9. Faith and values; philosophical, religious, and ethical belief systems; what is considered true and morally good, ultimate knowledge and trust; optimism, humor, generosity, expansiveness, love of sports, nature, travel, based on faith in life and the urge to reach farther. **"I trust, value and direct my life according to my understanding."** ♃ ♐ 9th House

10. Law—Karmic, natural, human-made; power above self-will; bureaucracy; puritan virtues—duty, responsibility, thrift, practicality, realism; ambition for reassurance of self-worth, security or to avoid guilt; sense of pressure from forces beyond personal control; crystallized structures from social institutions to bones and teeth. **"I carry out the Law."** ♄ ♑ 10th House

11. New opportunity for all people; rebellion **against** the old, constriction and control and **for** humanitarian principles; sudden, unexpected change to permit growth; explosive, individualistic, open, equalitarian; chaos or voluntary community. **"I seek new knowledge and brotherhood (sisterhood) for all humankind."** ♅ ♒ 11th House

12. Oneness with the whole; hunger for infinite love and beauty; creative imagination, fantasy; selflessness or escapism including drugs, alcohol and psychosis; the artist or savior-martyr; sensitive, compassionate, or passive-submissive. **"I dream of love and beauty and am absorbed in the whole."** ♆ ♓ 12th House

house/sign pairs share common themes, drives and issues. Similarly, each planet is said to "rule" a certain sign and house. That ruling planet symbolizes the same basic principles as the house/sign pair—but in a more active, significant and powerful sense. (Planets are like the verbs in a sentence; houses and signs qualify planets as adverbs qualify verbs.)

Because there are twelve signs and twelve houses, but only ten planets, some planets must do "double duty"—ruling two signs and houses. Mercury rules both Gemini/3rd house and Virgo/6th house and thus indicates principles associated with both house/sign pairs. Venus rules both Taurus/2nd house and Libra/7th house and is a key to principles associated with both of those pairs.

Astrology is inherently repetitive. What is most significant in the psyche and in one's life will be repeated in the horoscope. Recognizing the astrological alphabet helps us to see those reiterated messages. On pages 26-27 is a list of the planet/house/sign triplets that make up the astrological alphabet and the psychological issues and drives connected with each "letter" of the alphabet.

If you compare the previous list to the key words supplied earlier for planets, houses, and signs, you will note that the alphabet principles include the major themes associated with all the planets, houses and signs. Rather than learning twelve different signs, twelve different houses and ten different planets, many people find it easier to learn the astrological alphabet. Each of the twelve sides of life is represented by a planet, a house, and a sign.

Aspects: *Who Gets Along with Whom*

The fourth building block of astrology is aspects. Aspects refer to the relationships between the planets or between planets and points in the chart such as the Ascendant (or 1st house cusp). The relationships or aspects between the planets indicate the relationships between various drives and needs in our nature which are symbolized by the planets.

Every circle has 360 degrees and the circle of the zodiac is no exception. Thus each planet (or point in the horoscope) is separated from other planets (and points) by a specific number of degrees. Certain degree segments (0, 60, 90, 120, 150, 180) have—with time and trial-and-error observation of correspondences—been assigned meanings in astrology. (Some astrologers suggest that **any** number of degrees between two planets is significant. Historically, only certain degree segments were observed as offering useful information.) Most modern astrologers find that the six degree segments listed previously (0, 60, 90, 120, 150, 180) do "work" astrologically.

The aspect which is easiest to "see" in a horoscope is the conjunction, an aspect of zero degrees so the planets are seen together in the chart. (If, for example, a horoscope has the Sun at 13° Gemini 35′ and Mercury is at 13° Gemini 55′, we would

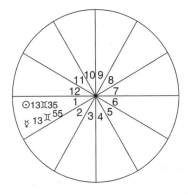

say that the Sun is conjunct Mercury. We could also say that Mercury is conjunct the Sun.)

The meaning of a conjunction is that the drives of the two planets are mixed. It is as if these planets are married or living together. In your horoscope, you do not get one without the other. They symbolize desires which are melded in your personality. The blending may be comfortable or not so comfortable—depending on the nature of the drives involved.

Someone with the Sun (where we need to shine and be recognized) conjunct Mercury (the mind, communication skills, need to learn), for example, might be very ego-invested in his or her mind. Positive attention for knowledge would be vital to that person. Appearing "smart" would be an ego need. Conversely, someone with the Sun conjunct Venus could be very ego-involved in either relationships (needing much admiration and attention from partners) or material possessions (measuring self-worth by what they own). People who do not have the Sun conjunct either of those planets are less likely to have intense ego investments in being admired and applauded for intellect, sharing, or possessions.

Remember, however, that Venus is associated with Taurus and the 2nd house in the natural zodiac and also with Libra and the 7th house. So, a Sun in the 2nd house or in Taurus, like a Sun conjunct Venus, could denote someone ego-invested in ownership or pleasure. A Sun in the 7th house, like a Sun conjunct Venus, might symbolize an individual who is ego-vulnerable in relationships. A Sun in the 3rd or 6th houses (or in Gemini or Virgo) probably identifies someone wishing to shine through the mind, as does the Sun conjunct Mercury. The major distinction is that planets [which are like verbs] point to more central, intense issues. Houses and signs are a less powerful statement of a similar principle. A Sun/Venus conjunction would represent more intense gratification and ego involvement through possessions and pleasures or relationships, than just the Sun in the 2nd or only the Sun in Taurus.

Interpreting a conjunction is not very different from putting together the meanings of a planet in a house or a planet in a sign. You are combining two of the twelve basic drives, two of the twelve sides of life (or two letters of the astrological alpha-

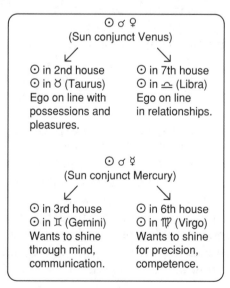

☉ ♂ ♀
(Sun conjunct Venus)

↙   ↘

☉ in 2nd house   ☉ in 7th house
☉ in ♉ (Taurus)   ☉ in ♎ (Libra)
Ego on line with   Ego on line
possessions and   in relationships.
pleasures.

☉ ♂ ☿
(Sun conjunct Mercury)

↙   ↘

☉ in 3rd house   ☉ in 6th house
☉ in ♊ (Gemini)   ☉ in ♍ (Virgo)
Wants to shine   Wants to shine
through mind,   for precision,
communication.   competence.

bet). Consider both sides: how might these two planets reinforce and support one another's themes and how might their basic drives conflict and compete with one other?

In terms of the meaning of a conjunction, look to the nature of the planets (or points) involved to determine likely positive or negative manifestations. Certain planets stand for drives which "get along" easily, that is they tend to want the same sort of things, and tend to pull in the same direction. When such planets conjunct each other, they suggest inner agreement, reinforcement and harmony. (Examples would include conjunctions between the Sun, Jupiter, and/or Mars.)

Other planets represent drives which are contradictory or at odds with one another. Where such planets conjunct each other, the individual must strive to somehow "make peace" between possibly warring factions. Integration takes more effort. (An example would include the Moon with Uranus.)

There are few hard and fast rules. Venus as ruler of Libra tends to conflict with Saturn as ruler of Capricorn, but Venus also rules Taurus which usually harmonizes with Capricorn. A Venus conjunction with Saturn can therefore show a good ability to be successful in the material world, whether in business or in a field of the arts. More attention is needed to maintain a comfortable, equalitarian relationship which Venus (as ruler of Libra) symbolizes while Saturn shows a desire to be in control. When Saturn aspects the planet of peer relationships (Venus), there is the danger (in that individual's relationships) that one partner might try to control the other, or neglect the relationship because of the importance of the career, or direct the work attitude (looking for flaws in order to correct them) into the relationship instead of keeping the critical focus for one's job.

The principles will be illustrated more fully later. At this point, it is important to realize that the picture is complex and that you will meet a variety of opinions in different astrology texts. There are writers who consider all aspects to Jupiter to be "good" and all aspects to Saturn to be "bad." It is true that Saturn calls for realism and effort while Jupiter encourages faith that we can have what we want without effort, but in the well-known parable of the grasshopper and the ant, the worker came out better than the one who trusted his luck. Of course, for fuller information, you would also consider the nature of the sign(s) and house(s) involved in your conjunction (and all other aspects that you analyze). Anything which is truly central in your nature will be repeated in the horoscope by different aspects or planet in house or planet in sign combinations. Notice what comes up again and again in these interpretations. Repetition reveals significance. (Familiarity with the astrological alphabet will help you to quickly and easily spot many repetitive themes.)

Ideally, conjuncting planets are separated by zero degrees. Few aspects, however, are exact to the degree. Astrology uses a concept called "orb" to handle that. The orb of an aspect refers to how many degrees **away** from exact the aspect can be, and still be considered relevant. (If, for example, an individual's Sun is at 5° Capricorn and the Moon is at 10° Capricorn, are the Sun and Moon conjunct? What if the Moon is at 15° or 20° or Capricorn? Is that still a conjunction?) Astrologers have differing opinions in regard to orb, but all agree that the tighter (closer to exact) an aspect is, the more important it is! So closer aspects are given more weight in any analysis. (A table of suggested orbs is provided later.)

As has already been indicated, a conjunction is not the only aspect which exists, but the conjunction is the most significant of all aspects. Other aspects (angular separations between the planets) provide additional information regarding the drives represented by the planets. Subject to the complications discussed briefly above, aspects other than the conjunction fall into two groups:

(1) **cooperative** (indicating parts of our nature which tend to combine easily, support and reinforce one another, where we may overdo) and (2) **challenging** (indicating parts of our nature which tend to be at odds with one another; where we have to work to make room for differing drives, for ambivalent needs). With **any** aspect, the nature of the two planets involved is **most** significant, but some additional subtle shadings are implied, depending upon the aspect involved.

One can consider the conjunction the fundamental aspect. Even if two planets make an aspect other than a conjunction, it is worthwhile to read the text interpreting a conjunction between them, as it will usually delineate the major issues and themes involved. Actually, it is a good idea to read all the descriptions of the planet-pairs which are aspecting each other in your chart. Even with a cooperative aspect, there may still be some issues you are working on, and you may have resolved the tension suggested by a challenging aspect so that you are handling the two sides of life quite successfully.

Five aspects other than the conjunction are considered important by many astrologers. Most are a division of the 360° circle by a whole number (e.g., division by 2, 3, 4, and 6). Following is a list of the six major aspects plus a few key words indicating the meaning of each aspect. Also listed is the symbol astrologers use for each aspect and the fraction of the circle which each aspect represents. Illustrations follow to graphically show the angular relationships between planets. (Other aspects exist besides those listed here, but these are the basics.)

0°: conjunction—unifying, blending, combining, living together, role models, intensification, concentration, focus ♂.

60°: (one-sixth of the circle): **sextile**—mild harmony; compatibility; may be opportunity, attraction or support ⚹.

90°: (one-fourth of the circle): **square**—conflict, competition, challenges, inner and/or outer tension, may point to turning points □.

120°: (one-third of the circle): **trine**—harmony, mutual reinforcement which could lead to excesses, easy flow, natural talents △.

150°: (five-twelfths of the circle): **quincunx**—difficult to combine, very different desires, seeming incompatibility, may feel like a forced choice is necessary, tendency to pull apart, may need to improve/adjust or to figure out what to keep and what to throw away ⚻.

180°: (one-half of the circle): **opposition**—polarities, natural partners, seesaw tendencies, potential for awareness (and projection—attracting other people who express disowned parts of

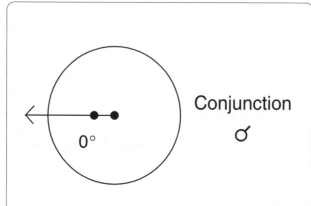

Conjunction

♂

Usually two planets are in the same sign and house.
Occasionally one will be very late in a sign (or house) and one
will be very early in the next sign or house.

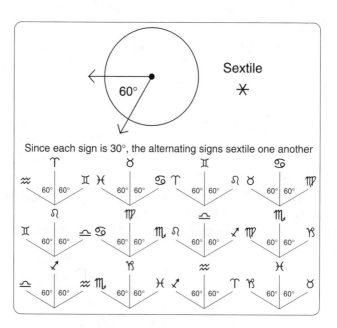

Sextile

✳

Since each sign is 30°, the alternating signs sextile one another

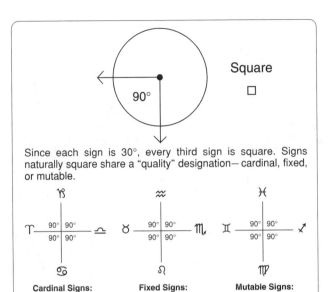

Since each sign is 30°, every third sign is square. Signs naturally square share a "quality" designation—cardinal, fixed, or mutable.

Cardinal Signs:
Aries, Cancer,
Libra, Capricorn

Fixed Signs:
Taurus, Leo,
Scorpio, Aquarius

Mutable Signs:
Gemini, Virgo,
Sagittarius, Pisces

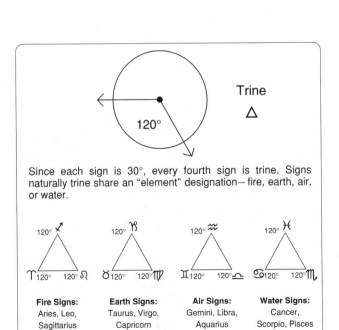

Since each sign is 30°, every fourth sign is trine. Signs naturally trine share an "element" designation—fire, earth, air, or water.

Fire Signs:
Aries, Leo,
Sagittarius

Earth Signs:
Taurus, Virgo,
Capricorn

Air Signs:
Gemini, Libra,
Aquarius

Water Signs:
Cancer,
Scorpio, Pisces

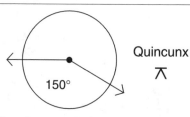

Quincunx ⩟

Quincunxing signs are 5 signs (150°) apart and different elements and qualities from one another.

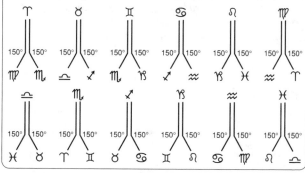

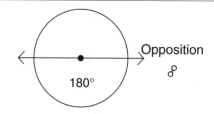

Opposition ☍

Opposing signs are 6 signs (180°) apart and share a quality (cardinal, fixed or mutable).

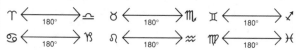

Cardinal:	**Fixed**	**Mutable:**
Aries/Libra	Taurus/Scorpio	Gemini/Sagittarius
Cancer/Capricorn	Leo/Aquarius	Virgo/Pisces

one's own nature), could flip from one extreme to the other until synthesis is reached ☍.

Following is a table of suggested orbs.

0°	conjunction	☌	8° orb (or 8 degrees + or -)
60°	sextile	⚹	3° orb (or 57 to 63 °)
90°	square	☐	6° orb (or 84 to 96 °)
120°	trine	△	6° orb (or 114 to 126 °)
150°	quincunx	⚻	3° orb (or 147 to 153 °)
180°	opposition	☍	6° orb (or 174 to 186 °)

Later in this text, you could look up example interpretations of your closest aspects. You can also experiment with simple keyword combinations for your aspects. Some sentences might sound a bit awkward. If so, a little thought will clarify matters. If, for example, the Sun conjuncts Venus, you might say: "Your life force is tied to your drive for pleasure." This suggests the person feels most vital and alive when indulging the physical senses, exercising aesthetic talents or engaged in activity with partners.

It is important to remember that all aspects can be reversed. Think in terms of an automatic "and vice versa" at the end of all your sentences. Thus, a Sun conjunct Mercury could be interpreted as: "Your self-esteem is tied to your ability to communicate." (Reverse: "Your ability to communicate is tied to your self-esteem.") This gets across the idea that the person gains pride and feels best about him/herself when communicating effectively. It also implies that the individual will **not** communicate well when feeling low in self-esteem.

In addition to the many psychological principles which aspects symbolize, they can point to issues in different life areas in the outer world which are associated with each planet. Aspects can be keys to how you might (or might not) get along with other people in your life. Following is a list of the people/objects in your life who can be represented by the planets.

Sun: loved ones (especially children/lovers); husband; leader; father; seller/promoter.

Moon: home; family; mother (figure); women; wife; the public; immovable resources; land; food; commodities.

Mercury: relatives; neighbors; short trips; brothers and sisters; means of transportation; trade/commerce.

Venus: self-earned money; possessions; the arts; partners.

Mars: personal action; men; competition; accidents; energy; physical body, mechanical objects, metal tools and weapons.

Jupiter: in-laws; grandchildren; long trips; higher education; sports; churches, libraries, law courts, publishing.

Saturn: authority figures; boss; older people; time; rules and roles; father (figure); societal structures, heights and falls.

Uranus: friends; groups; causes; science; technology; the new; progress; revolutions; astrology; sudden changes.

Neptune: mystical activities; drugs; glamor industries; film; secrets; illusions; psychic insights; inspired arts, healing arts.

Pluto: mates; hidden matters; occult studies; research; debts; pollution; obsessions; death/endings; unconscious complexes.

Cooperative (sextiles, trines) and challenging (squares, quincunxes and oppositions) aspects tend to be manifested more literally when other people are involved. Someone with a Moon-Mars square, quincunx or opposition, for example, is more likely to experience tension between men and women in his/her life (or at least be sensitive to such tension) than someone with a Moon-Mars trine or sextile.

Defense Mechanisms

People can and sometimes do attract outer conflicts as an unconscious mechanism for dealing with inner tension. Facing outer challenges may seem easier than dealing with inner ambivalences. If, however, we balance internally, outer relationships tend to flow more smoothly as well. Anyone with a Moon-Mars aspect (whether a conjunction, sextile, trine, square, quincunx or opposition) is facing inner issues around the integration of dependency and independence, separation and attachment, being alone and being together, spontaneous expression versus cautious holding in, and anger versus tenderness. The individual with a cooperative aspect is likely to find it somewhat easier to balance these different needs, than the individual with a challenging aspect, but both must face the Moon-Mars issues.

The three major defense mechanisms used by individuals to deal with inner conflict are **repression** (or denial), **projec-**

tion, and **displacement**. Repression means simply burying something in the unconscious and forgetting that we buried it. If we push something underground long enough, the most likely outcome is psychic stress and then (potentially) physical illness. Usually the illness is connected to whatever drive we are repressing. If we deny the Martian side of our nature, we may be subject to frequent headaches or colds; if we deny the Moon side of our nature, we may be subject to stomach problems. (Each planet is associated with different parts of the body, beginning with Mars and Aries for the head and ending with Pisces and Neptune at the feet. That, however, is a topic for another book. See, for example, the chapter on repression in *Healing with the Horoscope*.) If we find certain kinds of ailments recurring, however, it is worthwhile to query whether the issue might be related to unresolved needs and drives and not purely physical in manifestation.

Projection (like the projector of movies on a screen) refers to "projecting" our unrecognized needs or drives onto other people. Generally, however, this is not a matter of imagination, but rather a matter of unconsciously being attracted to people who manifest qualities we deny in ourselves. The psyche appears to abhor a vacuum and draws into our lives people who bring us face to face with what we have not developed within. The only problem is, the other person (living out our unrealized drive) is usually doing the expression to excess. As an example, the individual who totally denies his/her own Martian drive for assertion and self-expression may attract others who carry it to excess, perhaps in violence, perhaps in cutthroat competition, perhaps in extreme self-centeredness.

Projection offers us an opportunity to recognize what we have been denying and make a **moderate** place for it in our lives and psyches. The goal is not to become like the other person (who is usually overdoing what we have been underdoing), but to recognize the validity of that inner need and find a constructive outlet for it.

Displacement refers to doing the right thing in the wrong place. At times we may express our different drives and needs, but perhaps in circumstances which are inappropriate. That does not mean those drives or needs are "bad"—only that we need to find the "right" time and place to express them. As an example, the degree of assertion and aggression which would be appropriate on a football field is not appropriate for a quiet evening at home with friends or family. Each of us has a Martian side and must choose when, where, and how to express it constructively.

Aspect Review

When first learning aspects, mixing and matching key words can be instructive. You might say, for example, with a Jupiter-Saturn conjunction that your career (Saturn) is tied to (conjunct) travel, education or philosophy (Jupiter). You could also say that your world view (Jupiter) is likely to be (conjunct) realistic (Saturn). Another choice would be that father or authority figures (Saturn) are (conjunct) jovial, extraverted, confident, extravagant or optimistic (Jupiter). Or you might idealize (Jupiter) your father (Saturn) or be disillusioned by his failure (Saturn) to live up to your ideals (Jupiter). And there are many other combinations available! By mixing and matching aspect key words and planetary key words you can come up with additional possibilities. Be open to seeing the variety of potentials that astrology pictures.

Practice Example

Check what you've learned about spotting aspects with the horoscope below. Remember that each sign has 30 degrees and each degree has 60 minutes.

First, we consider **conjunctions**. Are there any planets occupying the same degree of the same sign? No. Are there any planets within 8 degrees (our allowable orb) of each other? No. There are, however, planets within 8 degrees of our horoscope angles. Mercury is 1° 28′ away from the 7th house cusp (also called the Descendant). [The Descendant is 25 Pisces 32 and Mercury is 24 Pisces 04. That is a difference of 1° 28′.] The Moon is 2° 10′ from the 10 house cusp (Midheaven). Saturn is 8° 0′ from the 1st house cusp (Ascendant). Mars is 5° 48′ from the 4th house cusp (also called I.C.).

We might expect, then, Saturnian themes (responsible, hardworking, career-oriented) in terms of identity and self-expression (the Ascendant). We would expect Martian themes (active, restless, assertive, independent) in terms of the home

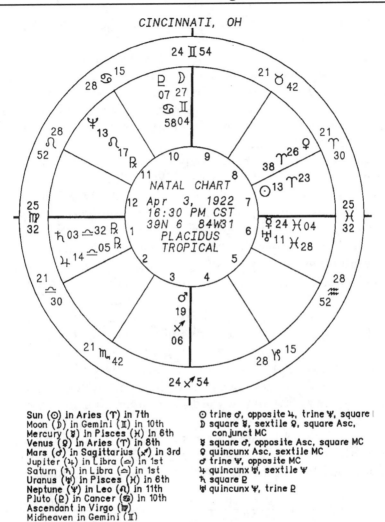

CINCINNATI, OH

NATAL CHART
Apr 3, 1922
16:30 PM CST
39N 6   84W31
PLACIDUS
TROPICAL

Sun (☉) in Aries (♈) in 7th
Moon (☽) in Gemini (♊) in 10th
Mercury (☿) in Pisces (♓) in 6th
Venus (♀) in Aries (♈) in 8th
Mars (♂) in Sagittarius (♐) in 3rd
Jupiter (♃) in Libra (♎) in 1st
Saturn (♄) in Libra (♎) in 1st
Uranus (♅) in Pisces (♓) in 6th
Neptune (♆) in Leo (♌) in 11th
Pluto (♇) in Cancer (♋) in 10th
Ascendant in Virgo (♍)
Midheaven in Gemini (♊)

☉ trine ♂, opposite ♃, trine ♆, square
D square ♅, sextile ♀, square Asc,
   conjunct MC
♅ square ♂, opposite Asc, square MC
♀ quincunx Asc, sextile MC
♂ trine ♆, opposite MC
♃ quincunx ♅, sextile ♆
♄ square ♇
♅ quincunx ♆, trine ♇

and family (4th cusp). We would suspect Mercurial issues (communication, thinking, and work, health, competence) to be significant in relationships. We would look for a lunar (Moon) focus (family, nurturing, emotional closeness, caring, protection) within the career (Midheaven).

Sextiles are 60° aspects. In this chart we have the Sun and Moon in signs naturally sextile each other, but the Sun and Moon are farther apart than the 3° orb we are allowing for sextiles. Venus and the Moon are not too far apart, however. The Moon is 60° 26′ away from Venus—well within our orb.

Also, Jupiter is 60° 48' ahead of Neptune—again an allowable sextile.

The Venus/Moon cooperative s spect (sextiles) ugsgests friendliness, sociability, charm, grace and attractiveness. The feminine is highlighted in that combination as both planets can signify women. The Jupiter/Neptune sextile suggests idealism, quest for something more, desire to rescue, save, or uplift in some fashion.

Squares (90°) are next. We note that the Sun barely makes a square to Pluto (with an orb of 5°25'). The Moon squares the Ascendant/Descendant axis (with an orb of 1° 32'). The Moon also squares Mercury (orb of 3° 0'). This individual may feel tension between thinking (Mercury) and feeling (Moon) and may be torn between nurturing and protecting (Moon), versus defending her own rights and needs (Ascendant) versus sharing the world with another person (Descendant). Pluto squares Saturn and the orb is 4° 26'. The Pluto squares to Sun and Saturn can be indicators of power struggles, especially with authority figures. It is usually helpful to channel the drive into competitive sports, business, or politics where we fight for causes in a constructive manner. Mars squares Mercury with an orb of 4° 58'. This suggests a quick mind, a quick tongue and possibly the ability to use words as weapons (debate, sarcasm, extemporaneous speaking, etc.).

Notice that all of the angles of this horoscope are closely square one another: the Ascendant (and the Descendant) square the IC (and the Midheaven) with an orb of 0° 38'. This configu-

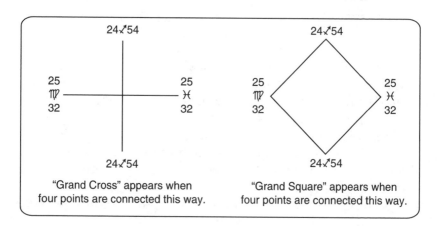

"Grand Cross" appears when four points are connected this way.

"Grand Square" appears when four points are connected this way.

ration, of four planets or points each 90° from the next, is called a **grand cross** or **grand square**. It indicates more inner conflict and challenge than four, unrelated squares. Since the angles occupy mutable signs, we would expect the issues to particularly revolve around issues of thinking, communication, and idealism. A mutable challenge includes tension between the real and the ideal—the necessities of getting along in the world, making a living and understanding others—versus our dreams and visions of utopia, something more, and something ecstatic or inspirational. A common manifestation is wanting more than is possible, never being satisfied. A more positive potential is a marriage of practicality and idealism so that the person works hard (and sensibly) to achieve his/her dreams over time.

The Sun **trines** (120°) Neptune very closely; the orb is zero degrees and only 6 minutes! (The Sun is just within the 6° [5°43′] orb of a trine to Mars.) Neptune trines Mars (orb of 5° 49′). Both Neptune aspects point to strong, personal idealism, romanticism, urge to rescue, compassion and potential grace in action or beauty in motion. Mars trine Sun suggests high energy, enthusiasm, courage and fighting spirit. We also note that Uranus trines Pluto (with an orb of 3° 30′). This can suggest the political reformer, the person who puts passion into humanitarian instincts, the individual who can balance their needs for independence and for emotional commitment.

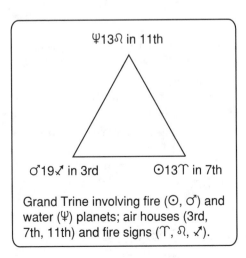

Grand Trine involving fire (☉, ♂) and water (♆) planets; air houses (3rd, 7th, 11th) and fire signs (♈, ♌, ♐).

This chart has a **grand trine**—three planets, each 120° [give or take our 6° orb] from the next (Sun, Neptune, Mars). Grand trines indicate strong inner harmony, talents and abilities (but also potential excess) more emphatically than three, unrelated trines.

Trines in fire signs (or involving Sun, Mars, Jupiter or 1st, 5th, 9th houses) point to confidence, extraversion, expression, faith, movement and initiation. Trines in earth signs (or involving Venus, Mercury, Saturn or 2nd, 6th, 10th houses) point to practicality, a literal focus, concern with tangible results, ability in the material plane. Trines in air signs (or involving Mercury, Venus or Uranus or 3rd, 7th, 11th houses) point to communication skills, capacity to detach and be objective, a focus on ideas and people. Trines in water signs (or involving

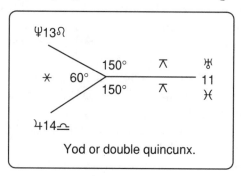

Yod or double quincunx.

Moon, Pluto, Neptune or 4th, 8th, 12th houses) point to sensitivity, intuition, inward tendencies, merging instincts, emotional depth.

Quincunxes are next (150°). Uranus forms two quincunxes. One is to Neptune (1° 49′ orb) and the other is to Jupiter (2° 37′ orb). You will recall that Jupiter and Neptune are sextile one another. This aspect configuration of two planets sextile each other and both quincunx a third is called a "yod" or double quincunx. It carries even more restlessness and instability than two unrelated quincunxes.

The yod of Uranus to Neptune and Jupiter suggests a challenge integrating idealism with independence, or compassion with detachment. Restlessness and constant activity are likely in the transpersonal realm (dealing with large issues and the wider reach of humanity).

Finally, we consider **oppositions** (180°). The Sun is closely opposite Jupiter (with an orb of 0° 42′). This opposition highlights emotional idealism, the importance of beliefs and values, the capacity to be swept away in "grand" projects, a need for excitement, expansion and a tendency to seek the best. Although they occupy opposing signs (Aries/Libra), the Sun is too far from an exact opposition to Saturn to count it (past a 6° orb). The Moon and Mars are naturally opposite in terms of their signs, but are outside our allowable orb. Similarly, Venus to Saturn and to Jupiter, although in opposite signs, are not within the 6° orb we are using.

For the curious reader, these aspects and the horoscope above belong to Doris Day—an actress noted for her family-oriented movies in which she played very feminine, charming roles. She is now a political activist on behalf of animals (founder of the Doris Day Animal League which campaigns against animal testing and abuses of animals).

Aspect Interpretations in YOUR Horoscope

When reading any interpretations of aspects, first read the interpretation **as if** those planets were conjunct. The conjunction is the most basic, fundamental aspect and its themes carry through with other aspects. For the other aspects, read also the interpretation of cooperating (sextile, trine) or challenging (square, quincunx, opposition) for the planets involved, but remember that other factors in the horoscope might suggest that life drives with harmony aspects still may require some attention, and you might have already integrated some of the conflict which were present at birth.

In all cases, we are dealing with trying to blend inner drives as well as different needs (and/or people) in our lives. The potentials inherent in any given placement might be overridden by other configurations in the chart. Particularly where challenges are involved, we are susceptible to repression, displacement or projection. As you read the interpretations for the various "pieces" of your chart, bear in mind that certain pieces will tend to suppress others. As always, repeated themes that recur again and again are most likely to manifest in your psyche and in your life.

CHAPTER THREE

THE SUN
THE SOURCE OF LIGHT AND LIFE IN YOUR HOROSCOPE

The Sun in Signs: *Receiving Recognition*

Here's a quick look at some of the possibilities implied by the zodiacal sign of your Sun.

SUN IN ARIES

- **YOU NEED TO SHINE THROUGH VALOR, BRAVERY.**
- **YOU SHINE ASSERTIVELY.**

This might indicate that you can gain favorable attention through being courageous or assertive. You are likely to seek direct, competitive action. You may be a natural leader, who tends to take charge and be center stage. (If carried too far, pushiness or arrogance is possible. You may be too forceful in expressing yourself or too rash in your undertakings.) You need to be proud of your strength of will and drive.

- **YOU NEED TO SHINE BY BEING FIRST.**

This can indicate that you naturally seek pioneering, ground-breaking activities or that it is vital to your ego (perhaps too much so) to be in the forefront. You need to be proud of your initiative, your ability to venture.

• YOU SEEK RECOGNITION ENERGETICALLY/ IMPETUOUSLY.

This might suggest you actively seek attention, but could sometimes be impulsive in your avenues. It also implies that your instincts (immediate impulses) might sometimes bring you into the limelight. You radiate forceful, confident vitality.

• YOU NEED TO SHINE IN YOUR TOTAL SELF-EXPRESSION.

This implies that you want to be admired for all that you are. Personal pride or shame could be central issues in your desire to be fully yourself. You want to be proud of everything you do.

SUN IN TAURUS

• YOU NEED TO SHINE COMFORTABLY.

Your quest for attention, limelight, or applause could be at odds with your desire for comfort, for pleasure without much effort. You may seek recognition in a manner which allows you to be relaxed and easygoing. You may want to be admired for your ability to be at ease.

• YOU SEEK RECOGNITION DELIBERATELY.

You are willing to be slow and steady in your pursuit of renown or attention. You may embark on a regular program to achieve the limelight, building for lasting results. Patience and persistence can lead to stardom.

• YOU NEED TO SHINE IN YOUR DEPENDABILITY.

You are likely to be proud of your dependability. If overdone, you might be too predictable and reluctant to change, denying your creativity. But to those who want steady performance, your regularities may be admired. You can gain recognition for your reliability and take pride in your stability.

• YOUR DRIVE FOR RECOGNITION MANIFESTS THROUGH SENSUALITY AND/OR POSSESSIONS.

You may gain favorable feedback through your handling of sensuality, money or possessions. You could be proud of what you own, or purchase only the finest of things. A sense of luxury is possible. You may shine at getting and/or giving sensual gratification or material goods.

SUN IN GEMINI

- **YOU NEED TO SHINE FLUENTLY.**
You may gain or seek recognition for your verbal skills. This could vary from the teacher/professor to the neighborhood gossip, from the punster to the user of an extensive vocabulary, from the chatterbox to the linguist, etc. You can be quite creative in terms of your perceptiveness and ability to compare, contrast, and find connections between concepts.

- **YOU NEED TO SHINE BY BEING VERSATILE.**
You are likely to be proud of your versatility (or ashamed of your tendency to scatter with multiple interests). Driven by wide-ranging curiosity, you may shine in diverse areas. A wide variety of talents, social contacts and hobbies aid your self-expression.

- **YOU SEEK RECOGNITION FOR YOUR MENTAL BRILLIANCE.**
You want to feel proud of your intelligence, rationality and logic. You are likely to be ego-vulnerable in terms of your mental and communication skills. Pride/shame issues are tied to your mind. You need to express yourself verbally and to gain favorable recognition for your intellect.

- **YOU NEED TO SHINE FOR NIMBLENESS/ FLEXIBILITY.**
You could achieve attention for your nimbleness, dexterity, adaptability, or good hand-eye coordination. (This can range from the skilled typist, surgeon, musician, etc., to the pickpocket.) You may be good at gymnastics or yoga. You could be recognized for your dexterity or flexibility.

SUN IN CANCER

- **YOU MAY SHINE THROUGH NURTURING WARMTH**
You could be very ego-involved with the giving of compassion and emotional nurturing. You may feel strongest when acting in a warm, motherly kind of way. You may be proud of your capacity to care, of your empathy and sensitivity. Your self-

esteem may be tied to your ability to provide emotional security to others. Your concern may be noteworthy.

- **YOU NEED TO SHINE THROUGH PROTECTION.**

You may be proud of your ability to take care of others. This can range from the very responsible parent to the super-patriot (guarding the homeland). You might feed people, clothe them, house them, guard them. If overdone, you could be arrogant in your assumption that you know what people need. You may be proud of and gain applause through your efforts to provide safety or to preserve the past. Your charisma and natural magnetism are most likely to emerge when you feel strong while protecting others who are weaker than you.

- **YOU ATTRACT OTHERS THROUGH SYMPATHY/ DEPENDENCY.**

You may seek and gain attention and love by being dependent, leaning on others, looking to them for support and appreciating their assistance. Weakness can attract people who gain pleasure and self-esteem from protecting and helping others. It is really easier and more satisfying to give than to receive. But in the end, to maintain healthy relationships, there needs to be both "give and take," so it is important that you continue to give love and gratitude in return for the assistance. For you, pride/shame are connected to mutual caring and genuine empathy.

- **YOU SEEK TO SHINE THROUGH FAMILY, ANCESTRY OR ROOTS.**

You are likely to be quite proud (or ashamed) of your family. You may be ego-involved with your ancestral ties, family background or genealogical roots. You might seek recognition and attention through a majestic or impressive home or be eager to praise your homeland. Your self-esteem tends to be on the line, subject to the state of your family, and you may take their behavior too personally or too much to heart. Yet you can be a great motivator, full of praise and admiration for those you love.

SUN IN LEO

- **YOU NEED TO SHINE THROUGH CREATIVE ACTIVITIES.**

You are likely to seek and/or gain attention through creative acts, whether by the procreation of children, by artistic creativity or by activities that put you in front of people, including drama, teaching, selling, promotion, etc. You may be very ego-involved with your creations (including the potential danger of looking to your children to build your own self-esteem, to do the creative things you wanted to do).

- **YOU SEEK RECOGNITION THROUGH RISK-TAKING OR EXCITING ACTIVITIES.**

You may be proud of your ability to risk, to try the new, to gamble or speculate for the potential of greater gain. You might gain recognition (positive or negative) from others for your involvement in exciting or thrilling activities.

- **YOU NEED TO SHINE THROUGH YOUR GENEROSITY.**

You probably want to be proud of your generosity, your ability to give whether on the material, emotional or spiritual level. When you give for the pleasure of giving, you only need to guard against giving too much and weakening the recipient. If you hope for admiration and gratitude, you become ego-vulnerable to people's responses. It takes faith, in yourself or in life, to be able to give. Your own confidence and your ability to encourage others can keep you in the limelight and can revitalize any activity.

- **YOU SHINE CHARISMATICALLY.**

You probably have natural stage presence. People are likely to notice you. Your dramatic instincts are strong though they may be used positively or negatively. (It is legitimate to build yourself up but not so constructive to do it by putting others down). You may want to shine in everything you do, and be too ego-dependent on constant attention from others, with your feeling of pride (or shame) too vulnerable to the responses of others. You can be vital, vibrant and exciting, with emotions which are heartfelt, spontaneous, eternally young, and which influence almost everything you do.

SUN IN VIRGO

- **YOU NEED TO SHINE FOR YOUR COMPETENCE.**
You want to be proud of your careful attention to details, your dedication to being thorough, organized and systematic. You may be driven by a need to be helpful, to be of tangible service to others, or you may seek to function effectively for the sake of doing it right. If you are too invested in your personal approach, you might feel that your way is the only correct way. Your pride/shame is strongly connected to your skills. You may be noted for your precision.

- **YOU NEED TO SHINE IN YOUR WORK OR HEALTH.**
You can achieve recognition for super-efficiency (or the exact reverse—inefficiency) in your job or in your health. Manifestations can range from the workaholic (who lives for his/her job) to the health food fanatic (who tells everyone how to be healthy) to the invalid (who gains the limelight by reciting a history of ailments, surgeries, etc.). It is also possible to refuse to work at a job which is unworthy of your talents, too ordinary, or fails to provide recognition from others and a sense of your own power. With acceptance of the true spirit of Virgo, you might work in a healing profession or in many forms of service which meet the basic needs of society. When functioning positively, you are admired for your contributions to the world.

- **YOU SEEK RECOGNITION FOR BEING PRAGMATIC.**
You are probably proud of your common sense, your ability to find realistic ways to accomplish goals and to enhance the functioning of people, tasks, and tools. Your capacity to be analytical and discriminating can help you see what will work. You may seek to constantly improve yourself (as well as repairing the world), realizing that it will take time and effort and can only be done one step at a time. You may gain attention for your patience, logic and ability to be reasonable.

- **YOU NEED TO SHINE FOR YOUR DISCRETION.**
In an ironic twist, you are likely to seek notice for your ability to avoid notice! You may gain positive feedback for your discreet handling of touchy subjects, or be applauded by others for your willingness to be dedicated, to serve, and to remain the power behind the throne. Your willingness to be humble could

hold you back from achieving public recognition. Your helpfulness and desire to assist others is considerable.

SUN IN LIBRA

• **YOU NEED TO SHINE FOR YOUR COOPERATION.**
You may feel proud of your capacity to cooperate with others. You may seek recognition for your kindness, fairness, impartiality, or capacity to see both sides of an issue and to find a compromise position. Your ego is often on the line in relationships. You want to be admired by other people, especially in one-to-one situations, including marriage, business partnerships and counseling relationships.

• **YOU MAY SEEK TO SHINE AT FENCE-SITTING OR DIPLOMACY**
You may sometimes be too other-oriented or concerned with the approval of other people. (Too much focus on pleasing others can inhibit your own self-expression.) You can be noteworthy in your handling of comparisons, contrasts and dualities, but might be so aware of all the relevant factors that you have difficulty in making decisions. You are likely to constantly seek balance in your relationships and in your life.

• **YOU SEEK RECOGNITION THROUGH AESTHETIC CHANNELS.**
You may achieve notice through aesthetic creativity, especially areas involving the visual arts (photography, design, decorating, painting, fashion). You may be proud of your fine taste or feeling for beauty. You may radiate grace, sociability and a refined approach to beauty.

• **YOU MAY SHINE IN COMPETITION/ONE-ON-ONE.**
You can achieve the limelight in relationships through competitive interactions, including sports, games, a competitive business, or (less comfortably) through "game-playing" in relationships as described by Eric Berne in *Games People Play*. In healthy competition, we win some and lose some and are aware that the goal is to have fun. Unhealthy competition includes fighting against members of one's own team or taking the results too seriously. In healthy interactions, both partners can admire each other.

SUN IN SCORPIO

- **YOU NEED TO SHINE PASSIONATELY.**

Pride and shame are intense emotional issues for you. In some ways, you are the most private of all people, yet you also crave an intimate bond with a mate. The sharing could include finances, possessions, sensuality, and/or sexuality. You may gain positive or negative attention for your handling of money, sex and power. Your seeking of recognition through your sensuality probably has an all-or-nothing flavor. Withdrawal could be tempting at times, but ultimately, you need to share your passion.

- **YOU NEED TO SHINE FOR YOUR POWER/ RESOURCEFULNESS.**

You may gain attention for your handling of power (use, abuse, misuse) or resourcefulness. You have tremendous reserves and inner depths which can work for the dark (destructive) or the light (life-affirming) side. You may exhibit impressive self-discipline and self-mastery.

- **YOU SEEK RECOGNITION FOR YOUR PENETRATION.**

You are likely to feel proud of your ability to look beneath the surface of life. Possible expressions could include an attraction to mysteries, archaeology, detection, the capacity to see layers within layers and to probe into the underlying motives of people. You are likely to be intuitive, sensitive to nonverbal messages and hidden agendas. You want to get to the inner essence (core) of people and their experiences and may seek an intimate experience of merging.

- **YOU MIGHT GAIN THE LIMELIGHT THROUGH COMPULSIVE PERSISTENCE.**

Your compulsive attention to certain details or issues might be noteworthy (in a positive or negative sense). You can be doggedly determined and willful in your pursuit of certain paths. Obsessions could block your self-expressive flow, or inhibit your vitality until you learn to recognize when is enough and how to let go. You may be tempted to push the limits in life, going to the very end (perhaps to the edge of death). Analyze your inner motives to discover whether you are proving your power or following a blind urge to finish whatever you have started. You can be enormously successful if your perseverance is directed toward constructive ends.

SUN IN SAGITTARIUS

- **YOU NEED TO SHINE FOR YOUR BENEVOLENCE.**
You are likely to seek positive feedback for your generous outlook. You may be proud of your openness of spirit and wholehearted thrust into life. You may also be noteworthy for your lavish scale of living whether in terms of money, fun, understanding or other activities. You tend to view things in **big** terms and could sometimes exaggerate or overdo. You may also share grandly with those around you. You may be proud of your positive attitude. You tend to radiate a friendly, open spirit, and could be quite magnanimous.

- **YOU SHINE THROUGH OPTIMISM/ENTHUSIASM.**
You may gain attention for your enthusiasm and optimistic outlook. You could find it easy to inspire others and probably have talent for promotion, sales, or anything expansive and broadening. If carried too far, this could manifest as overconfidence, carelessness, leaping to conclusions or wheeling and dealing without a practical base. You may scintillate in your faith. You are a natural cheerleader.

- **YOU MAY GAIN ATTENTION THROUGH UNLIMITED FREEDOM.**
You tend to value freedom on all levels, physical, emotional, mental, and spiritual. You can gain recognition as the avid sportsperson who keeps the body in motion; the chronic bachelor-bachelorette who has trouble settling down in one relationship; the perpetual student-teacher-travelor who constantly seeks new knowledge, or the preacher-guru-seeker for ultimate Truth. You could be proud of your independence and thrive in an atmosphere of openness and limitless possibilities.

- **YOU SEEK RECOGNITION FOR YOUR IDEALS.**
You need to feel proud of what you believe in and value. Issues of morality, ethics and justice strongly affect your inner sense of pride or shame. You need recognition for being moral, but excessively high standards could lead you to be self-righteous

or intolerant of the foibles of others. You aspire toward the heights in life. You are drawn to promote your ideals with others as well as pursuing them yourself.

SUN IN CAPRICORN

- **YOU NEED TO SHINE THROUGH RESPONSIBILITY.**
You take pride in (or are ashamed of) your handling of responsibility. You can successfully climb the hierarchical ladder to power, attention and the limelight by managing your share of the power as you go. You may be noticed for your willingness to take charge and get things done. Your inner vitality can be fed by tangible accomplishments.

- **YOU NEED TO SHINE TRADITIONALLY.**
You are likely to follow traditional paths in seeking attention. You may shine in your ability to fit the established mold. Your quest for recognition tends to be sensible, formal, and in line with customs. Caution and control temper your creative spirit. Too much pessimism, cynicism, or concern with what is "proper" might inhibit your self-expression. It is also possible to hold back for fear of failing or falling short. But with a realistic evaluation of what is necessary and what is possible, you can set reasonable goals and achieve them.

- **YOU SEEK ATTENTION THROUGH AUTHORITY OR AUTHORITIES.**
You may seek an authoritative role as an avenue for positive attention and admiration. Or, you may admire authority figures, or act in ways which you hope will bring favorable attention from those in power. You might overrate the importance of powerful people and undervalue the attitudes of "ordinary" associates. Pride/shame issues are close to the surface in dealing with the power structure. Sustained ambition can help you achieve your goals.

- **YOU MAY GAIN LIMELIGHT/ATTENTION THROUGH YOUR CAREER.**
You may gain prominence through your professional role in society. Your career is a potential avenue to feeling proud of yourself and gaining recognition from others (or you may feel ashamed of your vocation). You are ego-invested in your accomplishments and your self-esteem might be too dependent

on worldly measures of success. But success is very likely if you combine your potential creativity with clear goals and willingness to work in a self-disciplined way.

SUN IN AQUARIUS

- **YOU MAY SHINE UNIQUELY/INVENTIVELY.**

Your avenues for recognition or attention are likely to be unique to you. You may be admired as an individualist, criticized as an eccentric, or dismissed as simply quirky. You may invent other paths to the limelight or positive (and negative) feedback from others. Your self-expression is tied to a need for freedom to experiment. You are likely to pride yourself on not being like anyone else.

- **YOU MAY SEEK RECOGNITION REBELLIOUSLY OR INDEPENDENTLY.**

You may fight against standard formats for "success" or "fame" and seek recognition as a rebel. You may adopt a "maverick" approach to getting the limelight, perhaps being noticed despite yourself, or because of your opposition to tradition. You may be friendly with peers but highly resistant to anyone who attempts any kind of coercion. Patrick Henry was talking about you when he said "Give me liberty or give me death."

- **YOU MAY SHINE FUTURISTICALLY.**

You are likely to be ego-involved with progress, either proud or ashamed of your contributions to the future. You could achieve recognition through forward-looking activities or ideas, including work with new technology, avant garde science, space, computers or anything on the cutting edge of change. You could take a leadership role in groups or organizations which look ahead.

- **YOU MAY SHINE BY BEING RATIONAL.**

You may achieve recognition for your objectivity and logic. Your intellectual detachment and sangfroid may be noteworthy. You could apply your mental skills to any field of science, technology, new age ideas, research or teaching. You are likely to be proud of your independent mind. Your creativity might be directed toward innovative approaches to humanitarian causes and social welfare, being careful to analyze the options without any emotional bias.

SUN IN PISCES

• YOU MAY SHINE BY CREATING BEAUTY.

You could gain recognition through your artistic talents, or skills with the aesthetic side of life. Whether you are attracted to music, painting, poetry, drama, dance or any other artistic expression, you can build your self-esteem through your efforts to make a more beautiful world. Keep your expectations reasonable. The absolute level of one's skills is less important than continuing expression and further development of potentials.

• YOU MAY SHINE THROUGH YOUR COMPASSION.

You are likely to feel proud (or ashamed) of your compassion and ability to empathize with others. Your heart might bleed for the whole world, or you might be so personally sensitive that you feel even unintended hurts from others. Your self-esteem may require you to always be giving, healing and helping anyone who suffers. Remember that when compassion for others is carried too far, the savior can turn into a martyr. Sometimes, we can be most helpful by setting an example, demonstrating how to be a happy person, rather than crawling into the quicksand with a sufferer. Look for ways to encourage others, ways to help them develop their own strength.

• YOU MAY SHINE THROUGH PSYCHIC OPENNESS.

Your intuition and psychic insight may provide a tool for recognition and (positive or negative) attention from others. You may receive information through dreams, visions, thoughts, or impressions through any of the senses. It is important to test your impressions against experience and logic since the unconscious can also offer us wishful thinking and unrealistic fears. You may be attracted to magic as a tool to bring dreams into form in the material world. You may achieve center stage through your ability to live in both the physical and in the invisible worlds. Try to be clear about which experiences are mental creations, illusions, romance, drama, dreams, visions, and which are the kind of reality that does not go away no matter how much you don't believe in it. Your personal vitality may sometimes be affected if you let yourself be swept away by someone else's reality or by your own imagination.

- **YOU MAY SEEK RECOGNITION THROUGH SPIRITUAL OR MYSTICAL PATHS.**

You could be ego-vulnerable in your approach to spiritual, transcendent activities, feeling torn between normal ego needs for attention and mystical urges to be absorbed into something Higher. Humans need a healthy sense of self-esteem as individuals but do not need to put anyone else down to achieve it. When experiencing a state of "oneness," you may "absorb" the trials and tribulations of other people or you might just temporarily lose your own sense of self-expression and individuality. Alternately, there is a danger of feeling that you are the Whole, which can lead to the ego-inflation and grandiosity seen in some professional gurus. You need a place and a time to experience the Whole, with an equal need to be conscious and responsible as an individual when you are facing physical facts (such as driving a car, earning a living, caring for children). Life is always a balancing act. You **can** come from your own center and still share a Higher Reality. You may be inspired (or inspire others) through art, music, nature, religion, spiritual ideals. Beauty, art, nature, prayer, meditation and similar activities feed your inner vitality and spirit.

Remember, we have only considered some of the possibilities suggested by your Sun sign. Lots more could be said concerning this single factor, but it's time to take a look at where your Sun is placed in your horoscope.

The Sun in Houses: *Achieving Admiration*

SUN IN 1ST HOUSE

Your sense of self-esteem is central to your identity. You want to feel proud of everything that you do (your whole being). Your ego is on the line in terms of your personal behavior, appearance and capacity to assert yourself. You may be quite charismatic, instinctively dramatic—someone people naturally notice. You may rejoice in self-expression and pioneering activities. Your creativity might break new ground. You may instinctively take risks and seek to do more than you have done before. However, it is also possible to feel self-conscious or ashamed of how you present yourself in the world. You may be too susceptible to the opinions of others, craving their admiration. Your inner drive to be "larger than life" may cause you to freeze up and be afraid to try at times. When you release your natural spontaneity, you have much potential enthusiasm, dynamism and exuberance at your fingertips.

You need excitement and independence in your love relationships. You deal best with lovers and children who can feed your urge for activity, risk-taking and creative expansion. If these qualities are denied within you, your loved ones may be excessively self-centered, rash, independent, aggressive or impatient. If you share life's sparkle, kindling each other's zest and joyful spirit, you can bring much light, love and fun to one another.

SUN IN 2ND HOUSE

Your sense of self-esteem is tied to what you have and to your capacity to enjoy the physical world. You may be a creative artist, with a real flair for beauty. Your creativity might find form in sensual, tactile objects. Alternately, your self-esteem might be connected to your income. You may measure your worth and be proud or ashamed on the basis of your bank account or what you own. You may seek admiration for your possessions, buying only the "best" or most luxurious. Your dramatic instincts could flower in the realm of physical sense pleasures and gratification. You are likely to spend money on impulse at times, but can be quite generous as well. In general, you may rejoice in sensuality and the "good things" of life.

You need stability, physical comfort and pleasure in your love relationships. Mutual affection is quite possible with this placement. Giving and receiving love may flow naturally with children and others close to you. An easygoing attitude could contribute to positive exchanges with others. If you deny the placid, grounded side of your nature, lovers or children might enact it for you. They could be too hedonistic, self-indulgent, materialistic, stolid, boring, or stubborn. When pleasures are shared, you support each other's need for beauty and material gratification. You enjoy pleasing one another, are easily contented and find a sense of ease and comfort in one another's company.

SUN IN 3RD HOUSE

Your self-esteem is tied to the world of the mind and tongue. You may be quite proud (or ashamed) of how you think and/or how you communicate. Your ego is on the line in terms of your intellect and objectivity. You may strive to "star" in the classroom, and could be quite entertaining. Your dramatic instincts may express through word play, puns, word games (or intellectual snobbery, mental gymnastics and verbal power plays for attention). Exaggeration is likely, yet you can also rejoice in the exchange of information and ideas. With a quick mind and tongue, you can be onstage through any sharing of knowledge with others.

If you doubt and deny your mental ability, a relative (sibling, aunt, uncle, cousin, etc.) may play it out for you, often in excess. That individual could be too proud, too inclined to dominate the conversation, a verbal "show-off" or otherwise carry self-expression and being center stage to an extreme. You might bask in their reflected glory or gnash your teeth in envy. You are capable of very creative communication, gaining admiration for your speech or intellectual prowess if you own your very real skills here. You need to shine through your mind and capacity to learn, and you may also gain recognition for talent in using your hands.

You need mental stimulation in your love relationships. Magnetism is tied to an intellectual attraction in your case. You are drawn to variety, and the opportunity to always learn more. You appreciate a childlike freshness and lightheartedness. If these qualities are denied in you, your children or lovers may carry them to extremes. They might be flippant, excessively casual, scattered, superficial, gossipy or restless. If you are able to talk easily with your loved ones, you can learn much from one another (exchanging student and teacher roles), can communicate zestfully, and can encourage one another to risk whatever is necessary to gain more information and understanding.

SUN IN 4TH HOUSE

Your self-esteem is connected to home and family. The nurturing parent (usually mother or mother figure) in your household had a profound impact on your sense of pride and shame. The way you were (or were not) nurtured strongly affected your self-confidence, belief in yourself, creativity, and willingness to take risks in life. You might have had a very great love bond, with intense, joyful connections to family members. Or you might have had a parent who was childish, self-centered, arrogant, grandiose, dominating, or who constantly demanded attention (and center stage). Your early home shaped your capacity for zest, enthusiasm and a confident outreach into life. You may seek admiration for your warmth, nurturing or bonding capability. You are likely to have a strong family-feeling (proud or ashamed of family members) and you probably want children. You may rejoice in preserving, protecting, nourishing and giving love to others.

You need caring, security and a sense of emotional safety in your love relationships Your dramatic spirit emerges in private moments when you feel safe and secure. You can be quite creative in domestic and emotional realms. If the focus on protection, dependency and nurturing is expressed solely through your children or lovers, they are likely to overdo those qualities. They might be clinging, possessive, helpless or too emotionally intrusive. On the other hand, you may find support offered easily and freely by those you love, as you take turns taking care of one another. You are capable of making the deepest, most caring connections possible with those you love.

SUN IN 5TH HOUSE
Your self-esteem is tied to your creativity and your capacity to do more than you have done before. This placement indicates you need to pour out from your own center, expanding and accomplishing something to transcend the past. You need to take risks, in order to gain recognition or admiration for your self-expressive acts. With a naturally dramatic spirit, you could go onstage or be the center of attention in other ways. You might seek admiration for your emotional power or persuasive skills. You have the capacity to sway others through feelings; your inner child speaks to their inner child. Your zest, enthusiasm, spontaneity and fun-loving spirit can be quite contagious. You have natural skills for promotion, sales, teaching, recreation and/or anything that stirs excitement or involves risks, speculation, or the stimulation of emotions (e.g, through entertainment, stage, screen, etc.). You may be quite magnetic and charismatic.

You need excitement, joy and drama in your love relationships. Love, for you, feeds your sense of being alive. You are ego-vulnerable to those you love, intensely needing their positive feedback and attention. You are capable of a very great love bond. If your inner light is denied, your children or loved ones may overdo these themes. They could be ego-centered, hysterical, excitement addicts, or unwilling to share the stage. If both you and those you love share emotional warmth, you can be quite generous, powerful, magnetic and exciting. You will feed each other's willingness to risk for greater gain, to "go for the gusto," to seek joy in life. Loving, risk-taking and courtship feed your energy, vitality and enthusiasm for life.

SUN IN 6TH HOUSE

Your self-esteem is connected to functioning efficiently—either on the job or in your body (health)—or both. You may be either proud (or ashamed) of your level of health. You could rejoice in careful health habits, good nutrition, adequate exercise, or any other practices which promote healthful living. You might seek admiration for doing a good job, channeling your creativity into being efficient and productive. You may find joy in being competent, and express your dramatic spirit in your job. You may be willing to take risks vocationally. If you deny your onstage capacities, they might be carried to excess by colleagues or co-workers. People around you on the job might be demanding prima donnas, people who promise a lot and deliver very little, individuals who brag rather than doing, or people who chronically exaggerate. You need to feel that you are doing something worth doing and that you are doing it well. For full satisfaction, you also need positive feedback acknowledging your capacity to make a living and to maintain good physical functioning. You need respect for your effectiveness.

You need practicality and efficiency in your love relationships. It is important to you to do a good job. If you are not expressing that drive, your children or loved ones might overdo it for you. They could be excessively critical, judgmental, discriminating, nit-picking. They might work too hard (or not work at all). They could be health food freaks (or ill). A shared effort lets you and those you love work together. You all take pride in accomplishments and gain satisfaction through communal tasks which are handled sensibly and helpfully.

SUN IN 7TH HOUSE

Your self-esteem is tied to your relationships with other people, and you may be too vulnerable to the opinions of others. Positive feedback is especially important in your partnerships where you need to be admired, noticed and recognized. You may be proud (or ashamed) of your handling of relationships with others. You may seek admiration for diplomacy, fair play, balance and evenhandedness. In addition to your cooperative relationships, you might enjoy risk-taking, game-playing, or competitive activities. If you deny your own drama, charisma and natural self-confidence, a partner is apt to overdo it. S/he could be arrogant, exaggerative, egotistical, constantly demanding center stage. With integration, you are each other's best fans, encouraging one another to do more, admiring each other's accomplishments and being enthusiastic supporters of one another's efforts. You can rejoice in justice, equality, and beauty. You may also be proud of your talent for balance, design, color, line and form, and could enjoy creative artistic outlets.

You are drawn toward love relationships which feature ease, attractiveness, and pleasantness. You might sometimes focus too much on appearances (or attract loved ones who do so). Your children or beloved might be charming, vacillating or other-directed (or they could be naturally cooperative, attractive, sweet team players). Magnetism is tied to grace and charm within your family. You may shine through aesthetic talents, or through your flair for interpersonal relationships.

SUN IN 8TH HOUSE

Your self-esteem is tied to your capacity to dig beneath the surface in life (and in your own psyche) and to achieve self-mastery. You may seek admiration for your self-control, intensity or depth of insight. You could be proud (or ashamed) of your capacity to transform, regenerate and renew. You may rejoice in intense emotional exchanges, feeling that what really matters in life lies many layers down. Your ego could affect matters of sexuality and shared money and possessions. Power struggles over shared resources and pleasures are possible if either you or your mate is too ego-vulnerable and tries to overcontrol in these areas. Strong, passionate responses are likely in the realms of sex and money; you could be quite dramatic in dealing with financial and sensual issues. You are willing to face the "dark side" in yourself and others, mastering obsessive needs and drives. You may achieve recognition through your capacity to eliminate nonessentials and to creatively transform negatives into positives.

Your love relationships need an element of passion and should utterly fascinate you, with a compelling allure. An all-or-nothing tendency is likely in love relationships (and you may sometimes withdraw into a hermit or celibate lifestyle). If your own powerful inner urges are denied, children and/or lovers may express them in excess. They could be too intent on having their own way, demanding, manipulative, willful, or emotionally volatile. Yet you and those you love can be incredibly loyal and devoted to each other. You may experience magnetism on a gut level, with strong sensual and sexual overtones. You are learning to share possessions and pleasures, and to face the depths of your psyche with those closest to you. You can face the monsters (inside and outside) in order to achieve the heights of ecstasy.

SUN IN 9TH HOUSE

Your self-esteem is on the line in regard to education, religion, truth, or spiritual ideals. You may seek to prove your worth through amassing degrees, promoting a particular world view or philosophy, traveling all over the world, or being recognized as a guru or leader in metaphysics, ethics, or moral principles. You may seek admiration for your breadth of perspective and wide knowledge. You probably rejoice in exploring the world mentally (and often physically as well). Your creativity could be channeled toward adventures, expansion and big dreams. You may be proud (or ashamed) of your education, life philosophy or goals and values. You tend to seek the best, build your faith, be optimistic and trust in the future.

You need a sense of fun, expansion and idealism in your love relationships. You want love to be joyful, enlarging, broadening, and to always have a "happy ending." This can lead to expecting more than is possible of those you love (or they of you). It can also indicate seeing the highest potential in lovers, children, or grandchildren, and helping them to move toward a vision of brighter possibilities. You are willing to take risks for a greater return; you naturally seek the "big time." If you deny these enlarging potentials within, your children or beloved might carry them to excess. They might dream and never do, overextend themselves, exaggerate, expect the world to give them what they want, or just party a lot. They also could be philosophical, happy-go-lucky, or addicted to exploring. If these interests are shared, you encourage one another to visualize the best and work toward it. You feed one another's humor, confidence, faith and love of knowledge.

SUN IN 10TH HOUSE

Your self-esteem is tied to your professional standing and status in the community. You are ego-vulnerable in terms of your career and position in society. You want to be noticed and recognized, to gain a position of power and expertise. You may be proud (or ashamed) of your vocation and your contribution to society. Your capacity to handle your responsibilities strongly affects your self-worth.

Your authority parent (usually father or father figure) had a profound impact on your capacity to shine, to feel confident, to express your creative, zestful spirit. His example and up-bringing may have fed your self-esteem or squelched it. He could have presented a positive role model of confident achieve-ment, or a negative role model of excessive control, self-impor-tance or ego extremes. But despite any early parental impact, you now need to gain recognition and admiration for your responsible attitudes, practicality, and willingness to work productively, to do what is right. You find your magnetism through power, achievement, and "making it" in society. You rejoice in tangible accomplishments and measurable results. The more you achieve professionally, the more you feed your inner zest, enthusiasm, creativity and joy. Your dramatic spirit emerges in your professional efforts and career drives. You are willing to take risks to further your vocational accomplish-ments.

You focus on responsibility and dependability in love rela-tionships. In fact, you might overdo the parent role and take on responsibility which should be shared with others. You may measure love through deeds rather than words. Working to-gether with family members is a possibility or simply "working on" love—to improve and enhance relationships. If this is carried to an extreme, a "performance focus" could inhibit pleasure and enjoyment with those you love. A critical attitude (from you toward them or vice versa) might curtail having fun. Those you love could be ambitious, self-blocking or careful and dedicated workers. With integration, your love relationships can involve mutual contributions, with room for everyone to play as well as work; to entertain and to accomplish; to sparkle and to achieve; and to find positive excitement in their lives.

SUN IN 11TH HOUSE

Your self-esteem is tied to freedom, intellectual openness, friends and humanitarian principles. You may be proud (or ashamed) of your equalitarian outlook. You may seek admiration for your uniqueness, individuality and independence. Your creativity could be special, inventive and nontraditional. You may rejoice in new ideas, new experiences, new friends and the logical, detached intellect. You may pour your dramatic spirit into group activities or social causes and could be a leader within your networks. You can thrive on change and are instinctively innovative. If you deny your inner flame, friends may be too arrogant or flamboyant; the causes you get involved with could become histrionic and grandiose. But with integration, you can enliven logic with freshness and emotional enthusiasm; you can balance passion with detachment and a broad perspective.

You need freedom and space within your love relationships. You thrive in an atmosphere of tolerance, stimulation and open-endedness. You are willing to give this to those you love as well. If lovers or children carry those desires to excess, they could be rebellious, weird, aloof, overly intellectual or chaotic. Your style of loving is unconventional and motivates each person to do his/her own thing. You may encourage those you love to be independent, in order to have space for your own interests and activities. You are attracted to people who are themselves; not a carbon copy of you! You enjoy stimulation, change and the new. Your magnetism is tied to tolerance and being true to your inner essence.

SUN IN 12TH HOUSE

Your self-esteem is tied to your quest for infinite love and beauty. You might be a highly inspirational artist, whose creations lift people from the mundane realm into the sublime. You may dramatize grace, harmony, and the oneness of life. You may feed your inner vitality through healing or helping activities. You could seek admiration for your compassion, empathy, sensitivity and gentleness. Your creativity may be global, inclusive and intuitive. You may be proud (or ashamed) of your ideals, dreams and visions. If you are not actively transcending the past through beauty or healing work, you may succumb to the lure of escapism and seek your dream or "perfect world" through a pill, a bottle, a fantasy or other ephemeral traps.

You can rejoice in unity, in a connection to all of Life, yet need to express your personal ego and quality of specialness within a larger context. Ego issues are likely; you may repress your ego and self-confidence—or raise it to the infinite power (ego-inflation). You need recognition and positive attention within a context of Oneness and universal themes. You may lead or sway others emotionally through artistic acts or compassionate endeavors. Your dramatic spirit flows easily into channels of inspiration, healing and aesthetics.

You need a sense of beauty, romance, glamor (perhaps even illusions) in your love relationships. You are attracted to the lovely, the ideal, the graceful. You may dream a dream that humans cannot measure up to, or fool yourself into believing certain relationships are better than they actually are. You can easily be "in love with love." If your intuitive, seeking qualities are not expressed by you, your beloved and/or children may play them out. They could be martyrs, absent, confused, overly idealistic or escapist. If you can share the quest for inspiration with those you love, you may make beautiful music together (joined by an artistic connection), or you may work toward a shared vision (seeking a better or more ideal world). You can inspire one another without expecting godlike perfection. You can encourage each other's faith and trust in the goodness of Life.

The Sun in Aspect: *Esteem and Ego Issues*

The nature of the planets involved in any aspect is the most important factor. For any pair of planets, please read **all three** aspect delineations: conjunction, cooperating (sextile ✶, trine △), and challenging (square □, opposition ☍, quincunx ⚻). The conjunction is the basic, most fundamental aspect and its themes carry through with other aspects. The cooperating and challenging analyses will offer additional choices regarding of constructive and nonconstructive ways of handling the basic issues.

Remember that the life issues represented by cooperating aspects (or conjunctions) may still require some attention. We might overdo certain themes, or succumb to projection, repression or displacement in trying to balance our many, different drives. It is also quite possible that you could have integrated some of the conflicts (shown by challenging aspects) which were present at birth and are now manifesting potentials more reflective of the delineations in the cooperating or conjunction sections.

Other factors will complicate the picture. The potential inherent in any given placement might be overridden by other configurations in the chart. As you read the interpretations for the various pieces of your chart, bear in mind that certain pieces will suppress others. As always, repeated themes, which recur again and again, are the most likely to manifest in your psyche and in your life.

SUN CONJUNCT MOON

You are capable of much emotional warmth and likely to be strongly attached to your home, family, food and/or country. Because your feelings are powerful, you may take many things personally (perhaps when inappropriate). You tend to react emotionally to life and find security in loving and being loved (or feel insecure if that seems lacking).

Protective instincts are highlighted and you may naturally look after others, easily adopting a parental role. Your own early nurturing experience had a profound impact on your level of self-esteem. With a need to care for or to be cared for, maintaining an equalitarian stance may be challenging for you. A desire for family is probably marked.

An emotional balance is suggested between your expressive, outgoing side and your receptive, inward side. This can indicate an integration of extroversion and introversion—or feeling pulled between confidently reaching out versus cautiously guarding your sensitivities. You might be moody, or swing between holding in your feelings and emphatically expressing them.

The highest potential here is warmth, caring, empathy, emotional balance and great love for your nearest and dearest.

SUN COOPERATING MOON (✳ △)

Family and feelings are highlighted. You can be exceedingly warm and caring. Parental instincts are likely with a desire to care for and protect others (or looking to them to provide your care).

Harmony is suggested between your confident, expressive side and your cautious, sensitive side. You can be appropriately introverted or extroverted, depending on circumstances. You can blend "masculine" and "feminine" qualities and your mother and father may have been supportive of one another.

A good sense of emotional balance is likely; you can direct your loving instincts well.

SUN CHALLENGING MOON (□ ♂ ⚹)

Emotions are in focus and you may be torn between holding in your feelings versus freely expressing them. Introversion may vie with extroversion within you, or public roles could clash with private ones.

You may be unsure when to reach out confidently to life, taking risks, being creative, building self-esteem and when to hold back (guarding your sensitivities, protecting yourself or others, being receptive rather than active). You might choose active behavior when a more passive approach would work or vice versa. You might feel moody, weepy, or emotionally on edge. (This aspect can also signify tension between your mother and father and/or clashes with the opposite sex.)

Ego needs could affect the family matrix. It may be challenging to blend nurturing support and the need to shine, to be noticed and applauded. You may have felt you couldn't get the recognition you needed from your parents.

By staying in touch with your varied emotional reactions and choosing appropriate circumstances for your differing needs, integration is possible. This includes the potential for great warmth, caring, commitment and love.

SUN CONJUNCT MERCURY

You need recognition and admiration for your mental skills and capacity to be articulate. You may be quite clever, verbal, curious, witty or a dramatic conversationalist. You could say some things for effect—concerned with the impact of your information. If the Sun principle is stronger in you, you may sometimes think emotionally rather than logically. If the Mercury principle is stronger, you may detach into rationalization rather than react emotionally.

You might enjoy puns, sarcasm, word plays or other verbal forms of recreation. You are likely to be proud (or ashamed) of your knowledge. Your level of self-esteem is tied to your thinking and communicative abilities.

Variety probably appeals to you. You may be physically as well as mentally restless—potentially agile and in motion. You probably get bored if excitement seems lacking (but can find learning an exciting activity).

You may use your mind or tongue to sell, persuade, entertain or change existing opinions. You have a keen sense of humor and fun and are likely to have a youthful air and attitude. You think most clearly and are most articulate when being applauded, admired and noticed.

SUN COOPERATING MERCURY (✶ △)
(not possible natally)

SUN CHALLENGING MERCURY (□ ☍ ⚻)
(not possible natally) Mercury is never more than 28° from the Sun, so forms no major aspects other than the conjunction.

SUN CONJUNCT VENUS
Charm may be your middle name. You can be sweet, likable, courteous, pleasant, graceful and kind. You want to enjoy life and other people and strive to maintain harmony and ease. You are likely to be quite attractive to others.

If overdone, this theme could lead to flattery or a lack of sincerity. Style might be valued over substance. If appearances wield the power, "looking good" becomes everything.

Your feeling for beauty might be directed into any form of artistic creativity. You could be a romanticist, artist, poet, musician, actor, etc. Or, you may seek gratification through the physical senses and indulging the appetites. (A love of luxury and pleasure could be overdone.) In moderation, you appreciate aesthetics and enjoy the material world.

Other people's opinions may affect your self-esteem. You may **need** to be liked. You could invest your ego in a partner, depending on him/her for attention, support and affection. If this other-directedness is carried too far, you may feel "you're nobody til somebody loves you."

Your strengths are a skill at pleasing yourself and others, artistic/aesthetic talents, an enjoyment of material possessions and pleasures, plus a gratifying capacity for understanding what others (especially of the opposite sex) want.

SUN COOPERATING VENUS (⚹ △)
(not possible natally) Venus is never more than 46° from the Sun, so the conjunction is the only major aspect which can form between them.

SUN CHALLENGING VENUS (□ ☍ ⚼)
(not possible natally)

SUN CONJUNCT MARS
Courage is your watchword; you are willing to face challenges directly and forcefully. You can be quite energetic, forceful, brave, vital, eager, passionate, spirited and ardent. A physical outlet is advisable for your restless (perhaps impatient) nature.

If carried away, you can be blunt, combative, hostile, insistent on leading, rash, impatient and overextended (easily burning out).

You are a natural pioneer, providing the spark, the initiative, the enthusiasm to begin. (Finishing up is not your strength.) You thrive on excitement and may move quickly from one conquest to the next. (This can include a sexual Don Juan potential.) Sometimes the fun for you is solely in the chase, or you only want what you cannot have. Try to pick constructive challenges.

Your strengths are a high level of vitality, will, courage, enterprise and leadership abilities. You are attracted to power and are willing to take risks, yet also have a sense of fun and a high capacity for zest.

SUN COOPERATING MARS (⚹ △)
Energy and enthusiasm are likely assets for you. Passion, vitality and eagerness may be marked. You pour yourself easily into self-expressive activities and may find it easy to take risks. Your recuperative powers tend to be excellent; you can bounce back from almost anything.

If your desire for an adrenaline rush is carried too far, you could be rash, arrogant, pushy or foolhardy. You may have quite a creative spark and a natural sense of fun.

Your sexual (and other) drives are likely to be strong. You know what you want and have the confidence to pursue it in life. Challenges attract you and you can be skilled and incisive in crisis situations. Daring and adventurous, you need a high level of stimulation and excitement in life.

SUN CHALLENGING MARS (□ ✗ ⊼)

You may be too brave for your own good. Although high energy, vitality, courage and spirits are suggested, you might overdo in the quest for excitement. This could lead to rash, impatient, hostile or combative behavior. You could come across as very aggressive or competitive.

You are dealing with an inner conflict in regard to qualities defined as masculine by our culture. This could manifest as clashes with your own father or with males, or struggles in finding positive ways to express your own assertive, "me-first," forceful, dynamic and angry side. If you deny your personal rights and power, others around you are apt to overdo them or your "blocked fire" could lead to accidents or illness.

You have potential leadership skills and a natural inclination to pioneer. An eagerness to be first could be carried to the extreme of arrogance—or truly lead the way for people.

Your need for activity and attraction to an adrenaline rush could result in burnout. You may outrun yourself, pushing too much, too far, too fast, too often. You might have a quick temper, lack patience, or strike others as pushy and demanding.

With a positive outlet (sports, games, causes, competitive business) for your forcefulness and drive, you can inspire, persuade, teach, and lead others. Your zest, enthusiasm, creativity and courage can be valuable assets.

SUN CONJUNCT JUPITER

Exuberant, enthusiastic and expansive, you see life in larger terms. Few people can approach your *joie de vivre* ("joy in life"); you also do pleasure in a big way! Your inclination is to grow, expand and experience as much as possible. You seek success, fulfillment, and happiness on a large scale.

You can be very permissive, playful and affirming. This can go to the extreme of profligacy, exaggeration, bragging, arrogance, pie-eyed optimism and overconfidence. You may carry liberality, openness or generosity to an extreme.

Although physical well-being and vitality are likely, you can be undisciplined and immoderate which will affect the body eventually (burnout). Use your good judgment.

You may be ego-invested in your beliefs, values and opinions. If overdone, you could become a zealot. You are drawn to the heroic, larger-than-life roles, but can also overgeneralize, oversimplify, make assumptions, leap to conclusions and expect instant gratification.

Potential weaknesses are simply strengths carried too far! With a "more is better" attitude, you can too easily overdo. Yet you have real talent for persuasion, inspiration and education. You have a high level of faith, confidence, trust, enthusiasm, magnanimity, humor, tolerance and friendliness. You love being the best and promoting excellence in others.

SUN COOPERATING JUPITER (✶ △)

You have a natural urge to expand, to do more, higher, better, faster in life. Your vitality is probably strong and you tend toward optimism. You believe in yourself and in your capacities and are probably willing to take risks. Your openness to opportunities could seem lucky to others.

Your fun-loving spirit could be marked; you have a talent for joy and humor. You enjoy excitement and might be attracted to **big** dreams, schemes and ideas. Promotional abilities are likely; you could have talent for sales, persuasion, public relations, drama, or advertising. You may enjoy travel and are likely to thirst after more and more knowledge (especially about the **big** questions of what is really important in life).

Your urge for an adrenaline rush may sometimes carry you to extremes; moderation does not come easily. You might even feel: "Excess is not nearly enough!" It is possible to overdo the desire to shine, to be noticed, to live fully, to celebrate life, to play, to expand, and to be broadened by life.

Your enthusiasm easily sweeps others along. You are willing to plunge wholeheartedly into life and other people are likely to enjoy your *joie de vivre*.

SUN CHALLENGING JUPITER (□ ♂ ⚴)

You may carry the quest for excitement too far. Your urge to take chances, to risk, to live fully, to expand, to be noticed, and to constantly do more than before could be carried to an extreme. Grand passions might sweep you away. If you are immoderate, you could easily overextend yourself and make promises you cannot fulfill.

Ego clashes around beliefs, values, ethics and morals are possible. Your desire for admiration and recognition may be at odds with your faith or religious/spiritual principles. You might expect a lot of devotion and admiration from others. You may have to work to make room for trusting in something larger (with reasonable humility) while still feeling significant and noteworthy in your own being. Your world view and basic philosophy could affect your level of self-esteem.

Too much or too little pride is a possibility. You may come across as arrogant and pompous on occasion. Yet you are also capable of feeling, "If I am not perfect, I am nothing!" Although you are likely to have good vitality, you may sap yourself through conflicting values or excessive expectations. (Perhaps the grass is always greener where you are not.) Demanding perfection will simply set you up to feel inadequate. Your tendency is to want the best, the most, the highest, etc.

Positively channeled, your confidence, outreach and enthusiasm can persuade, sell, and promote almost anything. You can share humor, playfulness, creativity and the limelight with the larger world.

SUN CONJUNCT SATURN

You can accomplish incredible things and still doubt your abilities!

You have a natural drive to succeed, to lead, to achieve a position of power. A "fathering" archetype (strong, responsible, authoritative, looking after/advising others) is prominent in your psyche. You can be a model for others—a paragon, an example who sets the standard. (If overdone, you can be condescending, bossy and authoritarian.) You seek respect, and to become an expert or authority.

Yet beneath your drive to accomplish lurks insecurity. You **need** people's approval and respect for your attainments. You can be intimidated by authorities because you want so much to "make it" in order to feel worthy. You may only accept compliments from people you respect or whom you see as powerful—whether they are or not. (You may think that the comments of "ordinary" people don't mean anything or don't count.) Your father or father figure had a strong impact on your belief in yourself.

Because you tend to base your self-worth on outward measurements of "success," you can succumb to low self-esteem or be susceptible to guilt. You may be overly critical or judgmental of yourself. You may hold back in love relationships, feeling inadequate—or seek to dominate in order to feel safe. You might even give up sometimes—feeling success is just too hard or doubting your ability to cope with the world or with a relationship. Love and work might seem at odds with one another—each taking you from the other.

Yet the truth is that you **can** climb every mountain. You can accomplish an incredible amount, having a blend of enterprise and endurance; confidence and competence. You are a natural achiever and have the potential to make a real mark in the world. You can be responsible, practical and helpful in loving attachments, building a solid, lasting foundation of mutual admiration and appreciation.

SUN COOPERATING SATURN (✶ △)

You have potential leadership skills and the capacity to make a real contribution to the world. Your enthusiasm, creativity and confidence can combine well with your sense of responsibility, realism and willingness to work. You can achieve much through personal effort and dedication.

Your career or productive efforts may enhance your ability to shine, to be noticed and to express your creativity. Your risk-taking side and willingness to try for more can further your achievements. Older friends or mentor figures may contribute to your success.

You have the capacity to balance discipline and playfulness; you know when to labor and when to relax. You also can integrate love needs and work needs: maintaining a commitment to both loved ones and a productive career.

By a judicious mixture of constructive criticism and praise, you can reap the best results. You are able to harness excitement and enthusiasm as well as hard work and dedication. You can combine common sense and confidence.

SUN CHALLENGING SATURN (□ ☌ ⚻)
You can achieve something noteworthy if you get out of your own way. You have the potential to ground your creativity and to work your way to a position of authority or expertise. But, you are likely to feel pulled between very different drives in your nature: your cheerful, confident side versus your somber, cautious side; your extroverted, outgoing side versus your inhibited, self-critical side and your arrogant "royal" side versus your humble, self-effacing tendencies. You may also experience some tension between love and work—relationship desires competing with achievement needs.

By choosing appropriate times and places to express each need, you can be highly effective and live a fuller, richer life. Instead of doubting yourself, criticizing your needs, or being defensive because you fear rejection, you can use your practical side to break your goals into manageable pieces and work your way up the ladder of success a step at a time. If you fall down, you can always get up again. You are potentially indefatigable. Each successful experience will build your self-assurance.

Instead of feeling love takes you away from work (or vice versa), you may commit to spending a certain amount of time/energy on each area and carrying through as promised. Instead of feeling guilty about one because you are thinking of the other, you can learn to focus fully and joyously on loving (when you are doing that) and on productive achievement (at the right time and place).

You can love responsibly, seriously, with a deep commitment and you can achieve with joy, zest and enthusiasm.

SUN CONJUNCT URANUS
Creativity is life for you! Naturally innovative, inventive, progressive, you seek thrills and excitement. Unique self-expression is central (but could go to the extremes of rebellion or eccentricity). You may take pride in being different or special. (You could be defiant and singled out in uncomfortable ways.) Your essence flows easily toward the new, the future, and the unusual.

Stimulation is important to you (mental and emotional) so you may dislike routine. You are likely to seek exciting or unusual friends—or ones to stroke your ego. Although you believe in equality, it is important for you to feel special in your social group.

You can be warm, passionate and dramatic one moment and cool, intellectual and nonchalant the next, so people may find you unpredictable. The truth is, you tend to feel torn between your mind and passions and may blow hot and cold in relationships. As long as you maintain a sense of freedom and openness, you'll probably do OK. If you close off your options or feel total commitment is being demanded, you may flail about, seeking escape or retreat into a rationalizing logic. Heed both your heart and your head, expressing both love and freedom needs, and all will be well.

SUN COOPERATING URANUS (✶ △)
Creativity comes easily to you, with an inventive, original streak. Unique and individualistic, you thrive in an atmosphere of tolerance and openness. Drawn toward the future, you have visionary potentials.

Excitement is essential in your life (both mental and emotional). You may be drawn toward groups, political action, teaching or other activities that put you in the forefront of progress and innovation.

You have the capacity to turn friends into lovers and stay friends with lovers after the romantic attachment has ended. You need both passion and detachment, attachment and separation in your relationships. By balancing your love and freedom needs, you can have the best of both worlds. If you do not integrate your head and heart, you could come across as erratic in relationships: first hot, then cold—or attract others who play out one side of this polarity while you do the other side.

You may have strong personal magnetism. You thrust eagerly into life, seeking stimulation, broadened perspectives and the thrill of the new.

SUN CHALLENGING URANUS (□ ⚹ ⊼)
You find excitement stimulating, but may sometimes be drawn to negative forms of it. Ego clashes are possible, or risk-taking might be overdone. If your search for stimulation is carried to an extreme, you could be seen as an upstart or troublemaker.

You are working on the balance between your intellect and your passions. If unintegrated, you could swing from intense emotions to detached aloofness. You might experience relationships as "come closer, go away." You could feel torn between a desire for love, attachment, closeness and a yearning to be free, independent and unconfined. Your head and heart might be at odds with each other. By making room for both in life, you can have more satisfaction.

You may also feel some conflict between your need to shine, to be special, to be noteworthy and recognized as someone above the crowd, versus your belief in equality, fair play, and everyone being on the same level. Equalitarian principles could clash with the desire to be King or Queen of the Hill.

Friends may vie with loved ones for your time and energy or the demands of the wider world, the needs of humanity, might seem to pull you away from commitments to those you love. Both are essential.

You have a flair for looking ahead and can be naturally progressive, innovative, creative and inventive. You can deal constructively with change and flux. You are drawn toward the new and different in life.

SUN CONJUNCT NEPTUNE

You can see a vision beyond the ken of most mere mortals. Romantic, idealistic, spiritual, artistic, your creative imagination can inspire others. You have a flair for magic, illusions, dreams, images, roles and masks. You can be a skilled actor/actress, artist (or dramatic hysteric or martyr). Persuasive talents are likely; you affect people's emotions.

You are also open to the feelings of others (and may even pick up illnesses or moods). This quality can include mediumistic (channeling) abilities, but also carries the danger of being emotionally controlled/manipulated by others (too susceptible to outside influences). You may deny your ego, feeling weak, fragile and vulnerable—or raise the ego to an infinite power (identifying with God in terms of religious, healing or spiritual capacities). A middle ground allows you to tune into the Infinite for inspiration, but not be swept away or submerged.

Your view of love inclines toward romance (which may be tragic). You tend to be in love with love and could don rose-colored glasses in regard to loved ones. (You may worship false "gods.") Do not depend on a human being to give your life total meaning (nor attempt to "be everything" to someone else). Those paths lead to disappointment and disillusionment. You can inspire to a divine standard in life through art, beauty, spirituality, etc. Utopia is a legitimate goal, but do not expect it immediately or from yourself or from your loved ones.

Look for positive ways to be "swept away" rather than succumbing to con games, escapism, deception, drugs, or other forms of illusion/delusion. A shared focus on art, beauty, spirituality, mysticism, charities, religion, or any form of constructively inspiring activity allows you (and others) to touch the Infinite and be uplifted while still accepting yourselves as fallible, growing human beings.

SUN COOPERATING NEPTUNE (✶ △)

Your creative capacities are strongly marked. You may have considerable artistic/aesthetic talent and could achieve recognition through your handling of beauty. You may have high ability in the visual arts, perhaps attracted to filmmaking or similar ventures. You might exhibit dramatic instincts, with a flair for magic, promotion, illusions, sales or other persuasive fields where you sway people emotionally.

Idealism is likely to color your love relationships. You may seek (and "see") the best in your lovers and children. If overdone, you could be disillusioned when the fantasy fails and the people you adore prove to be only too human and fallible. In moderation, this quality allows you to visualize the highest potential of those you love, to support and praise their assets, and to generally encourage positive outcomes.

Potentially you can blend pride and humility optimally. You understand the necessity of good self-esteem and appreciate your own capabilities, but you also are tuned into the Universe, sensing the oneness of life and your place in a larger Whole. The blend allows you to both lead and follow, in a complex, graceful dance of appropriateness.

Joy, splendor, aesthetics, creativity and charisma are likely assets. You bring dreams to vivid life, inspiring others with their beauty.

SUN CHALLENGING NEPTUNE (□ ☍ ⚻)

You are likely to have strong talent for creating beauty in some form, but may avoid manifesting your skills because real world attainments never measure up to the ideal inside your mind and imagination. You may feel frustrated when reality constantly falls short of your inner dreams. Your challenge is to persist even when the world or your creation is not as lovely as your internal images. You may be talented in fields such as entertainment, promotion, sales, public relations and advertising.

You are working on the balance between pride and humility and may sometimes go to either extreme. You could slip into excessive ego and believe that the world ought to revolve around you, perhaps to the point of deceiving others, hiding inner motivations to present your "best" side. You might also succumb to self-denial and self-sacrifice on behalf of those you love. Feeling misunderstood by your parents and/or loved ones could add to your lack of faith in yourself. You might be tempted to avoid confrontations and protect yourself by playing weak, sensitive or needy. Seek the middle ground of healthy self-esteem combined with a good dose of empathy for the needs of others.

Romantic ideals might affect your love relationships. If you demand more than is humanly possible (in love with love) from yourself or others, disappointment is likely. You could fall into escapism or rescuer/victim interchanges. Seeing and appreciating the best in others can be healthy, as long as the adoration contains a dose of reality (clarity and objectivity) as well.

You probably want to be inspired and swept away by passionate experiences (and have the capacity to touch the hearts and souls of others). You are likely to have charisma and a native, whimsical charm along with marked creative capabilities.

SUN CONJUNCT PLUTO

You have an inner core of will: an indomitable spirit. Intense and powerful, you may feel driven to accomplish the impossible. You can be the reformer, undaunted by the odds—daring in the face of death (or any extreme challenge). You are passionate—in every sense.

Power is a likely issue in your life and you must find the middle ground between abuse of power (toward self or others) and denial of strength. You tend to attract extremes and may face life-or-death issues. You could feel impelled to destroy and tear down in order to then build up and regenerate in a new form.

Power struggles could have begun with Dad (or other authority figures) and are likely to continue until you have a constructive outlet (sports, games, business, fighting for causes, climbing a career ladder) for your competitive, dominating side. It is vital to differentiate between the situations where you should wield power as the king (Sun) and the situations when you should share power as an equal (Pluto). If you do not use your power drive, you may attract people who use it against you. Or your blocked power could turn against your own health. If you do not learn how and when to share power, you are likely to spend your whole life in power struggles which could involve almost everyone around you.

You tend to be sensitive to issues of loyalty and betrayal. When you commit to someone/something, it is total. Sex, money, power and ego are likely to be mixed in your life—and fodder for confrontations. You may use sarcasm, irony or satire to attack and could succumb to jealousy or possessiveness (or face the above through loved ones). There is a tendency to keep score, so gratitude, acknowledgments, and paybacks become important.

Life may not be easy for you, but it is probably intense. You live and experience on levels deeper than those perceived by most people. You can face the dark side of life (and people—including yourself). You may be drawn to hidden or taboo areas, yet you will gain mastery. You will overcome. You are a survivor.

SUN COOPERATING PLUTO (✶ △)
Your emotions are likely to be quite intense, and your passions (sexual and otherwise) quite strong. You seldom do things by halves: total commitment is your style. You may, however, feel torn between your desire to shine, to be recognized and to pour out into the world versus your drive for self-control, self-mastery and internalization. Life provides opportunities for both if you choose wisely.

You can deal naturally and instinctively with power issues. Leadership skills are quite likely. A competitive outlet (sports, games, business) could help ensure you do not fall into power struggles with those closest to you. If your personal will and forcefulness do not have a constructive channel, you may fight with loved ones, particularly over issues of money, possessions, sex and pleasures.

You will probably seek excitement and intensity in your love relationships (and negative excitement and strife are possible at times). You may sometimes tear down in order to rebuild and rejuvenate attitudes or interchanges that have died or become stale. Superficialities have no appeal for you; "all or nothing at all" could be your motto where attachments are concerned.

You may have skill in financial matters and could be fortunate in terms of investment or inheritance. You are likely to have great personal endurance and survival instincts.

SUN CHALLENGING PLUTO (□ ☌ ⚹)

You have a strong will and tremendous passion, but may sometimes sit on your intensity. Emotional volatility is quite likely. If you try to confine your feelings, you could sometimes explode emotionally. You need to strive for balance between your tendency to hold a lot in and be secretive, to dominate and control, versus your urge to flow, to express and pour out into the world. Moderation is not easy for you.

You are likely to be quite sensitive to issues of loyalty, betrayal, acknowledgment and justice. You may succumb to paybacks, score keeping or subtle forms of seeking revenge. Irony, sarcasm or covert, manipulative attacks could be used to further your causes. People may see you as having a chip on your shoulder. You need a constructive outlet for your drive for power, such as competitive sports, business or games. Executive or leadership capacities are probably talents. If you overdo this power drive, you could feel that "might makes right." Conversely, if you do not express your desire for mastery, you may unconsciously draw in other people who abuse power or misuse force.

Because you seek the deepest levels in life, you may be drawn to life-and-death issues or situations. You are inclined to go to the end, to the death, to the furthest, deepest experiences in life. You seek a soul mate—someone who can share the deepest, darkest secrets of your psyche, the most buried recesses of your inner depths. Sometimes the implied vulnerability is too much and you retreat from it all into a hermit role. Yet you hunger for emotional intimacy and sharing.

You have the capacity to survive almost anything. Your inner core of strength is incredible. You may be fascinated by and attracted to the dark side in life, but part of the motivation is to overcome it—to transform and transmute negatives into positives. This is no easy task, but you came into life looking for challenges!

CHAPTER FOUR

THE MOON
NURTURING AND NEEDINESS
IN YOUR HOROSCOPE

The Moon in Signs:
Categories of Caretaking

MOON IN ARIES

You tend to feel things immediately and may express your feelings with equal speed. At times, this can lead to a quick temper. Your moods can also shift rapidly and may sometimes be hard for others to keep up with! You may feel safest when being courageous, active, assertive or self-reliant. Although warm, you do not want to be confined emotionally and can sometimes seem hot/cold to others. You are willing to nurture in your own distinct way, with an emphasis on action. You are likely to have high spirits, with a fresh, spontaneous and pioneering quality.

MOON IN TAURUS

Your emotional reactions tend to be slow, steady and predictable. You may find security in physical possessions, money, sensuality, nature, or beauty. Your sense of touch might be well-developed with an appreciation of tactile experiences such as good back rubs. Fine food and drink may also appeal. You can be quite faithful and affectionate, but gravitate toward keeping things the same. You might incline toward stubbornness, but can be very loyal and dedicated.

MOON IN GEMINI

Your emotional reactions tend to center around the world of the mind and communication. You are likely to seek security in variety, trying to satisfy an insatiable curiosity, but the people nearby, relatives and neighbors, could also be important keys to security. Though your interests may be scattered, you have a talent for quick perception and for responding to a variety of stimuli. You can be a good observer of others and tend to be rational and reasonable rather than heavily emotional. You may connect with your emotions by verbalizing them (or sometimes rationalizing them away). You are likely to be restless and active and may use your hands as well as words to communicate.

MOON IN CANCER

Your feelings are deep and strong, but you are unlikely to reveal them to the world—either to protect yourself or to avoid hurting others. You may enjoy nurturing others or you could expect others to take care of you. Warm and emotional attachments are a likely focus. Your home and/or family may be very important to you. You probably have an emotionally intense bond with your mother, but it could be negative or positive (or a little of both). You may seek to hang on to what you have to maintain emotional and physical security. You can be extremely caring and supportive.

MOON IN LEO

Your emotional reactions tend to be fiery and dramatic. You have an instinctive stage presence and may even monopolize the limelight on occasion. Admiration and attention matter a lot to you, so you might be ego-vulnerable to flattery or feel "down" when not getting a positive response. You may be quite magnetic and generally have a feeling for children (having never lost your inner child and sense of fun). You can be quite generous, enthusiastic and encouraging of others.

MOON IN VIRGO

You are likely to have a "need to be needed." If carried too far, you could end up feeling you are indispensable and could carry far too much of the load in work and other situations. You tend to be more practical than emotional, and may be a bit insecure or shy in relationships as a result of self-criticism or a fear of being criticized by others. Your talents lie in organization and thoroughness, but your desire to have things "right" could lead to being overly critical or to being critical in situations which are not your "job." You find security in doing a good job, in analyzing the world, and in making constant improvements (repairs). Self-doubt and self-criticism can be mitigated by focusing on efficiency in the world rather than turning yourself into a job. You nurture efficiency in yourself and others. Dedicated and willing to serve, you are ever ready to lend a helping hand.

MOON IN LIBRA

Your emotions gravitate toward beauty, grace and harmony. You can be quite affectionate, good natured and charming, and are generally popular with others. You may sometimes appear chameleon-like, adopting the attitudes of those around you, which could make you seem fickle or capricious. If you are too caught up in "looking good" (graceful, charming), you might inhibit your emotional responses and block real intimacy. Because you need relationships, you may sometimes have trouble being alone. Emotional connections with others are important to you, although you may feel torn between nurturing and/or being nurtured versus relating as an equal and a peer. Because fairness matters to you, you might weigh matters too much and be indecisive. You have an intuitive grasp of polarities and a desire to seek a synthesis (middle ground). Beauty soothes you and diplomatic skills are likely.

MOON IN SCORPIO

You are likely to have very intense feelings, as well as considerable skill at sensing the feelings of others. Your awareness of "hidden messages" and layers beneath the surface can be a useful talent but could also be used to manipulate others or to conjure fearful fantasies. With your natural sensitivity, you probably have above-average psychic ability. You may need to work out power issues with your mother, or another mother figure, or in your role as mother. For you, nurturing and being nurtured are tied to intense emotional experiences, yet a fear of vulnerability or losing control could lead you to repress emotions. Security is vital to you; letting go (emotionally or financially) may not be easy. If your security is too dependent on another person, you risk being trapped by jealousy or possessiveness. But you also are capable of great loyalty and tremendous endurance. You are a natural survivor, able to surmount what would defeat many people, able to keep on to the end.

MOON IN SAGITTARIUS

You are likely to seek security in adventure! You react enthusiastically to life, and may be drawn to travel, books, philosophy or metaphysical explorations to feed your inner psyche. You might sometimes slip into arrogance about your world view, or in preaching your beliefs to others. You are probably most content when progressing toward future goals or promoting ideals. You are apt to idealize feelings, your home or motherhood. This can range from wanting more than is possible from any of those areas and being perpetually discontented, to only seeing the best in your loved ones. You may get emotional support from traveling, from nature, from exploring, or just from being independent. You are probably naturally friendly, gregarious and tend toward optimism. You can be casual, offhand, even careless (with the implicit faith that God is taking care of things so you don't have to), but you are also capable of inspiring others by your faith.

MOON IN CAPRICORN

Your emotional attitude tends to be serious and grounded. You can be quite determined and self-controlled, but may have to guard against pessimism, against too much attention to what is or might be wrong in a situation. The basic insecurity which leads to such feelings can stem from a lack of unconditional love in childhood. You may feel that your early nurturing experience was harsh or judgmental rather than supportive, or your parents could have simply emphasized the work ethic. Perhaps you had to be strong in order to cope, or were forced to face reality at a young age. You may feel too responsible, that no one else will do it right. You are likely to find security through working hard, being dedicated, responsible and/or seeking a position of status or power. You may seek to control your emotional responses, and your drive to be an authority could inhibit intimacy and emotional exchanges. You probably feel most comfortable as the responsible provider, dedicated caretaker or person in charge. You are likely to have organizational skills, talent for business, and a practical approach to handling assets.

MOON IN AQUARIUS
You are likely to have some humanitarian instincts and may become involved in social causes or politics. Although friendly and open to almost anyone, your style is cool and detached rather than warm and personal. If your drive for objectivity is carried too far, you might alienate yourself from your own feelings or from other people. You probably feel secure with unconventionality, the new, the unusual and the innovative. You will often react eccentrically or unpredictably. You may swing between nurturing warmth and rampant individualism and personal freedom. You can treat family like friends: equalitarian and tolerant. You may be casual about domestic matters. You nurture through the mind, encouraging people to envision alternatives and to consider their options. You support others by encouraging their freedom and feel nurtured if they recognize your independence in return.

MOON IN PISCES
You are apt to be very sensitive, dreamy, imaginative and possibly artistic. You may be intuitive, able to tune in to the feelings of others as well as your own. Because you want to believe in an ideal, a romantic image, you could sometimes fool yourself emotionally, or get too emotionally involved in trying to rescue other people. (People might take advantage of your caring nature.) You might be too vulnerable. Because you easily tune in to others, you can lose track of your own feelings and reactions. You can nurture and heal others and may wish to serve a spiritual ideal or to assist the downtrodden. You need a connection to the universe, a sense of oneness with life, to feel secure. You need some alone time to process feelings and achieve serenity. Artistic outlets including music, or being near water, can also be helpful. Meditation or unfocused daydreaming can help you maintain peace of mind.

The Moon in Houses
Seeking Safety and Security

MOON IN 1ST HOUSE

Your identity is tied to home, family, mother (figure) and emotional needs. Mother is a role model (positive or negative) for self-assertion, independence and your behavior. You may want to be like her—or the exact opposite. Positively, mother could have been active, courageous, pioneering and liberty-loving. Negatively, mother could have been self-centered, rash or angry. Family connections are a significant influence in your sense of self. Your early nurturing experience (or lack thereof) had a profound impact on who you are. Your family either supported or challenged your initiative, vitality and ability to fight.

Emotional needs are central in your self-expression. You may be primarily focused on meeting your own needs, clinging, dependent, childlike, on the one hand, or extremely self-sufficient on the other, avoiding the vulnerabililty of dependency. Alternately, you could be very intent upon meeting the needs of other people (maternal, protective, nourishing). Because you want to do any caretaking on your own terms, you could sometimes end up being the sole parent or helper. It is important to keep a balance in your life between nurturing and being nurtured.

On the one hand, you have a strong urge to be emotionally supportive. On the other hand, you most want to protect and conserve freedom, directness and your own independent action. So, your caretaking style may seem "hot and cold" to some. You may be a bit moody—pouring out, then withdrawing inside. You might be very emotionally attached and then pull away for your own space. You need a home environment that encourages people to do their own thing. You feel most secure emotionally when being yourself. You are learning to nurture yourself and others in ways which affirm personal strength and power.

MOON IN 2ND HOUSE

Your emotional security is linked to possessions and pleasures. Sensuality is accented, and you may be inclined to indulge in terms of food or other forms of physical gratification. You **need** physical contact, caresses and sensations. Tactile gratification is a form of nourishment for you. A sense of safety could also be sought through collecting possessions. It may be very hard for you to let go of things, especially as you tend toward sentimental attachments to much of what you own. You are likely to want to protect and conserve your monetary and physical resources. Saving for a rainy day is fine, but don't nag yourself about every little financial fluctuation. You might be too dependent on physical goods for feeling protected in life. Or, you may nurture others through providing comfort, material security or possessions.

Your mother (figure) is a role model (positive or negative) for handling the sensual, material world. She might have been easygoing, pleasure-loving or artistic. She could have been materialistic, self-indulgent or stolid. Your family would tend to accentuate ease and contentment or gratification and stubbornness. The past either solidly built or stiffly challenged your capacity for pleasure, comfort and security. You function best in a domestic environment which is attractive, comfortable, predictable and secure. Your feelings tend to be deliberate, persisting and enduring. You can be very loyal, affectionate and attached to family. Your emotional balance is fed by beauty and material safety.

MOON IN 3RD HOUSE

Your emotional security is linked to thinking and communication. You may seek to protect and conserve ideas, information and knowledge. You may hunger for information and nourish understanding. Your mind and feelings tend to be intermixed and your emotional needs may overwhelm objectivity on occasion. With integration, you can get your thinking and feelings into a harmonious balance. Your communications are apt to be strongly influenced by your mood of the moment. Protectiveness is often part of the communication style. When feeling nurturant, you believe: "If you cannot say something good, don't say anything." When you feel safe, you can be quite talkative (often in close family gatherings). When not secure, you may not open your mouth. You learn best in a sheltered setting and may understand much viscerally or unconsciously before realizing consciously that you **do** know it.

Your mother (figure) was a role model (positive or negative) for the world of the mind. She could have been lighthearted, verbal, flippant, scattered or bright. She could have been a peer, easy to talk to and share with on a casual, equal basis (almost like a sister). It is also possible that another relative (sister, brother, aunt, etc.) provided some of your nurturing— or you nurtured relatives yourself, playing out the maternal role in your early life. In some fashion, you are likely to nurture or depend upon relatives (including siblings). You can easily turn more casual contacts into a "family" feeling, becoming warm and emotionally attached to those in your immediate environment. Your family probably bred flexibility, awareness, curiosity and wit and may have encouraged (or necessitated through challenges) your language skills or dexterity.

MOON IN 4TH HOUSE

At least one of your parents was a significant role model for emotional closeness and attachment (most likely your mother figure). Your feelings are strongly affected by the influence of your mother figure. She (or your father if he was the uncondi- tional love parent) could have been extremely nurturing or quite dependent. If the former, you could have experienced Mother as warm, sensitive, and caring. If she carried those qualities to an extreme, she might have been too maternal (smothering or overly protective). If one of your parents lived out the dependent option, s/he could have seemed clinging, childlike, and emotionally needy. You may have felt that you had to parent your own parent (be the strong, supportive, helpful one). The experience let you learn about vulnerability and caring or being cared for. The past either supported or challenged your capacity to give and receive tender, loving care.

Your emotional security rests on your home, family and close ties. Safety, security and protection are apt to be priori- ties (perhaps too much so at times.) Your nesting instinct is well-developed. You may nurture or depend on your family, pets, plants, anyone in your home, or possibly extend your protection to life in general or to the planet. Your family may breed sensitivity, deep feelings, caring and protectiveness. You tend to remember feelings, hurts, sensitivities and emotional nuances. You probably protect or conserve your feelings, re- sources, needs and security. Your home or domestic environment needs to be warm, supportive, protective and private. You could be quite intuitive or psychically open.

MOON IN 5TH HOUSE

Your emotional security is tied to being recognized, admired and applauded. You may only feel safe when you are receiving love, or you may substitute taking center stage and getting attention. If carried to an extreme, you might only feel secure when everything revolves around you. Emotional warmth is accentuated; you are likely to have a strong family feeling, wanting to be a parent, to nurture, to be creatively involved with loving relationships. Maternal instincts are marked, whether you are male or female. You may mother your lovers and/or children, or seek loved ones who will mother you. (Mutual caretaking works best.) You can be quite exuberant, vital and lively. You remember experiences of joy, expansion, pride, excitement and love. You are "fed" by romance.

Your mother (figure) was a role model (positive or negative) for handling power, the limelight, risk-taking and extraversion. She could have been dramatic, flamboyant, generous or egocentric. She might have craved excitement or power, with gambling instincts or a drive to speculate. She could have been extremely loving, dynamic and charismatic. "Unfinished business" with your mother may be faced through your children or other love relationships. You might have a child or a lover who pushes the same emotional buttons that your mother did. The past either strongly supported or forcefully challenged your creativity, willingness to risk and drive for self-expression. You thrive in a domestic environment which is larger than life, brings you pride, and in which you can be noticed or find stimulation and excitement.

MOON IN 6TH HOUSE

You seek emotional security through productive efforts. You are likely to feel safest when accomplishing tangible results, with careful attention to details. You may nourish and preserve efficiency, a critical attitude, or health. Your emotional focus tends to be quiet, humble and dedicated. You remember health issues, minutiae and anything requiring repair or improvements. Your feelings center around practical issues and fixing things up. You nurture in pragmatic ways—taking care of business. You may depend on co-workers or play a maternal role toward colleagues. If you adopt the caretaking role, beware of your need to be needed. You might be **too** helpful, assisting others whether or not they desire it. You may fall into the indispensability trap, believing no one else can handle things as well as you can.

Your mother (figure) could have been a positive or negative role model for work and health. She might have been capable, hardworking, and effective. She could have been ill, self-effacing or overly critical. Issues in your family centered around doing a good job and maintaining healthy physical functioning. Any health problems are strongly connected to your emotional life. Your stomach could be sensitive to emotional upsets, and good nutrition is particularly important for you. Unfinished feelings with mother (and the nurturing you did or did **not** receive) could contribute to ailments. You need a positive emotional support system where you both give and receive assistance. The past either strongly supported or challenged your pragmatism, humility and discrimination. You appreciate precision, restraint and practicality in your home environment. You may organize domestic matters or consider homemaking as your job.

MOON IN 7TH HOUSE

Your emotional security is wrapped up with other people. You are likely to depend on them to nurture you, or be attracted to people you can look after and protect. You may be quite charming, graceful, polite or kind. You may tend toward "polite lies" to avoid hurt feelings (your own or those of other people). You are moved emotionally by grace and beauty. You tend to remember imbalance, interactions with others and what is attractive. You naturally want to form attachments with others and can be quite empathic.

Your mother (figure) was a positive or negative role model for partners. She could have been an equal, more like a partner than a parent (authority figure). She may have been cooperative, attractive, diplomatic, artistic or refined. Or, she could have been vacillating, too other-directed or competitive. A grandparent may have played a nurturing role for you at some time. Your capacity to share was strongly influenced by your early nurturing experience. You could unconsciously choose a partner who tries to mother you (or expects you to mother him/her). A partner is likely to push the same emotional "buttons" that your mother did, bringing up old feelings about vulnerability, caretaking and emotional support, so that you can resolve them. Your past either solidly supported or heavily challenged your sense of justice and fair play and your ability to be an equal in relationships. You function best in a domestic environment which is beautiful, harmonious and balanced.

MOON IN 8TH HOUSE

Your emotional security may come through intimacy or you may avoid emotional vulnerability and seek security through self-control. You are naturally intuitive and can merge (almost without thinking) with a mate. You and a partner may tune into one another easily (although this can feel intrusive or overwhelming at times). You also feel a strong need for self-control so you may be torn between your merging instincts and your hermit side that wants to focus on inner insights and self-mastery. You may protect and conserve hidden knowledge, monetary resources, or sensual/sexual pleasures. Financial safety is probably important to you. You are likely to depend upon self-mastery, material resources or a mate. You feel strongly about issues of purification, transformation, regeneration and forgiveness. Your emotional style is intense and can be all-or-nothing. You tend to remember almost everything and may sometimes find it hard to forgive (yourself **or** others).

Your mother (figure) could have been intense, resourceful and interested in life's deeper meanings, or she might have been power-hungry, game-playing and manipulative, or she could have been timid, fearful, dependent, blocked and hermit-like. Your early nurturing experiences (or lack of them) strongly affected your capacity for intimacy and a close, emotional connection with another person. You tend to attract a mate who will bring up the same feelings you faced with your mother—issues of vulnerability, emotional closeness, privacy and addiction. The challenge is to avoid the extremes of total absorption/dependency on one another or total withdrawal, and to find the middle ground of deep commitment and respect. Your family may have bred power, manipulation, intimidation, retreat or sharing. The past either firmly supported or challenged your capacity to forgive and let go. You function best in a domestic environment which can face and handle deep, emotional issues. You tend to look beneath the surface where feelings are concerned, and to deal with root causes.

MOON IN 9TH HOUSE

Your emotional security is sought through education, travel, exploration, expansion and/or faith. In an ironic twist, you may enjoy testing your safety needs with adventures. You tend to nurture (and depend upon) concepts, beliefs systems and ethical principles. You may protect and conserve knowledge, nature and understanding (of higher ideals). You are "fed" by learning. Your emotional approach tends toward optimism, confidence and a trust in the future. You may remember philosophies, world views and metaphysical ideas or you may retain personal goals and values.

Your mother (figure) could have been idealized, idealistic, adventurous, witty, religious, or out for a good time. Mother might have been too busy traveling, studying, writing, teaching, saving the world, etc., to do much nurturing. She might have overdone "truth" and bluntness. She might have been supportive, but felt trapped and wished to explore the wider world, seeking and questing. Or, she may have integrated freedom (searching) drives and her compassionate, caretaking needs. She strongly affected your beliefs and values as a positive or negative role model. You may choose freedom to pursue your vision rather than settle down with a home and family. Or you may take your home with you and live in foreign countries, or bring the world into your home with foreigners, books, or wide-ranging discussions. Or you may idealize the "mothering" principles and want the perfect family. (Your own family may match your great expectations, but you are more likely to feel let down by mere human beings. You could like the best, the brightest, and the most wonderful where nurturing and caretaking are concerned.) Your family may have bred exploration, expansion, faith and trust. The past strongly affected your ethics, morality and faith. You function best in a domestic environment which features intellectual stimulation, exposure to other cultures, broadened philosophical perspectives or a happy-go-lucky, eager enthusiasm for life.

MOON IN 10TH HOUSE

Your emotional security is tied to your status, role in society, and achievements. You are likely to either preserve or rely upon rules, structures, cause-and-effect, or authorities. You tend to control your feelings, channeling them into practical results, especially into anything which will further your career. Your vocation may involve nurturing, land, the public, women, commodities, food, shelter, clothing or anything tied to the mothering experience or your mother's example. (This can be a "nurturer of the world" indicator.) Security (emotional, financial, vocational, physical) is important to you. You need a sense of safety in the world and may prefer the predictable. You remember duties, limits, laws and needs. You are likely to be quite cautious, responsible, realistic and possibly susceptible to guilt.

Your mother (figure) was a role model (positive or negative) for handling power in the world. She could have been a professional, working hard outside the home, dedicated, responsible, realistic and authoritative. Or, she might have been inhibited, blocked, frustrated and limited (perhaps even to the point of you having to parent your own parent). She could have used power wisely to make things happen in the world, or tried to dominate and control others. She is a strong influence in terms of your attitudes toward a career, responsibility, authority and the power structure. If you have unfinished business with her, authority figures (including your boss) might push the same buttons until you become conscious that you are no longer dealing with your mother. A tenth house Moon can sometimes indicate one parent playing both roles (authority figure and nurturer), or parents who are similar, or the need to take on early responsibilities, sometimes to parent your own parents. Keeping a balance between unconditional love ("I love you because you are") and conditional love ("I love you because you perform adequately") might have been a challenge for your parents. They might have overdone emotional support or judgments and demands. Your family brought up issues of responsibility, the need to perform, and obligations. The past fiercely supported or challenged your strength, power, authority and control. You function best in a home environment which is organized, sensible and stable.

MOON IN 11TH HOUSE

Your emotional security is tied to new age knowledge, technology, friends or communal associations. You are "fed" by the new, the unusual and the different. You may protect and conserve opportunity for all, humanitarian principles and tolerance. You are likely to nurture and be nurtured by friends, causes, and social networks. Your caretaking style is intellectual and a bit detached rather than warm and emotional. You are concerned with broad issues, but may be quite objective in more personal realms. You tend to treat friends as family (warmer, more caring) and family as friends (with space and objectivity), so your emotional responses can be viewed as rebellious, inventive or unconventional.

Your mother (figure) was a role model for individuality and progress. She could have been equalitarian (more like a friend than an authority), open, bright, unusual or involved with the cutting edge of change. She might also have been erratic, unpredictable, cool, aloof and detached. Your mother was dealing with a freedom/closeness clash around nurturing. She could have felt torn between her desire to care for her home and family and her urge to be independent and involved in the wider world (transpersonal issues). You are facing the same motifs in terms of your own nurturing instincts. You may feel torn between your domestic role versus the pull of causes, new age activities, and the beckoning vistas of the outer world. Your family may breed individualism, change, open-endedness and unusual approaches. The past soundly supported or challenged your uniqueness, humanitarian principles or openness to the new. You function best in a domestic environment which is unstructured, unusual, ever-changing or full of stimulating friends and ideas.

MOON IN 12TH HOUSE

Your emotional security is tied to the universe and feeling connected to the whole. You are naturally intuitive, and drawn toward experiences of transcendence. You want to be uplifted, swept away, to merge with something Higher. You may seek to protect and conserve the highest, the most ideal and the most beautiful in life. You remember fantasies, visions, dreams and inspirations. You can be quite gentle, compassionate, idealistic, kind and sensitive. You understand the unity of all life and have a natural empathy. You tend to romanticize and idealize nurturing qualities and may strive to be the all-loving, all-giving figure who runs the risk of ending up in martyred self-sacrifice. Or, you may seek a cosmic caretaker—looking for someone else to provide unconditional love, assistance and protection for you. You are "fed" by inspirational experiences (whether artistic or helping/healing), but guard against being carried away with trying to "be everything" for someone else or expecting "Heaven on Earth" yourself.

Your mother (figure) provided a (positive or negative) role model for handling the quest for infinite love and beauty. She might have been artistic, a savior (rescuing and assisting others) or a victim. She could have been lovely, idealistic or self-sacrificing. Her example affected you strongly on unconscious levels and you may want to do some work with journals, dreams, visualization or other nonverbal means to bring your deep feelings up into consciousness and release them. Be sure your emotional responses are your own. Your family bred imagination, artistry, an attraction toward mysticism, martyrdom or escapism. The past heavily supported or challenged your capacity to seek the beautiful and idyllic in life. You function best with a home which is like a sanctuary: beautiful, soothing and a retreat from the traumas of the material world. You need some time alone to meditate or work through your inner feelings and impressions, including getting rid of emotions you pick up from other people. Your Higher Self is close to the surface of your awareness and can provide assistance, illumination and uplifting encouragement.

The Moon in Aspect: *Parenting Principles*

The nature of the planets involved in any aspect is the most important factor. For any pair of planets, please read **all three** aspect delineations: conjunction, cooperating (sextile ✶, trine △), and challenging (square □, opposition ☍, quincunx ⊼). The conjunction is the basic, most fundamental aspect and its themes carry through with other aspects. The cooperating and challenging analyses will offer additional choices regarding of constructive and nonconstructive ways of handling the basic issues.

Remember that the life issues represented by cooperating aspects (or conjunctions) may still require some attention. We might overdo certain themes, or succumb to projection, repression or displacement in trying to balance our many, different drives. It is also quite possible that you could have integrated some of the conflicts (shown by challenging aspects) which were present at birth and are now manifesting potentials more reflective of the delineations in the cooperating or conjunction sections.

Other factors will complicate the picture. The potential inherent in any given placement might be overridden by other configurations in the chart. As you read the interpretations for the various pieces of your chart, bear in mind that certain pieces will suppress others. As always, repeated themes, which recur again and again, are the most likely to manifest in your psyche and in your life.

MOON CONJUNCT MERCURY

You have the capacity to blend thoughts and feelings. Your mind is apt to be influenced by your emotional state. You may be skilled at sensing the moods of others and might understand public temperament. You may have talent for figuring out, explaining and communicating about emotions. You are likely to communicate best in a secure environment, or with those close to you. You may nurture people through words.

Your thinking may be intuitive at times. It could appear changeable to others as you shift moods or as your sensitive antennae shift and you pick up more information. You can be quite sympathetic and receptive, but may also seem indecisive, fickle or wavering to people. If feelings overwhelm thinking, misunderstandings may arise. Yet you can also find security in knowing. You may be nourished by thinking and/or communication and feel safest when being rational. Accuracy requires a blend of intuition and logic. A good memory is likely.

Restless and perceptive, you may have skill at mimicry or imitation. You could be very active in your neighborhood, with relatives or in the nearby environs. You need mental and emotional stimulation.

MOON COOPERATING MERCURY (✶ △)

You are able to integrate your rational and emotional sides, using both thoughts and feelings. Your rich, inner world may inspire your communications. You are likely to express ideas clearly, with logic as well as emotional impact. You may have talent for explaining concepts to the public. You can be an effective speaker, sensing how to reach people.

You can communicate caring, protection, nurturing, and emotional support well. People probably find you easy to get along with as you tend to be sociable and friendly. You are likely to be perceptive and open to stimulation and information from many sources.

MOON CHALLENGING MERCURY (□ ☍ ⚼)
You may feel torn between logic and emotions or thinking and feeling. Your gut may argue with your head. If neediness, vulnerability or sensitivity overwhelms your rational side, misunderstandings with others are possible. You may take things too personally on occasion.

You can be quite clever and shrewd, but might also be high-strung and restless. You tend to respond to many different stimuli and could sometimes feel bombarded by the world.

Conflicts with family members are possible, particularly if insecurities get in the way. You communicate well when feeling safe, but may clam up (or chatter as a protective distraction) when you feel threatened or intellectually unclear (deluged by feelings).

When you bring together your emotional and rational sides, you can explain touchy issues well and communicate skillfully in the realm of feelings. You may be quite glib, empathic and helpful.

MOON CONJUNCT VENUS
You have a strong sensual nature and need tactile connections. You may equate food with love and nurturing (or with safety) and could overeat (or overfeed others). You are likely to seek comfort, love and tangible beauty. You may collect lovely things or seek security through money and possessions.

You can be quite sweet, compliant, gentle, accepting and charming. You may nurture tenderly. You can be passive and might wait for others to assist you (being receptive or even playing helpless). Yet you could also enjoy taking care of others. Your relationship with your mother or mother figure is likely to strongly affect your later love relationships. You may turn partnerships into parent-child associations.

Your home can be a source of pleasure or beauty. You may enjoy socializing at home or create an abode of grace and comfort. Family and being cherished matter much to you. With your instinctive courtesy, most people want to be your friend.

MOON COOPERATING VENUS (✶ △)

You can be quite charming, graceful, loving and attractive to others. You probably have a flair for dealing with emotional matters with kindness and empathy. Courtesy comes naturally to you, and most people want to be friends with you. You can radiate calmness and support. You may be very discomforted by discordance or acrimony.

Physical and emotional security probably appeal to you. This could be expressed through creating beauty, collecting possessions, eating or other forms of sensual gratification.

Relationships are apt to be a vital forum for emotional support. You respond well to others and need feeling connections. Home and family are apt to be important.

MOON CHALLENGING VENUS (□ ✗ ⊼)

You may feel torn between seeking emotional versus physical security. One may seem to take away from the other. Family conflicts over money, loyalty, comfort, or love are possible. You may feel you pay a price for caring or that others take advantage of you. Perhaps a parent is at odds with your choice in partners. Perhaps financial clashes affect your domestic routine. Perhaps different views of love make a stable commitment challenging.

Your relationship with your mother (or mother figure) is apt to influence your capacity to love, to enjoy life, and to handle money successfully. You may be susceptible to emotional manipulation or being manipulative to protect yourself in those areas and need to be sure you have "finished up" any feelings related to the past (especially your early life). There is no need to repeat a negative pattern; rather it is important to learn from the past in order to create a more constructive future in your relationships.

By coming to terms with old feelings about nurturing and emotional support, you can create a sense of inner comfort, security, trust and a willingness to share feelings, pleasures and resources with others, equally and lovingly.

MOON CONJUNCT MARS

You are capable of a great deal of emotional warmth and caring. Until you resolve the tension between your nurturing nature and your drive for freedom, you may feel torn between them. You could identify with nurturing and help others whether they want it or not—or identify with dependency and take closeness on any terms. You might carefully consider nurturing options to avoid feeling trapped—or take care of others only when/where you feel like it. You might fight with your family, feeling cornered and hemmed in, or being unable to accept nurturing from others (fleeing any vulnerabilities). You might even cling to people in subtle ways while denying dependency, or avoid commitment while denying that you need independence.

The relationship with your mother or mother figure had a strong impact on your sense of identity, your self-assertion and your handling of anger. You may feel rage at your mother, at women, nurturing, nurturers or children til you come to terms with your own ambivalences in this area. You might have a quick temper, emotional explosions or sullen, suppressed rage until you learn the moderate, ongoing expression of feelings (neither holding back too much nor pouring out excessively).

Misplaced aggression is possible (unbridled emotion) or impulsive acts followed by second thoughts. You may spend time defending yourself against threats which do not materialize.

With integration, you tend to care deeply for others, feeding their independence and self-reliance. You can commit to family and close loved ones, but maintain your personal freedom and room to express yourself as a separate individual at the same time. Your emotional reactions are strong, but you can balance expression and holding in, choosing appropriate moments for each.

MOON COOPERATING MARS (⁎ △)

You are capable of great warmth. Your drive, assertive needs and basic energy support your caring nature and desire to nurture. Similarly, your willingness to protect and assist others feeds your physical vitality and desire to take action. You have a healthy balance between inward tendencies and outward thrust.

You have the capacity to get along well with your mother (or mother figure). She could have encouraged your sense of independence, your courage, willingness to do, to be and to express yourself. You can balance nurturing, dependency and doing your own thing. You are able to get close to people and still maintain your personal integrity and sense of individuality.

MOON CHALLENGING MARS (□ ⚹ ⊼)

Emotional clashes or even explosions are possible. You are likely to feel torn between your desire to seek safety, to protect yourself and/or others versus your assertive, expressive side that demands immediate responses. You may feel pulled between "letting it all hang out" emotionally versus holding things inside and waiting until it is safe to express how you feel. If tension builds up too long, emotional moods swings, outbursts, or sulkiness and resentment are possible.

You may have clashed with your mother (or mother figure). Tension is likely between freedom needs and a desire for emotional closeness. Perhaps you felt she was too suffocating, clinging, possessive or protective and you yearned for more independence. Perhaps you felt she was too independent, self-centered, angry or assertive and was not sufficiently nurturing or warm. There is the potential of imbalance between dependence and independence. To maintain committed relationships, you will have to learn to compromise, making room for both attachment and separation.

Your emotional reactions tend to be strong. The challenge is to seek constructive outlets for your fighting spirit as well as for your desire to assist, depend upon and get close to others. A reasonable blend of security and risk is essential in your life.

MOON CONJUNCT JUPITER

You can be exceedingly good-natured, tolerant and kind. You may reach out to others through emotional warmth, honesty and generosity. You may nurture on a wide scale (perhaps when others do not want it) and could exaggerate feelings or make assumptions about people's emotional states. You might overindulge (yourself and/or others). You are likely to value feelings, security, family, and may give any of them too high a priority in life, or you may expect too much of them and be perpetually disappointed.

Your mother or mother figure probably had a strong impact on your faith, beliefs and world view. You may have idealized your mother (or motherhood)—or seen her as indulgent, idealistic, religious, intellectual, overextended, a generalizer or not around much. She affected what/who you trust and your moral/ethical principles. She influenced (pro or con) your capacity to believe in something/someone. You may overvalue nurturing, family, ancestry, safety, food or feelings.

You might make the world your home with an interest in foreign cultures and a desire to adventure and explore. Or, you might bring intellectual stimulation, books, foreigners or spiritual discussions into your abode. You could have been educated at home, boarding school, or learn much through the emotions. You are working on the balance between roots and faraway places; between exploring and nesting urges; between security and risk-taking. You are capable of protecting while broadening people's horizons.

MOON COOPERATING JUPITER (✶ △)

You are able to blend nurturing needs and an adventurous spirit. Your warmth, caring, protectiveness and desire for emotional security reinforce and assist your quest for meaning and search for something higher in life. Your optimism, faith, values and ideas feed and further your desire for emotional connections to others.

You may have skill in dealing with people as you can combine emotional sensitivity with intellectual curiosity. You tend to be good-natured, friendly and helpful. You are likely to be sympathetic to others and encourage them to see and work for the best in life. You have a knack for accentuating the positive.

Your interests are apt to be broad and you may be well informed in a wide variety of areas. You are drawn to both the familiar and the foreign or faraway. Your home may be enhanced through other cultures, intellectual stimulation, religion, philosophy or any spiritual path. Your secure emotional foundation encourages you to explore, adventure, and seek exciting, broadening experiences in the world. You can maintain roots while wandering the world, and make a home for yourself in the midst of exploring.

MOON CHALLENGING JUPITER (□ ⚼ ⚻)

You may feel torn between the near, familiar, safe, secure and the faraway, unknown, risky and adventurous. This could include the pull between your roots and the wider world, or between playing it safe and taking chances. Both sides of your nature need acknowledgment to preclude either being overindulged.

Conflicts with your mother (or mother figure) around beliefs, ideals, values and/or religion are possible. Your world views may have clashed. Your life philosophies could be at odds. The issue of expectations (too much, too little, the wrong kind) is probably significant in your nurturing relationships. If carried too far, you may demand more than is possible from family members (or from yourself as a nurturer) and hence promise or expect more than can be delivered. Overindulgence could be a familial issue. You might be generous to excess or compulsively honest. You could prefer seeking the "easy" way in life. Visualizing the best is the first step. Then you must figure out the practical steps needed to help bring your dreams into being.

Your positive spirit can contribute to building a more secure, supportive domestic environment. Your faith and trust in the future can help to work through and resolve the past. By combining compassion and confidence, you can make the most of your opportunities.

MOON CONJUNCT SATURN

There is a strong parental streak in your nature. You have the potential to blend warmth, compassion and caring with responsibility, practicality and a willingness to work hard. You can be quite helpful and productive.

You can learn from your own parents who were working on the balance between conditional and unconditional love. If they overdid conditional love, they may have been harsh, critical, demanding. You could have felt hurt, abandoned, rejected, lonely, cut off or shortchanged. Or, they might have been blocked, ill, inhibited, inadequate and you might have even parented your own parents. If they overdid the unconditional love, they may have been overly protective, and unconsciously encouraged weakness in others. If they integrated this polarity, they could be nurturing and practical, supportive and sensible (as can you). Sometimes, the presence of Moon and Saturn in the same sign/house is an indication that the parents are similar in some basic ways. Sometimes, it indicates that one parent is playing both roles.

The past is likely to be very important to you. Excessive guilt is a possibility. Safety, security and the familiar tend to appeal. If the principle of caution and facing limits is overdone, you could feel defensive, moody, crabby, self-pitying, shy, and afraid to express emotions or even to discuss emotions with significant people. You might feel neglected, depressive, or worry about being a burden. You might feel critical toward your mother or toward women. You might be cut off or alienated from others until you develop more faith and trust in others, in yourself and in expressing feelings.

There is a tendency to seek security through status, authority, predictability and habits. You can be quite reliable and responsible. You may feel some tension in dividing your time and energy between home/family versus career/work in the world. You are working on the balance between dependency and dominance; emotions and pragmatism. By making room for both, you can be sensibly supportive, competently compassionate and gentle as well as strong.

MOON COOPERATING SATURN (✶ △)

Your safety instincts are excellent. You can be thoughtful, conservative, careful, productive and appropriate. You are able to blend physical and emotional tasks, to be effective in both realms.

Your worldly success may be enhanced by a parent. You are willing to work your way to the top and plan sensibly for advancement. You can be quite prudent and may have talent in a number of business realms, or in working with the public. You are able to blend domestic and professional demands and might even work with family members, carry on a family business, work out of your home, or work in a field involving "home" (e.g., real estate). Work with emotional matters is also possible, or feeding, clothing, housing, or comforting people.

You deal well with tasks because you address emotional needs as well as material issues. You can keep people supportive of one another while still getting the job done. You are an empathic manager.

This aspect suggests harmony between your parents. They could have agreed with one another and taught you about the balance between emotional needs and pragmatic, real-world demands. They may have integrated competence and compassion, empathy and effectiveness. You have the potential of bringing together dominance and dependency, of blending a comfortable home and family with work and success in the world.

MOON CHALLENGING SATURN (□ ☍ ⚹)

You are apt to feel some degree of tension between your emotional needs and your focus on getting the job done. You may feel torn between home and family needs versus your drive for material accomplishments. You could vacillate between dominance and dependency, between compassion and hard-nosed realism. You are learning to compromise, to keep room for both sides.

Tension between your parents is a real possibility. They might have clashed over work issues, emotional needs or been estranged from each other. They might have fostered too much dependency or not nurtured well, perhaps pushing too hard for you to be strong and cope from a very young age. As a result, you could have some lingering insecurity about getting what you want in life. This can lead to intense ambition and achievement or to feeling that the world has all the power and that you might as well give up. You might be afraid to be vulnerable, not trusting others to be there for you emotionally or demanding unqualified love and acceptance from others (the unconditional support you always wanted from Mom and Dad and didn't get). You may be overly susceptible to guilt or to feelings of responsibility for those closest to you. You might avoid emotional matters, feeling that is the best way to maintain control. You could be touchy, moody, suspicious or feel that real intimacy eludes you. Since you tend to be serious, depression or inhibition is possible.

The challenge is to constructively blend your emotional and pragmatic nature, not denying either one, but incorporating both into life. By blending caring with competence, you can be productive as well as emotionally close, keeping room for emotional connections along with worldly achievement.

MOON CONJUNCT URANUS

You may have unusual emotional experiences, or even sudden outbursts. You are apt to be excitable, unpredictable, unsettling and possibly even erratic at times. You are blending emotional needs with a strong drive for independence and individuality. The combination can lead to sudden breaks with the past, disruptions in nurturing, or conflicts between attachment and separation. Your lifestyle or habits may be unusual. You could have a unique approach to emotional needs.

Your early nurturing experience affected your capacity to be a free soul. You may have experienced your mother as a friend, as an intellectual, as aloof or as unpredictable. She may have seemed too possessive at one moment (when you wanted freedom), then inadequately protective the next (too detached when you wanted closeness). You could have swung between hot and cold with each other. You are apt to feel ambivalent about nurturing—unsure how much you are willing to give up your independence in order to closely commit to someone else. Caring may seem restrictive or confining to you.

You may turn family into friends or friends into family. You may find it easy to nurture friends (and to be nurtured by them). Or perhaps you have lots of female friends and a tendency to meet interesting women. You might feel at home in the world, fitting in anywhere, gaining an instant rapport with anyone regardless of background. You may look to your friends and your mind for security, safety and solutions—and could even intellectualize, rationalize and explain away emotional needs and issues.

You could be quite intuitive, with real flashes of insight, especially about people, emotions, or trends in the wider world.

MOON COOPERATING URANUS (✴ △)

You may have intuitive flashes, combining logic and intuition in a spark of insight. You can put together the mind and emotions, allowing them to serve and enhance each other in finding creative solutions to problems.

Your mother (or mother figure) may have encouraged your sense of individuality and uniqueness or herself been highly individualistic. Your early nurturing experiences fed your need to be different and unlike anyone else. Your home could have broadened your perspectives, exposing you to many different alternatives in life. Your nurturing parent probably supported your need for freedom.

You can combine security needs with risk-taking urges and make the best of both. You are able to blend thoughts and feelings as well as adventurousness and safety-seeking. You can make an emotional contribution to groups and causes, especially forward-thinking ones. You abhor injustice and may have sympathy for the underdog. Your understanding is above average as you bring together the intellect and the emotions.

MOON CHALLENGING URANUS (□ ☍ ⊼)

Although psychic flashes are possible with this combination, you may feel they are more disruptive than helpful. You are working to effectively combine the mind and emotions and they may seem at odds with one another. You might overdo emotional impulses at the expense of the intellect—or rationalize and intellectualize away your feelings. Seek a middle ground.

You may have experienced conflicts with your mother (or mother figure) around the issue of freedom and individuality. Perhaps she was independent or aloof when you wanted nurturing support. Perhaps she was clutching and clinging when you wanted to do your own thing. Perhaps she was disturbingly unpredictable. If you do not resolve your inner tension between attachment and separation or closeness versus freedom, you may have similar push/pull experiences with children or partners.

You also might feel pulled between friends and family— each seeming to take time/energy away from the other—until you make room in life for both. You could feel tension between security needs and the urge to take risks. You need a fundamental sense of safety within a matrix of change, innovation and progress. You are drawn toward both the past and the future; a healthy blend contributes to a richer life.

MOON CONJUNCT NEPTUNE

You are apt to be dreamy, idealistic, imaginative, sensitive and romantic. You can be quite compassionate, kind, empathic and sympathetic, but may succumb at times to passivity or escapism. You are likely to be open to psychic impressions and may sometimes be too subject to external influences. It is very important for you to stay grounded, checking your intuitive feelings against logic and the material world.

You could idealize mothering, nurturing, your mother, homeland, or emotions in general. Your mother (and your view of nurturing) could be artistic, ill, elusive, mysterious, spiritual, rescuing or escapist. You might make security, safety or the home into an ultimate value. You could put your faith in emotions—or feel overwhelmed by the power of emotions. You are more apt to operate on a feeling (than an intellectual) level. You could also deny, rationalize, see life through rose-colored glasses or be overly suggestible and gullible. Your longing to merge, to blend, to be a part of something higher could lead you to inspiration—or temptation.

If your sensitivity and compassion is overdone, you could fall into self-sacrifice or martyrdom or take many things personally, feeling defensive. You may be manipulated by unconscious needs, unaware of many of your deeper feelings and reactions.

You have the capacity to tune into public needs and desires and may have talent for advertising, film or other media dealing with images and emotions. You are drawn toward mystical experiences but may also find outlets involving water and/or chemicals. Living near water may prove soothing. You tend to feel deeply and are moved to help others.

MOON COOPERATING NEPTUNE (✶ △)
You are apt to be quite sensitive—both to your own feelings and to the emotional needs of other people. Naturally compassionate, you want to help, and some people might take advantage of your good nature, playing on your empathy.

You may be psychically open and could have intuitive talent. Artistic abilities are also likely, along with an urge to assist, to help, to heal others. Philanthropy and similar efforts come naturally. A safe emotional foundation ensures that you will not be excessively drained when you reach out and want to rescue others.

Your mother or early home life could have encouraged your idealistic nature. This might have been a healthy focus on spiritual ideals, compassion or aesthetics. An alternative is a home involving escapism, victims or a lack of clarity where you were motivated to improve the situation. Your deeper feelings are roused by issues of family, emotional closeness and caretaking. Be sure you have a constructive outlet for any need to be needed and that you also feel comfortable in expressing your own personal needs. Your feeling for beauty can enhance your home environment and spiritual ideals may contribute to your emotional connections with other people.

MOON CHALLENGING NEPTUNE (□ ☍ ⊼)

Sensitivity is likely to be a challenge in your life. Perhaps you are overdoing the openness to feelings and impressions from others. Perhaps you need to "tune out" a bit and be less willing to become involved for the sake of others.

You may have experienced conflict with your mother (or mother figure) around issues of faith, ideals, escapism, illusions, beauty, or wish fulfillment. The challenge is to gain a sense of inspiration through family interactions without trying to "play God" (rescue) other family members and also without expecting them to "be everything" for you. A shared aesthetic perspective or healing goals can work wonders (and help avoid negative paths such as drugs, alcohol, etc.).

Passivity is a potential if you do not see an "easy" way to go for what you want. You may be afraid to push or openly assert yourself. You might see what you want, particularly in emotional situations, rather than what is there.

Psychic talent is a real possibility, although you may not always like what you pick up. You could sometimes be **too** receptive, particularly to anxieties and insecurities. The challenge is to believe in yourself and your emotional responses without taking everything personally—and also to trust that the universe is good without becoming gullible and **only** seeing the good in others. You can give much to the world, but must also take care of yourself!

MOON CONJUNCT PLUTO

Your emotions are deep and strong, but rarely revealed upon the surface. Because you feel so intensely, you may strive to maintain control through secrecy or even manipulation. Your feelings may seem overwhelming. Emotional fanaticism is possible; unconscious energies might dominate your psyche. You can, however, be incredibly loyal, quite psychic and even prophetic.

You first experienced emotional intensity in the relationship with your mother or mother figure. She may have been powerful, manipulative, compulsive, healing, controlling, abusive, competitive, possessive, addicted or empathic. The bonds between you may be very difficult to break; a symbiotic association is possible. The tendency is to experience the relationship as very good or very bad. You might also fall into power struggles with other women. You are apt to inspire intense emotional interchanges.

Your powerful feelings can be used as a force for transforming your life. You may have to separate nurturance from control; they are easily mixed in your psyche. You might link pain and healing, or hurting and then being taken care of. Sex could be confused with nurturing. If emotions (yours or someone else's) seem overwhelming, emotional blackmail is a possibility. You are likely to be alert to clues, innuendoes, hints, and might hear preferences as demands. You can be quite canny and watchful (even suspicious).

When positively directed, you are capable of deep commitment, incredible healing, intuitive insights and profound transformations. You are willing to face the dark side of the psyche and do what is necessary to turn negatives into positives.

MOON COOPERATING PLUTO (✶ △)

You are able to handle emotions constructively and may be quite sensitive, psychic and aware of life's underlying patterns. You can tune into your own inner depths and those of other people, sensing subterranean issues, drives and needs. You may be quite empathic.

You have the capacity to balance nurturing drives with the urge for control and mastery, choosing appropriate times for each. Emotional closeness is important to you; your level of commitment to relationships is very deep. When you care about someone, it is total.

Your mother (or mother figure) may have encouraged you to deal with issues of addiction, self-mastery, intimacy and the sharing of resources. Your inner emotional security makes it possible for you to share deeply, to risk vulnerability, to touch souls with another human being.

You are quite aware of people's hidden agendas and unconscious motives, picking up on subtle cues and clues in their language and behavior. You respond to process—not just content. You have talent for working with emotions, for dealing with the unconscious, for using intuitive insights. You may also be capable of galvanizing individuals or groups of people into transformation.

MOON CHALLENGING PLUTO (□ ☍ ⚹)

You are likely to deal with intense emotional issues in your life. Feelings (your own or those of other people) may seem overwhelming at times. You may have to face obsessions, compulsions or driving, unconscious needs. Issues around addiction are possible.

Conflict with your mother or mother figure is possible. She may have competed with you, sought total control, been manipulative, very dependent, or used emotional blackmail. Interactions with her probably taught you about facing the unconscious, dealing with strong emotional complexes and handling issues of self-control and self-mastery.

Psychic openness is a potential talent, but it may sometimes seem negative or overwhelming, until you gain a sense of being in charge of it. You are apt to be quite sensitive to nonverbal cues, but could be overly suspicious or defensive, perhaps inclined to see attacks which are not there.

You can tune into the underlying patterns in life and within the psyches of other people (as well as yourself). By using your insights and emotional forcefulness wisely, you can have profound effects and be a catalyst for transforming the lives of others as well as your own life.

CHAPTER FIVE

MERCURY
CONCEPTS AND COMMUNICATION IN YOUR HOROSCOPE

Mercury in Signs:
Intellectual Interchanges

MERCURY IN ARIES

Your mind and tongue are apt to work quickly (sometimes impulsively). You may have a talent for debate or extemporaneous speaking, and you might use words aggressively (biting, ironic, sarcastic). You are likely to communicate directly, forcefully, with confidence. (You may sometimes be insensitive to others—in too much of a hurry, interrupting, etc. which can inhibit a true exchange of ideas.) You think for yourself and learn best through personal experience. You may need to be active in order to learn. You are likely to seek out new ideas and be willing to take mental risks. Self-will colors your perceptions. You are likely to be interested in courage, self-reliance, freedom and self-expression.

MERCURY IN TAURUS

Your mind and tongue tend to work deliberately and steadily. You may sometimes get stuck in mental ruts, but can be very practical and grounded, with a good, retentive mind. Skills in business are likely, or in any activity that puts your common sense to work. You may learn through tactile contact or through physical manipulation of the world. You may sometimes limit your perceptions due to a desire to learn slowly and carefully. You want to bring ideas down to earth, and are likely to be interested in money, sensuality and physical comforts.

MERCURY IN GEMINI

Your mind and tongue tend to be restless and facile. You are likely to be quite articulate and might sometimes tend to talk (or gossip) too much. You have a skill for verbal expression and can communicate quickly and cleverly. Sometimes your ideas and speech are a bit superficial, because you have the urge to communicate your perceptions immediately or because you are trying to cover too much ground. Curious about everything and ever eager to learn, the world is your school. You are likely to be logical, rational and able to offer information on almost any topic. One of your skills is making connections between con-cepts. You are prone to friendly interchanges with others and may ask innumerable questions. You could have a high degree of nervous energy which flows into speech, gestures, writing, or manual dexterity in some form. Physical dexterity and flexibil-ity are also likely.

MERCURY IN CANCER

You do not say everything you feel as you are apt to avoid hurting yourself or hurting others with careless comments. You can be protective of your thoughts. You nurture ideas and encourage them to grow up before sharing. You use emotions as well as logic and may let sensitivities sway your decisions. Subconscious fears, habits or prejudices might inhibit your objectivity or openness to the new. You could have a good memory and above-average psychic ability. You learn through absorbing experiences, making emotional connections. You are likely to be interested in family, food, the home, the land, the public or security.

MERCURY IN LEO

Entertainment could be your forte. You may have dramatic talent and could be skilled at sales, advertising, promotion or anything using your mind/tongue to persuade people. You may gain attention through your mind and tongue and probably want people to admire your thinking or style of communication. You can speak with energy, pride, liveliness and charisma. You use drama and humor in your communications. You learn best when excited and "turned on" by a topic. Your ego-involvement with certain concepts could lead to fixed thinking or limited objectivity, but you can be quite dynamic and magnetic in presentations. Your interests could include power, children, fame and creativity.

MERCURY IN VIRGO
Your mind and tongue are probably precise, thorough and analytical. Your communications may be logical, helpful, critical, negative, skeptical, practical or humble. You are apt to put your mind to work, to use your mind in your job. You may well ground the intellect through writing or technical crafts, converting ideas into tangible form. Talents for organization are probable, but your discriminating focus could slip into excessive criticism if overdone. You learn best with an organized sequence and logical presentation. Your concern for details might sometimes lead to "not seeing the forest for the trees." You are likely to be interested in health, nutrition, competence and your job.

MERCURY IN LIBRA
Your mental approach tends toward balance. You can argue both sides of a question (to ensure fair play). You can also be charming and diplomatic; your language might even be poetic and flowing. Your aesthetic sense colors your speech. You can communicate adeptly, diplomatically, elegantly and in a balanced manner. Logic, objectivity and equality appeal to you; you may fence-sit from trying too hard to include all points of view. Fairness and synthesizing polarities are important to you. You could be interested in people, the law, the arts. You need feedback from others, to clarify your own opinions and probably consider taking turns and mutuality highly important in relationships. Your tact and impartiality can help you to connect with others.

MERCURY IN SCORPIO
Your mental approach is intense and probing. A natural detective, you tend to ferret out hidden motives and tune into

underlying messages. You communicate passionately and intensely. Many of your messages are nonverbal, and you can form intimate bonds through your communications. You are not interested in superficialities; what you say comes from the depths of your psyche. You think about secrecy and silence, sometimes deliberately withholding information. (This might handicap connections to other people.) Your mind is apt to be thorough and organized, but powerful emotions (and obsessions) can sway your thinking. You seek root causes and may be unflinching in your quest for information. You might be drawn to detection, research or ferreting out secrets. You may be interested in anything that looks beneath the surface: archeology, psychotherapy, the occult.

MERCURY IN SAGITTARIUS

Your mental approach is broad and quick. You communicate enthusiastically, openly and optimistically. Your desire to be direct, truthful, generous and broad-minded helps you to make connections with other people. Your mind seeks the overview and the big picture (perhaps through religion, philosophy, spiritual ideas, etc.). Your thinking and reasoning are influenced by long-term goals rather than specific details or short-term needs. Honesty may be a major focus. You are likely to be quite articulate and gregarious. Your thinking tends to be optimistic and you may sometimes leap to conclusions, overgeneralize or exaggerate. You can inspire people with your ideas. You are naturally inclined to learn and to teach others what you know, having an instinctive connection between learning and teaching. You also could be involved in writing, the law, or travel.

MERCURY IN CAPRICORN

Your mind and tongue are likely to be serious and sensible. You tend to communicate cautiously and might doubt your mental ability when young, needing to prove to yourself that you have a good mind. Sometimes this doubt is associated with limited educational opportunities in childhood and it can be overcome by more study in adulthood. When you are sure of your knowledge, you can speak with an aura of expertise or authority and may choose a career involving the mind. It is also possible to slip into rigid thinking at times. Your reserved, formal, authoritative or self-sufficient qualities may sometimes inhibit interchanges with others. Your natural logic and cautious planning are apt to be oriented toward material success or personal responsibilities. Your thinking is probably well-organized and you may have talent for business. You learn through persistence, dedication and steady progress. You want results from what you know and what you learn (practice must back theory). You can be a bit pessimistic at times (focusing on limits rather than potentials), but your basic ambition should keep you striving to attain more intellectual expertise and to gain respect for your mind.

MERCURY IN AQUARIUS

Your mind and tongue tend to be unconventional (perhaps to the extreme of sometimes shocking people). You tend to communicate intelligently, objectively, openly and independently. You use language individualistically (sometimes rebelliously). You think for yourself and resist other people's answers. You learn best by questioning authority and seeking unique experiences. Your mind is experimental, innovative, and future-oriented; you want to explore all possibilities, keeping options open. You may sometimes leap from idea to idea (an intuitive flash or brainstorm), though this can also run the risk of producing fragmented or erratic thinking. You probably have excellent verbal skills, can be quite objective, and may be able to talk to anyone. You like to make connections on an individual basis, while still appreciating group process. Your interests are likely to include anything new age, unusual, different, technological or progressive.

MERCURY IN PISCES

Your mind and tongue tend to be sensitive and intuitive. Due to compassion, you will express your intelligence sympathetically. When feeling safe, you can be very talkative; otherwise you clam up. You may be poetic or your language could be lovely. You are likely to communicate idealistically, imaginatively, or evasively. You can make connections with people on a nonverbal level, and may be psychically or spiritually tuned in. You may uplift others through your thinking or communicating. You probably have a wonderful creative imagination and may create beauty with either your mind or your hands. Your interests tend toward areas that are inspirational: art, nature, the spirit, etc. You could incline toward fantasy, evasion, avoidance or denial if what you perceive does not match your inner ideal. "What if" might cloud your reasoning process. Yet, you can be quite flexible in your thinking, have a wholistic approach, and a natural talent for synthesizing and seeing the whole.

Mercury in Houses: *Rational Realms*

MERCURY IN 1ST HOUSE

Your mind (and tongue) may work rapidly. You can learn quickly, especially through action, but may be impatient if ideas are slow to click in (for you or others). Your communication style tends to be rapid, spontaneous, direct, and may be impulsive. You can use words as weapons (biting, ironic, sarcastic) and think well on your feet or in crises. You are likely to be quick and clever, but may be easily distracted. You probably have a natural lightheartedness or flippancy with a casual spirit. Your identity is tied to your mind; you think of yourself as a rational, logical person. Communication and perception are important bulwarks of your self-expression.

Your consciousness is self-oriented, concerned with independence and assertion. You are likely to think about liberty, action, and doing your own thing. You notice courage, initiative, vitality and enthusiasm. You are curious about who you are, the new, bravery and independence. Your interests may include sports, skilled coordination, forthright self-expression or courageous ground-breaking. If you have not integrated your freedom-oriented side, relatives (including siblings) may live it out to excess—be too independent, acerbic, aggressive or eager.

"I think, therefore I am" is quite appropriate for you.

MERCURY IN 2ND HOUSE

Your mental approach is oriented toward comfort, ease, beauty and pleasure. You may prefer to learn easily and smoothly, not wanting to "work" at it. Yet the use of your mind can be—for you—a sensually gratifying experience. Your communication style is probably slow and steady, but pleasant and attractive. You may create beauty with language. You may make money through your intellect, through verbal, communicating, or perceiving skills, or through eye-mind-hand coordination and finger dexterity. You are also likely to spend money on education or possessions which are mentally stimulating.

Your consciousness centers on possessions, physical pleasures and/or beauty. You tend to notice comfort, happy endings, sensual gratifications and material rewards. Your curiosity could focus around beauty, ease, satisfaction or material security. Your interests may be artistic, hedonistic or financial. You can be logical and rational about monetary matters. If you have not integrated the sensuous side of your nature, relatives (including siblings) could be laid-back (perhaps even lazy), sensual, materialistic, attractive, artistic or comfortable. You can be lighthearted and objective about beauty, sensuality, pleasure or finances.

MERCURY IN 3RD HOUSE

Your mind is extremely restless, eager to explore in many directions. You want to learn everything and constantly seek information. You think (and can talk) about anything and everything. Your communication style is varied and versatile. You are likely to be quite articulate. Your curiosity is extremely marked, with a natural yen to learn, teach and spread information. You can be quite perceptive, rapidly picking things up, but may be a bit prone to nervous tics or twitches. You need constant stimulation from the surrounding environment and could get bored easily. You may be quite dextrous, flexible and adaptable.

Your consciousness is open, aware and interested in everything around you. If you have not integrated your mobile, restless side, your relatives (including siblings) could be very scattered, bright, talkative or adaptable. You can be lighthearted about thinking, communicating and learning, and may be easily distracted. Because your interests are many and varied, you could be overextended or superficial. You notice many things and are skilled at comparisons and contrasts. You are almost always processing information.

MERCURY IN 4TH HOUSE

Your mental focus is rooted in emotional needs. You can learn through absorption, assimilation, intuition and memorization. Your intellectual and communicating abilities are strongly influenced by your childhood experiences, especially the degree to which you felt secure. The parent (usually mother figure) who was supposed to be supportive and sensitive on a feeling level had a strong impact on your capacity to think and communicate. That individual is a significant role model (positive or negative—what to do or what **not** to do) in terms of the world of the mind and tongue. Your communication style could be somewhat reticent; you probably talk when you feel safe and secure (often in a "homey" atmosphere).

You are likely to think about feelings, security, home and family. Rational processes lead you naturally into emotional realms. You may be curious about vulnerabilities, commitment, roots, heredity and parenting instincts. You probably notice emotional bonds, family interactions, domestic demands and people's soft spots. If your own feeling side is not integrated, your relatives (including siblings) might be too nurturing, dependent, needy or emotional. Your interests could revolve around the home, your homeland, genetics, ancestry, the past or nurturing/dependency issues. You are likely to seek constant stimulation in your home and might be restless there or might move often. Your consciousness centers on emotional issues and security drives, yet you can consider family, home, and feelings from a rather objective viewpoint.

MERCURY IN 5TH HOUSE

Your mind is drawn toward excitement, vitality and expansion. You learn through dramatic examples, the adrenaline rush and onstage activities. You probably think about pride, fame, power, joy, and creative self-expansion. You want to shine, to be the center of attention, and to achieve recognition through your intellect or communicating skills. Your verbal style is probably dramatic, exciting, entertaining, lively, or exaggerative. You are seeking mental stimulation with lovers and children. If you deny your own perceptiveness or intellectual prowess, those you love might be verbose, scattered, easily bored or overly rational. You can enjoy the thrills of mental competition and could be skilled at word games or other mental gymnastics. Flirtation (especially on the verbal level) may come easily; you enjoy words of courtship and romance. You want to have fun in communication. You may be quite witty.

Your consciousness centers on issues of self-esteem and positive feedback. You notice admiration, generosity, egotism and confidence. You may be curious about creativity, shame, children, magnetism or ego needs. Your interests probably revolve around drama, children, speculation, recreation or self-expressive activities.

MERCURY IN 6TH HOUSE

Your mind is apt to be serious, dedicated and intent on doing a good job. You can learn through focused attention, careful handling of details and a willingness to work. Your mental approach is apt to stress efficiency, practicality, self-restraint, productivity and a critical eye. If you carry the focus on analysis and discrimination too far, you could put physical stress on your body, overdoing a careful attention to detail. You are curious about how things work and the ways and means to improve people and/or situations. Your interests revolve around health, healing, service, competence and efficient functioning (in the body and on the job). Your communication style is exacting, precise and studied. You can be quite critical about how language is used, wanting just the **right** word at any time. You may be overly critical of your intellectual capacities and could judge yourself as unequal to others who seem more eloquent, educated, etc. It is important to count your assets and not just flaws!

Your consciousness centers on productive efforts and quiet efficiency. You notice where the flaws are and how to fix them. You tend to think about your work and your health. You need mental stimulation and variety in your work, or boredom could easily set in. If you deny your more causal, flippant side, co-workers could overdo being scattered, superficial, lighthearted or restless, or you might be subject to nervous tics and twitches. Your mental, verbal or writing skills may be an important part of your job routines and you are likely to have talent in many types of craftsmanship, including mechanical skills (able to take things apart and put them together properly). You have a natural flair for puzzles of any variety and a good instinct for repairing things.

MERCURY IN 7TH HOUSE

Your mental approach is to weigh, balance and seek equality. You probably think about justice, relationships, fair play and even-handedness. You are apt to be curious about interpersonal interactions, aesthetics and the process of give-and-take. Your interests revolve around people exchanges, visual beauty and harmony. You tend to learn what is pleasurable and may prefer not to "work" at it. Your communication style is likely to be diplomatic, tactful, charming or other-oriented. Your words may flow forth with grace and harmony. However, you might also possess a competitive streak, and could enjoy debating or other forms of verbal contests. You could even be a good "devil's advocate," willing to argue for principles you do not hold personally in order to make sure that both sides are represented.

Your consciousness centers on relationships, balance and beauty. You can be lighthearted about people exchanges and loveliness; you need stimulation (especially intellectual) in your partnerships. If you deny your more casual, flippant side, you may attract a partner who is scattered, overly rational, cool, or too restless to settle down. You may unconsciously look to your partner to stimulate your thinking, or to initiate communication. Social contacts will be an important part of your relationships. You may enjoy the art of negotiation (perhaps comparing and contrasting a bit too much with others). You have a natural skill for meeting people on their own level and understanding their point of view.

MERCURY IN 8TH HOUSE

Your mind is deep, penetrating and intuitive. You learn through intense emotional experiences, self-mastery, and obsessively getting to the bottom of things. You are probably curious about hidden knowledge, death, passion and transformation and transmutation. When you study something, you take it to the limit. Your communication style is intense, probing, confrontational, relentless and/or secretive. You see knowledge as power and may withhold information if you feel it is in your best interests. You might be drawn toward hypnosis, mind control, propaganda, advertising or other forms of intellectual power. You are likely to have above-average psychic ability.

Your consciousness centers on elimination, insight, intensity and purification. You probably think about power, mastery, passion, boundaries, secrets, waste and regeneration. You can be rather objective about intensely emotional issues, including sexuality and shared possessions, finances and pleasures. You may enjoy "playing" with resources, trying out a variety of options, restlessly moving money here and there. If you deny your more casual and flippant side, a mate may express those qualities in excess: be overly rational, scattered, superficial, restless or verbose. Yet communication and mental stimulation make up the glue that holds your intimate bonds together. Your mind is that of a psychotherapist: probing inner drives and desires, seeking to illuminate the deepest and darkest recesses of the psyche (your own and those of other people).

MERCURY IN 9TH HOUSE

Your mind is concerned with issues of faith, philosophy, education, travel or anything expansive and broadening. You learn through principles, broad perspectives, overviews and generalities. You think about the meaning of life and are apt to be curious about faith, beliefs, values, goals and world views. Your interests tend to be philosophical, spiritual, expansive or wide-ranging. You tend to "think big," and are apt to be optimistic. Your communication style is probably outgoing, gregarious, humorous, lively or adventurous. You may be prone to "foot-in-mouth" experiences on occasion or jumping to conclusions. An appropriate motto might be "Be sure mind is in gear before putting mouth in motion." You could enjoy argument for the sheer intellectual stimulation and may be a skillful rationalizer. Ethical issues (especially too much or too little honesty) could affect your written and verbal exchanges.

Your consciousness is restless, expansive and always wanting more. You can be a natural student, teacher, writer and traveller. If you pursued higher education, you may have studied many different things! If you have not actualized your own faith, trust or expansiveness, your relatives (including siblings and grandchildren) may be overly confident, outgoing, ethical, religious, spiritual, perfectionistic, funny or rash. You seek the stimulation of always learning more, going further, understanding more fully, and expanding your horizons.

MERCURY IN 10TH HOUSE

Your mental approach is apt to be serious, dedicated, work-oriented, responsible or inhibited. You learn through experience, perhaps not believing you can do something until proving it to yourself by succeeding. You are probably curious about the laws of life, the structure of society and the issue of limits: what one can and cannot do. Your mind, communicative abilities, dexterity or perceptiveness could be an asset in your career. Your authority parent (usually father figure) had a profound impact on your capacity to think and communicate. If his role model was negative, you may be excessively self-critical in regard to the use of your intellect. If he was a positive role model, you may slip easily into the role of expert where communication is concerned; you **sound** authoritative! If father carried mercurial themes to excess, he could have been flighty, unable to settle down, scattered, too casual or cool or aloof rather than protective and responsible. Your mental capacities are tied to your experience of dominance and authority.

If you have not yet internalized your own sense of power and effectiveness, your communication style is apt to be cautious and conventional (perhaps even blocked). If you have a sense of yourself as an authority or expert, you are apt to be a professional communicator, with your mental capacities a major part of your career. You can be an excellent manager of information, and may have a knack for understanding who can best handle which responsibilities. Your consciousness revolves around necessities, demands, obligations and practical accomplishments. You tend to notice rules, limits, authority, control and realism. Your interests are apt to be career-oriented, or to further a sense of accomplishment and power. You need variety and intellectual stimulation in your work.

MERCURY IN 11TH HOUSE

Your mind is apt to be original, inventive, individualistic and perhaps even rebellious. You can find new and different pathways of thought and are not afraid to go beyond traditional boundaries. Although you may be quite unconventional in terms of thought, behavior is another matter. You learn on your own, in a unique fashion, with a broad, eclectic approach. Your communication style is unique, unusual and may be unpredictable. (You may sometimes say things just for the shock value—or to prove to people that their stereotypes and pigeonholes are not working.) You are apt to be quite restless mentally, and can get bored easily. You need quite a bit of variety and stimulation, and could be a networker, picking and connecting information from a wide variety of sources. You are probably interested in people from all walks of life.

Your consciousness is open to many options and capable of inventive leaps. You think about humanitarian issues, the future, technology, friends and the new and different. You could be involved in politics and social causes. You notice originality, independence of mind and progress. You are curious about change, friends and anything on the cutting edge or of the "new age." You can stimulate and be stimulated by the thinking of others, and can "leap-frog" onto ideas from those around you. Your friendships tend to be sociable, with much intellectual stimulation and conversation. Your interests are many and varied, centering around a theme that is unique, unusual, humanitarian or eclectic.

MERCURY IN 12TH HOUSE

Your mind is drawn toward the experience of Oneness and union with all of life. You can learn through empathy, absorption, intuition and merging. If you have inner faith, you tend to think about the web of life, interconnections with others and the patterns in the whole. If you lack inner faith, you may be very focused on your own interests and on guarding against too much sensitivity to the world. You are probably curious about beauty, faith, psychic understanding and nonverbal knowing. Your interests may revolve around aesthetics, healing and helping, rescuing and saving, or (if your inner faith is weak) escaping and running away.

You tend to notice kindness, compassion, beauty and self-lessness, but also may constantly contrast the ugly reality of the world with your beautiful dream of how the world ought to be. Your communication style may be soft, poetic, confused, illusory or beautiful. You probably have a vivid imagination, flair for fantasy and capacity to blend logic and intuition. When your psychic impressions get mixed with logic, a lack of clarity is possible. When you are tuning into the cosmos, others may find your communications confusing or incomprehensible. Your challenge is to combine the rational and irrational, taking the best of both.

Your consciousness centers on dreams, visions and a quest for infinite love and beauty. You are apt to think and dream a lot about utopias. You may face both the positive and negative side of seeking an ideal through relatives. You are susceptible to the thoughts and feelings of others and may sometimes pick up input like a "psychic sponge." Learn to clarify what is yours and what is not. It is important to take some alone time (call it meditation or whatever) to go inside and clean out any garbage—leftover frustrations, fears, guilts, hurts, etc. Once you have learned what you could, and done what you could about past experiences, give them to the Infinite and let them go. You can absorb too much from others and need to regularly purge it. Faith and beauty can complement your thinking and logic to create mental wholeness.

Mercury in Aspect: *Mental Matters*

The nature of the planets involved in any aspect is the most important factor. For any pair of planets, please read **all three** aspect delineations: conjunction, cooperating (sextile ✶, trine △), and challenging (square □, opposition ☍, quincunx ⚻). The conjunction is the basic, most fundamental aspect and its themes carry through with other aspects. The cooperating and challenging analyses will offer additional choices regarding of constructive and nonconstructive ways of handling the basic issues.

Remember that the life issues represented by cooperating aspects (or conjunctions) may still require some attention. We might overdo certain themes, or succumb to projection, repression or displacement in trying to balance our many, different drives. It is also quite possible that you could have integrated some of the conflicts (shown by challenging aspects) which were present at birth and are now manifesting potentials more reflective of the delineations in the cooperating or conjunction sections.

Other factors will complicate the picture. The potential inherent in any given placement might be overridden by other configurations in the chart. As you read the interpretations for the various pieces of your chart, bear in mind that certain pieces will suppress others. As always, repeated themes, which recur again and again, are the most likely to manifest in your psyche and in your life.

MERCURY CONJUNCT VENUS

You may be skilled at using beauty in language (poetry, songwriting, etc.). Crafts or creative writing could appeal. You could make money through communication, writing, verbal arts, graphic arts, or sales. You are sensitive to beauty and may find it easy to communicate love and affection.

You can be quite affable, compliant, accommodating and pleasant. If overdone, you could slip into being apologetic, dualistic, duplicitous, hypocritical or imitative. Appearances matter to you and you are likely to know what one is supposed to want and say (and be able to say it). You can be quite persuasive and charming and may have a pleasant voice. You enjoy communicating.

Your thinking is apt to be influenced by concerns for beauty, comfort and ease rather than just logic. Learning may be a source of pleasure for you, but you might also avoid arduous studies, preferring topics you can pick up without effort. You want to enjoy the mind and the tongue, expecting them to bring more pleasure into your life. You might be attracted to youth, to younger people or to ideas. Conversation tends to flow smoothly for you. You know how to put others at ease.

Your thinking and communications may revolve around relationships, possessions, or money. You are likely to attend to (focus on) pleasure in life—whether from things or from people. You are sensitive to the beauty of your surroundings and have the capacity to contribute to that appeal.

MERCURY COOPERATING VENUS (✶)
Social graces may come easily to you. You have a knack for putting people at ease, and may be quite charming. Compromise and cooperation could be natural for you.

Your mind, hands, or communication skills might contribute to your income. You could make money through crafts, writing, speaking, sales, entertainment, transportation, finger or hand dexterity or other agile activities.

Easygoing and agreeable, you tend to gravitate toward pleasant activities and might avoid confrontations. Your skills are suited for projects that flow smoothly and comfortably; this combination is not inclined toward arduous labor.

You may have skill for dealing with people, a knack for discussing important issues in relationships with tact and sensitivity. You can be affectionate and caring as well as objective and logical, blending the best of each in interpersonal encounters. You probably have a flair for people.

MERCURY CHALLENGING VENUS (□ ⚹ ⚻)

Not possible natally. Mercury and Venus are never far enough apart to form a square, quincunx or opposition.

MERCURY CONJUNCT MARS

Your mind and tongue are apt to be quick and sharp. You may be fond of argument or debate and could be a skilled extemporaneous speaker. Verbal aggressiveness is possible; you could have a tongue like a sword and not be afraid to use it. You might be sarcastic, blunt, outspoken, sharp, witty or quarrelsome but it is also possible to think about verbal aggression without actually saying it. Competition (especially with relatives) is possible. Your quick wits could also make you a good comic.

Because your mind works swiftly, you can think on your feet and respond rapidly to crises. You learn quickly, are constantly active mentally, and may be skilled at repartee. You are likely to be quite alert. Your fast response time can mean going off in several directions at once, or being nervous and rash. You may sometimes speak without thinking, or forget in mid-thought. Because you process ideas so quickly, you could be susceptible to interrupting others. You might talk in bursts or sprints. You can be quite energetic and vigorous in your thinking. You can assert yourself verbally, act on your own ideas and have a forceful intellect.

You express yourself primarily through the world of the mind, tongue and hands. You might have good coordination, be mechanically skilled or generally adept and versatile. You probably identify yourself as a thinker and/or a talker. Expressiveness comes naturally to you. Some restlessness is likely; you need variety and lots of stimulation in life.

MERCURY COOPERATING MARS (⚹ △)

You have the capacity to balance thinking and doing. You can choose when to act and when to observe. Courage and confidence support logic and rationality (and vice versa). Your energy flows easily into verbal activities.

Variety is important in your life. With a strong streak of curiosity, you need mental (and other) stimulation lest you get bored. You can also get other people excited about ideas—turn them on. Change and movement are essential. You can react quickly to situations and may have good coordination (except when moving **too** fast). Mechanical skills are possible or you might be talented with crafts.

Because you can react rapidly, you may be skilled at debate or extemporaneous speaking. Verbal expression can be a favorite form of assertion. You might fight with words literally in terms of biting sarcasm, irony, argumentativeness or verbal attacks. You probably deal well with crises. Your quick-wittedness may be channeled into a shrewd business mind or a sense of humor and skills with repartee.

Your openness to life and experiences can come across as a youthful attitude, and your freshness may appeal to children. You could do well in sales, politics, journalism or other fields which require rapid assessments of the people and situations surrounding you. You thrive on activity.

MERCURY CHALLENGING MARS (□ ⚹ ⚻)

Your mind and tongue are apt to work more swiftly than average. Thinking on your feet is an attribute that can contribute to skill in persuading or convincing others. Impulsive speech is also possible; you might speak more quickly than is wise on occasion. Some strife with relatives is possible if balance is lacking in your degree of assertiveness. Having lots to do at family gatherings can be helpful.

If you do not have a satisfactory outlet for your competitive spirit, you could use words aggressively rather than assertively—in arguments, verbal attacks or sardonic humor, bitter irony or sarcasm. Your natural urge is to express yourself, particularly verbally, so you need a forum which will allow you to constructively pour out. You could debate for the pure pleasure of it. (If there are other inhibitory patterns in your chart, the challenge may be simply to allow yourself to say what you think and how you feel.)

Your active, spontaneous side may be at odds with your rational, logical side. This can feel like tension between doing and observing, and you may sometimes swing between impulsive actions (and accidents if extreme) and overanalysis, weighing alternatives. By integrating thoughts and deeds, you can have the best of both. It is important to know when to think, when to speak, and when to take action.

Your mind is apt to be quite restless and you need variety in your life. You can easily become bored with routine. Seek out circumstances that feed your hungry curiosity and desire to learn.

MERCURY CONJUNCT JUPITER

A life of learning and imparting what you have learned is the one for you. You probably enjoy studying, teaching and/or traveling, with a restless, eager mind that seeks the broadest horizons in a quest for answers and meaning from life. Probably blessed with a good sense of humor, you can be witty, informative, a good conversationalist, playful and intellectually generous (in offering and in being open to information).

Constant mental (and physical) activity is a possibility in your life; you could have the shutterbug mind that never seems to click off. You may have trouble settling on one pursuit or study as your diverse interests draw you in many different directions. Able to grasp the wide overview as well as details, you can appreciate the small and the large issues of life.

You may be particularly interested in issues of philosophy, religion, ethics, morality and truth and spend time discussing these topics. A talent for foreign languages is possible. You could be drawn to publishing, education, travel, broadcasting or gathering and distributing information. Communication is the breath of life to you, but talking may feel more natural than listening; give others a turn too. You can be an inspirational and persuasive speaker and do well in fields such as teaching, public relations, promotions or sales.

Because you tend to think big, you could overextend yourself, especially in what you want to learn or communicate to others. You could be a dabbler or dilettante. You are inclined to focus on the positive and may ignore the negative. You may overidealize the mind and succumb to rationalizations, intellectualizations. You can leap to conclusions, overgeneralize from your data, or exaggerate. Your mind works quickly (and often your mouth as well); you may be too blunt at times ("foot in mouth").

You are likely to be optimistic, insatiably curious and on the go, constantly seeking intellectual stimulation.

MERCURY COOPERATING JUPITER (✶ △)

Your mind is likely to be quick and restless, with multiple interests and a constant, driving curiosity. You may enact the role of perpetual student, teacher or traveller in your life, constantly seeking mental stimulation, new knowledge and broader horizons.

You can translate concepts from the wide to the specific and may have linguistic talent as well. Communication skills are marked, with a quick wit, playful spirit and tendency to accentuate the positive in life.

You may sometimes scatter your forces, because your interests encompass so many different areas. Higher education could enhance your efforts if you are able to focus on one subject. The truth may be a significant issue in your life, whether through a blunt, tactless honesty or a tendency to exaggerate, or to see the best, or to use your tongue to promote your own beliefs and values. Verbal expression is accented; you may need to learn to listen more, but tend to be a fascinating conversationalist with a wide array of knowledge at your fingertips.

With a mind and tongue that can function more quickly than average, you could be skilled at anything requiring comprehension or communication. You thrive in an atmosphere of variety and constant intellectual stimulation.

MERCURY CHALLENGING JUPITER (□ ⚹ ⊼)

Mental restlessness is likely and a desire to be on the move, mentally and/or physically. Your mind is apt to be pulled in many different directions, and you may have trouble finding a focus on occasion. You could feel torn between the details and the overview; between the near-at-hand and far away, or between information versus wisdom, between the world "as it is," and your ideal of how it ought to be. You seek constant mental expansion and activity.

Truth (or morality, ethics, religion) may be an issue in your life. Perhaps you are ruthlessly blunt ("honesty at all costs") or have tendencies toward the con artist—pitching pipe dreams—or using truth in other ways for personal ends. Perhaps you see so many sides to "truth," that you have trouble believing any one. Your rational side may war with your desire for an absolute spiritual, religious or philosophical faith. Your optimism and desire to know and understand everything could lead you to sometimes jump to conclusions, exaggerate, speak too quickly or see only the positive potentials.

You probably have talent for any communication fields, including broadcasting, journalism, sales, media work, promotion, etc. For fulfillment, your restlessness and need for variety must have constructive outlets in life. You can learn a great deal, and teach and inspire others as well!

MERCURY CONJUNCT SATURN

This combination suggests a serious, grounded mind that is able to be thorough, organized and practical. It can, however, indicate someone who doubts his/her mental abilities. The impact of the father (or father figure) is particularly relevant in your handling of thinking and communication. If he was critical, harsh, judgmental and demanding—or if you simply felt you could not measure up to his example—you are likely to feel anxious, insecure, perhaps even phobic about your capacity to think, to talk and to use your head. If he was a constructive role model, he taught you to be sensible, skeptical and to use your mind to work in the world.

Once in a great while, this aspect indicates actual blocks in thinking or communication skills. More commonly, it shows a lack of inner faith in your mental abilities. You may also, in undervaluing your own mind, put blind faith in the orthodoxy, authority figures, or pundits at large. With discipline and work, however, you can build a solid foundation for yourself. Only by actually **doing** it (by using your mind and your verbal skills) will you prove to yourself that you **can** do it. Your accomplishments build faith in yourself.

After working through early challenges, this combination can denote the professional communicator—someone whose career involves thinking, talking, writing or using the hands. Your mind is your potential gift to the world, the contribution you can make to society.

You can access a rational, sober, thorough mind with a cool head for business. You are likely to prefer the concrete and practical to the abstract. You can do research and solve problems methodically, with careful, considered thought. You may appreciate lists, outlines and formats, but might give too much weight to having the **right** answer. You are likely to use words carefully, take education seriously, and learn well from experience.

MERCURY COOPERATING SATURN (✶ △)

Your thinking can be quite organized, practical and systematic. You deal well with lists and may have business acumen. You can be quite analytical, methodical, and precise with language and thinking. You have a good sense of appropriateness and can operate well in formal settings. Your judgment tends to be steady with good concentration and excellent timing.

Verbal skills, finger dexterity, adaptability, thinking, relatives, or communicating may contribute to your professional achievements. You are willing to put effort and discipline into mental pursuits.

Your memory could be good. You are likely to be most interested in practical matters which can further your career. Contacts and those you know might be of assistance to you vocationally.

Logic and rationality are accentuated in this combination. You are able to be objective, sensible and unmoved by emotions. (If overdone, this quality could seem too dry, humorless or literal-minded.) You have the instincts of a scientist: check observations against reality and test ideas before accepting them.

MERCURY CHALLENGING SATURN (□ ⚹ ⊼)

Your mental prowess may be inhibited by criticism or doubts. A father or authority figure could have seemed stifling, judgmental, or harsh in regard to your thinking or communicative abilities. You might retain some underlying insecurities about your intellectual capacities, or feel verbally blocked. You can be disciplined, responsible and efficient in your use of the mind and tongue, if you trust in your abilities and act despite inner doubts.

You may feel a sense of conflict between your flippant, casual, lighthearted and variety-oriented side, versus your desire for commitment, follow-through and seriousness. Life requires both the ability to work and to play; to focus and to scatter; to socialize and to get down to business. The inner tension could also be between flexibility versus rigidity or between youth and age. Integration means using the best of both.

You may experience difficulty "hearing" others because you sometimes fall into a rut mentally, or perhaps you feel others ignore or minimize your input (don't "hear" you). Building your inner sense of faith in your abilities will help smooth outer challenges. You can use your mind, tongue or hands to further your career and have the capacity to be thorough, organized and systematic in your intellectual dealings.

MERCURY CONJUNCT URANUS

Originality in thinking and speech is a keynote of this combination. Regardless of how much you show to the world, your inner reasoning is highly individualistic and innovative. (This can go to the extreme of the rebel, the iconoclast or the individual whose thought processes are inevitably odd or unusual.) Your speech or writing could be idiosyncratic. Yet you are likely to be rational, objective, impersonal—living in the head.

You could have sudden flashes of brilliance (even genius)— and sudden flashes of off-the-wall thinking as well. You may leap to conclusions, interrupt, overgeneralize or rationalize. Problem solving is a likely talent; you can view challenges from a totally new perspective, standing a problem on its head to come up with an innovative solution. You can reassemble, reorganize, and reform concepts. Brainstorming may be a way of life for you. You are curious and seek solutions to everything, naturally experimental, inventive and innovative.

Networking is an appropriate forum for your talents. You can be interested in anyone and anything, particularly the widest reach of humanity, groups and progressive ideas. You can probably talk to anyone, no matter what their level or background in life. You are apt to be naturally equalitarian, instinctively treating people as peers. You may be drawn to politics, science, writing, computers, electronics, math, technology or anything new.

Variety is important to you; your boredom threshold is much lower than average. If you are in a stifling situation, your restlessness may unconsciously attract "surprises" (to the point of disruptive events). By deliberately keeping your life full of change, mental challenges, and new experiences, you can optimize your intellectual freshness, your productivity, and your enjoyment of life. You seek mental excitement.

MERCURY COOPERATING URANUS (✳ △)

The mind is doubly emphasized here. Your thinking and perceptions may make sudden leaps, skipping steps but intuitively grasping the right answers. You might even have flashes of genius. Mental stimulation is vital in your life, particularly a sense of constantly stretching and challenging your intellectual muscles.

You can be quite logical, rational and objective. A natural observer, you may sometimes watch life's fascinating parade without feeling a need to **do** anything. Knowing and understanding might be enough, or knowing and talking.

People contact is important in your life; you need the stimulation of other minds and ideas. You could be a skilled networker. Naturally equalitarian, you can relate to anyone and everyone. You may make valuable contributions to groups, organizations and causes.

Your communications and thought processes are apt to be original and innovative. This can sometimes include rebelliousness or inappropriate impulses to go against tradition. Generally, however, you can be a wonderful brainstormer and a skilled problem-solver. You have a knack for bringing in an overlooked or rare perspective, another alternative or a new viewpoint. Your tremendous need for variety helps you to see many viable choices in life.

MERCURY CHALLENGING URANUS (□ ⚹ ⊼)

This restless combination needs constant mental stimulation and lots of variety in life. Otherwise, nervous tics, twitches or even accidents are possible. You thrive in an atmosphere of change and intellectual challenges. Your mind needs constant mountains to conquer, but may sometimes operate in bursts and spurts.

Your individualistic thinking may occasionally lead you into overdoing the role of the rebel or revolutionary. You might throw out the old simply because it is old (even if still useful). You are likely to be most interested in the new, the progressive and the futuristic.

Communication conflicts are possible, particularly if you feel your individuality is being slighted. Clashes with relatives or friends could occur, especially around questions of freedom and fairness.

Logic or rationality could be an issue in your life. Most commonly, a cool, detached attitude can be overdone and strike others as callous or uncaring. More rarely, you may have difficulty calling on your capacity to be an observer of life when it is appropriate to stop with that.

By harnessing together your originality and perceptiveness, you can be quite a creative problem-solver. You can open your mind (and other people's minds) to alternatives and options.

MERCURY CONJUNCT NEPTUNE
Your imagination is likely to be highly creative. You have the capacity to blend logic and intuition, combining rationality and psychic impressions for the best of both worlds.

You may have talent for flowing, graceful language (e.g., poetry), music, songwriting or other artistic/aesthetic outlets. If the desire for grace, ease and harmony is overdone, you could fall prey to "little white lies" or deception to avoid unpleasantness and any violation of your ideal imagery. A general linguistic flair is possible. Perhaps you can "pick up" accents like a chameleon. A flexibility of mind is indicated; you can easily visualize alternatives and possibilities (and have a high tolerance for ambiguity).

You need inspiration and desire to transcend ordinary thought patterns. You may be concerned with spiritual ideas and ideals. You could fantasize (indulge in magical thinking) or seek magic words and rituals. You may think and communicate in metaphors and symbols. You can learn through revelation, absorption and intuition.

Because you are "wide open" on one level, you may sometimes feel overwhelmed by sensory or other input. You might be more susceptible to drugs, alcohol, etc., than the average person. You could have a sensitive nervous system and may occasionally have difficulty "shutting out" the world. Trying to process too much information from too many different sources could result in uncertainty or confusion. It may take effort to keep ideals and imagination differentiated from the physical world and common sense. If you allow logic and intuition to fight each other, you might deceive yourself (or fall for the fantasies of others) due to wishful thinking, or overvalue common sense at the expense of your "gut" impressions. A synthesis will work best. You can be skilled at blending the conscious and unconscious sides of the mind for psychotherapeutic or healing work, for artistic expressions, or to permit mystical experiences.

MERCURY COOPERATING NEPTUNE (⚹ △)

You may inspire others through speech and/or writing. Your words may flow with grace and beauty. You could be talented in terms of singing, songwriting, playing a musical instrument, linguistic abilities or other aesthetic skills. You may create beauty with your hands, e.g. through hairdressing, crafts, etc.

You are able to bring unconscious, psychic impressions into conscious awareness and communicate them. This is an excellent quality for the skillful therapist or the professional psychic. Your capacity to combine logic with intuition can be an asset in any field: once your mind has collected all the rational data available, you can then act on instinct.

Because you can paint lovely word pictures, you could have skill in sales, advertising, media work (or lies and deception). You are likely to seek harmony in communications and may be susceptible to a "sob story" when your sympathies are aroused, or set yourself up for deception by wanting to only see the best in others.

You are able to tune into another world, and could enjoy sharing with others the creatures of your imagination, the fruits of your impressions and your special, whimsical magic.

MERCURY CHALLENGING NEPTUNE (□ ⚼ ⚻)

Your imagination is one of your best assets, but can seem a liability at times. You are likely to be open to otherworldly vistas, tuning into spiritual, mystical, idealistic (or unreal) images. This can be an asset in many aesthetic/artistic pursuits (including songwriting, playing a musical instrument, singing, hairdressing, crafts, linguistic talent, etc.).

Your capacity to paint lovely pictures with words could also support work in the fields of public relations, advertising, sales, promotion, the entertainment world, etc. If the illusory qualities are overdone, you might lie or unconsciously deceive others through a need to "make nice" and keep things on a "pleasant" or idealized level. Susceptibility to drugs, alcohol or other escapist paths is possible. The membrane separating truth and fiction is very permeable in your mind; imagination and reality tend to easily blend.

If the passive tendencies of this combination are overdone, you could be susceptible to daydreaming or fantasizing rather than doing. Due to a sensitive nervous system, you tend to take in a lot of input and may end up overwhelmed, confused or absent-minded. You need to make clear priorities in your handling of information. You cannot absorb everything and have to decide what needs your attention the most at any given moment.

Your mind is potentially poetic, visionary and inspired. Your communications may have a touch of magic. You can assist and uplift others.

MERCURY CONJUNCT PLUTO

Your mind is capable of incredible depth, comprehension, thoroughness and focus. You can concentrate fully on gaining essential information and may be sensitive to subtle clues and perceptions which escape others. You naturally search for root causes and underlying motives; surface answers are much less interesting to you than what lies beneath. You are an instinctive therapist with an urge to understand what drives both you yourself and others, seeking insight into motivations.

You are likely to be curious about hidden matters and could be drawn toward occult studies, politics, hypnosis, mind control, detective work, history, research, archaeology or any realm which gives your probing intellect a forum to dig, question and seek deeper answers. On the mundane level, you could be interested in joint resources, dealing with fields such as bookkeeping, insurance, investments or financial planning. Alternately, you might be attracted by sex, therapy, magic, death or any taboo areas.

You can be quite focused in your thinking, but may also cling too hard to opinions. Others may see you as fanatic on occasion, or you could be susceptible to obsessions or compulsive, repetitive mental patterns. You can be quite insightful, subtle, persuasive, sly, cunning, careful and thorough in your thinking and communication.

The potential power of language may matter greatly to you. It is possible to use words to control others or to avoid speech for fear of its power. Blackmail, intimidation or manipulation may be tools of the trade for you (or for others against you) in terms of language. You might engage in satire, polemics, sarcasm, teasing or irony. You may believe that knowledge is power, and be attracted to confessions. You can be quite incisive and decisive in your thinking.

You may think a lot about power: its use and misuse and such themes could color your interactions with others. Early relatives (or anyone you relate to) may bring up power themes with you as you struggle to own your own strength without using or being used by others.

Your mental skills lie in acute perceptiveness, exacting organization and a determination to finish, to get to the bottom of things.

MERCURY COOPERATING PLUTO (✶ △)

Your powers of concentration and focus can enhance and aid your perceptiveness. Able to take in lots of data, you can still organize it and use it systematically. You are likely to have talent for business (particularly financial realms), for research, for psychotherapy and for anything which requires an in-depth, mental approach. You may use words as therapy, for healing.

You see knowledge as power and may use words to intimidate, manipulate, overwhelm others (or experience this from the world). You could be drawn to fields such as advertising or sales work. Occult studies, politics, hypnosis or other forms of mind control could appeal to you. You may be fascinated by the dark side of life and tend to investigate areas that others would avoid, see as taboo, or shrink from in horror.

You can be quite analytical, easily cutting to the core of a matter. You may have a penchant for getting to the heart of any matter, and tend to seek underlying motives rather than relying on surface appearances. You may seek (and give) clues and hints, enjoying mysteries, puzzles and intense scrutiny to ferret out secrets.

You may wield power through your use of thinking or communication. Because your rationality and logic are backed with emotional intensity and a strong, tenacious will, you can be more than ordinarily persuasive, amazingly efficient and totally organized.

MERCURY CHALLENGING PLUTO (□ ♂ ⊼)

You are dealing with the conflict between breadth and depth, between variety and concentrated focus, and between openness and secrecy. You may feel pulled between intense scrutiny, a single-minded determination to get to the bottom of matters, versus a light, flippant, casual approach to life.

You can be quite open and naturally communicative and then clam up, obsessing about hidden agendas and self-protection. You may feel torn between directness and seeking a back door route to what you want. You can be intellectually competitive and may compare your thinking, knowledge or verbal skills to those of others.

Because you see power in the use of knowledge and communication, you could incline to verbal manipulation, intimidation, sarcasm, satire, innuendoes, or obsessiveness (or deal with any of these in others). Assigning blame, justification and excuses may be central issues in your life.

You can be quite a powerful communicator. Mentally resourceful and verbally intense, your handling of information is likely to be potent. What you know and say (and what you **don't** reveal) has a strong impact.

CHAPTER SIX

VENUS
PLEASURE AND POSSESSIONS
IN YOUR HOROSCOPE

Venus in Signs: *Enjoying Exchanges*

VENUS IN ARIES

You are likely to enjoy activity and doing things **once**, but repetition may bore you. You can be assertive in relating to people and probably appreciate courage. Your desire nature is emphasized; sensuality comes naturally to you. Your handling of money and possessions tends to be direct, forceful and/or impulsive. Freedom and novelty are important issues in your love relationships. You enjoy **beginning** relationships (and may prefer the early states to later ones). You probably express affection impulsively, directly, and honestly and prefer an enthusiastic, energetic response from others. You like independence, initiative and action in yourself (and others).

VENUS IN TAURUS

You are likely to enjoy physical gratifications (food, drink, possessions, finances, sensual indulgences). You can deeply enjoy sensations, appreciate nature, and savor the five senses, especially touch. You are probably relaxed and easygoing in relating to people and appreciate loyalty and stability. You express affection physically, steadily (and are sometimes possessive). Your drive for pleasure is strong and might lead to excessive self-indulgence. Your handling of money and possessions is apt to be sensible, but you may overvalue comfort, luxury and/or attractive physical objects. You want comfort in your love relationships and respond to sensual energy from others. Your appreciation of beauty and artistic talents can lead to personal satisfaction and success.

VENUS IN GEMINI

You are likely to enjoy mental stimulation and learning. You can be lighthearted and casual in relating to people and probably appreciate good ideas. You express affection playfully, youthfully, verbally, lightheartedly. You might feel closeness through talking and sharing perceptions. Your handling of money and possessions is likely to be objective and logical. You want good communication and intellectual give-and-take in your love relationships. Flirting or engaging in superficial relationships may occur due to a desire for variety and new stimulation or to a desire to keep things cool, to avoid too much emotional intensity. You are attracted to intelligence and a quick wit.

VENUS IN CANCER

You are likely to enjoy home, food, nurturing and/or dependency. You can be sensitive and protective in your relating to people and appreciate emotional warmth and attachments. You tend to express affection protectively, tenaciously, nurturingly and kindly. You find pleasure in security. Your comfort level may depend on feeling like part of a family. You prefer to share within a very closely attached (clannish) group. If you lack faith, moodiness, timidity, overprotection (of self or others), or stinginess may inhibit your potential for closeness and ability to enjoy life. Your handling of money and possessions is probably cautious. You want to nurture and/or be nurtured in your love relationships. Closeness for you involves dependency, caretaking and receptivity.

VENUS IN LEO

You are likely to enjoy the limelight, attention, admiration and applause. (Sometimes you might be too ego-centered or driven

to dominate in relationships.) You may have natural magnetism and sex appeal. Others often find you exciting. You tend
to express affection dramatically and wholeheartedly. You can
be quite magnanimous, loyal, playful and magnetic when in
love. Your handling of money and possessions is apt to be
generous, extravagant and speculative. You want zest, enthusiasm and an adrenaline rush in your love relationships. Your
pride and urge for recognition affect your capacity for closeness.

VENUS IN VIRGO

You are likely to enjoy competence, precision and doing things
right. You can be exacting, discriminating or critical when
relating to people. You tend to express affection pragmatically
(doing things for people/serving them), modestly, or timidly.
(Criticism, feeling indispensable or too much rationality could
inhibit passionate response.) You find pleasure in functioning
efficiently and in being helpful or repairing things, situations
or people. You tend to enjoy analysis, precision and organizing
details. You probably feel more comfortable with logic and
common sense. Your handling of money and possessions can be
quite practical and thrifty. You want common sense and a
willingness to work in your love relationships.

VENUS IN LIBRA

You are likely to enjoy art, harmony and people. You can be
charming, diplomatic and graceful in relating to people. You
express affection with elegance, charm and consideration. Fairness, balance and gentleness contribute to the subtle dance
between self and other. Excessive concern for peace and tran-
quillity could lead you to avoid unpleasantness; not facing
issues inhibits intimacy. You find pleasure in balance and in
beauty (aesthetics); you appreciate symmetry and may wish to
harmonize polarities. Your handling of money and possessions
is probably cooperative (but could be competitive). You want
affection, beauty and ease in your love relationships, and to be
sure there is equal sharing between you and your partner.

VENUS IN SCORPIO

You are likely to enjoy intensity and getting to the bottom of
things. You can be demanding, forceful and unflinching in your
relating to people. You may express affection passionately,

with consuming, obsessive feelings. You probably find pleasure in figuring out hidden motives and meanings. In order to feel closeness, you need to penetrate deeply into the relationship, and make an absorbing emotional bond. Secrecy or a reluctance to trust others (not wanting to let your guard down) can hinder love or social needs. Sharing the sensual, sexual, or financial world without overindulgence or denial may be a challenge. Engaging in a give-and-take with others can generate transformative, transmuting energy. You want loyalty and to be swept away, seduced, fascinated, and absorbed in love.

VENUS IN SAGITTARIUS

You are likely to enjoy travel, philosophy, education or anything which broadens your horizons. You can be friendly, expansive and philanthropic with people. You express affection generously, grandly, extravagantly, confidently unless you are disillusioned when your ideals are denied. You value honesty and can be quite broad-minded in terms of love. You probably get pleasure from ideals and ideas. Because you enjoy exploring and adventuring and because you seek an ideal relationship, you may have trouble settling down to just one relationship. Your comfort and harmony require the freedom to roam and explore and always look for something better. Your handling of money and possessions is apt to be optimistic (perhaps rash) and could lead to getting overextended. You want **the best** in your love relationships. You and a partner must agree on goals, values and world view; philosophical harmony is essential.

VENUS IN CAPRICORN

You are likely to enjoy being responsible, practical and competent. You tend to relate seriously, formally, with some reserve. You express affection cautiously, soberly (and sometimes dutifully or perfunctorily). You find comfort in control, and could sometimes inhibit pleasure or love needs due to fears, limitations and inner doubts. You can get pleasure from achievement and status in the world. Your ambitions, status, or conservatism may affect your love and social urges. Your handling of money/possessions is apt to be businesslike, pragmatic and well organized. You want predictability and fidelity in your love relationships. You want to be **sure** before making a commitment in partnership, but are willing to work hard to make the relationship endure.

VENUS IN AQUARIUS

You are likely to enjoy being unusual or different in some way. You tend to relate casually, erratically, or with openness and tolerance. You probably express affection experimentally, freely or unconventionally. You can get pleasure from being unique. Your handling of money and possessions may be progressive, intellectual, unpredictable, changeable or rebellious. You want freedom and friendship in your love relationships—and not to be tied down. At times, you could seem too cool and aloof to others; you can come across as impersonal and detached. You may enjoy stimulating intellectual exchanges with a partner. You prefer something or someone a bit outside the usual in love relationships.

VENUS IN PISCES

You are likely to enjoy being compassionate, tenderhearted, and helpful. You could relate to people by taking the role of either a rescuer or a person looking for help. You may express affection idealistically, romantically, sympathetically, or evasively. You have a deep desire for magic and romance in love. A lack of clarity about what you want or a failure to be objective in your observation of others can set you up for disappointment, deception or disillusionment. You find it easy to idealize love and loved ones. A lack of discrimination could lead to frustrating attachments. You want a beautiful dream in your love relationships; you yearn for a soul mate and you may be psychically attuned to a partner. You can also receive much pleasure from art, nature and inspirational matters. Your handling of money and possessions may be idealistic, dreamy, or escapist. Look for ways to use your artistic and philanthropic talents to make a better and/or more beautiful world.

Venus in Houses: *Sensual and Satisfying*

VENUS IN 1ST HOUSE

Your identity is tied to sensuality and beauty. You may be physically attractive and/or graceful. You probably have artistic talent, or at least a strong feeling for, and some ability to create beauty. You may enjoy dancing, or other forms of beauty in action. But you are also likely to be oriented toward comfort and sensuality. You might be strongly drawn to eating, drinking, sex, or other sensual pleasures, or focused on money and material possessions. You find it easy to like yourself as well as to enjoy the physical world.

You find comfort in being yourself and doing your own thing. You probably enjoy direct and open self-expression. Security, for you, means the freedom to be yourself and the ability to enjoy yourself. (At times, this can go to the extreme of passivity or laziness. You might expect life to flow too easily, without personal effort.) Your possessions may be almost like part of your identity, and they make a statement about who you are. Your money could come through entrepreneurial routes, or involve personal initiative, energy, or a pioneering and independent spirit. You want close, personal control over finances and may partially define yourself through what you earn and own.

You are seeking to balance assertion and accommodation, personal desires and interpersonal needs. Equality, in your eyes, is related to the freedom to act, to be, and to do in your own fashion. Your partner may be active, assertive, courageous, vital, independent or impulsive or just extremely important in your life. Your social interactions are likely to be a give-and-take dance between freedom and closeness, separation and union, liberty and sharing.

VENUS IN 2ND HOUSE

This placement strongly emphasizes beauty, sensual pleasures and physical security. Artistic talent is quite possible, particularly in areas which involve a sense of touch (sculpture, pottery, gardening) or music. You are likely to be quite comfortable, settled and easygoing (but may sometimes be too stable and rooted). Because of your desire to always have beauty and comfort, you may have trouble dealing with strife. You have a strong attraction to sweetness and comfort. You probably enjoy physical gratification, money, possessions and tangible beauty. You may rely on material security and financial safety to feel good and could even marry to obtain wealth. Security, for you, is related to what you have and can enjoy. Your possessions are a source of pleasure and reassurance for you. You would prefer to be surrounded by lovely objects. You probably earn money in order to enjoy life and might prefer not to work too hard. You can handle tasks gracefully, but are **not** oriented toward physical labor. You probably work well as a team member, in cooperative endeavors. When doing something you enjoy, you are a steady, reliable worker.

Your social interactions are likely to be comfortable, easygoing and laid-back. You expect "true love" to run smoothly. Your partner may be sensuous, financially comfortable, hedonistic, self-indulgent, stodgy or physically attractive. Shared pleasures and mutual gratification will be important between you.

VENUS IN 3RD HOUSE
You find pleasure in the mind, communication and learning. You may enjoy discussions and mental activity, but could also be a bit lazy and want to think only as long as it is comfortable. When it is no longer easy, you might politely look for something more enjoyable. Yet you are capable of much grace, beauty and ease in the intellectual realm. You could express beauty through language (e.g., singing, song-writing, poetry) or enjoy the dissemination of knowledge. You are likely to seek a partner who is bright, scattered, versatile, flippant or communicative and mentally stimulating. (You might literally fall in love with a teacher or someone who feeds your love of information.)

You may earn money through or with your mind, voice, hands or tongue. (This could range through the teacher, the singer, the Vegas dealer, the ventriloquist, the craftsperson, work in the media, etc.) Your possessions are also likely to be mind-related. You can find comfort and security in the intellect and may depend upon rationality or logic. You could have a beautiful speaking voice and may overdo tact (to the point of untruths) because you dislike unpleasantness in social exchanges.

You are attracted toward beauty and comfort in relatives (including siblings) and neighbors. If the people around you overdo this theme, they could be physically attractive, artistic, hedonistic, lazy, stubborn or excessively materialistic. The people in your immediate vicinity offer role models (positive or negative) for your handling of the urge for pleasure, gratification, possessions and stability.

VENUS IN 4TH HOUSE

This placement emphasizes a desire for security and stability. Your home may be a source of pleasure and/or beauty. It may have an emphasis on physical possessions and sensuality. Above all, you want your nest to be comfortable, attractive and pleasant.

Your mother or nurturing figure may exhibit Venusian qualities: stable, secure, artistic, comfortable, and/or stubborn, plodding, self-indulgent or materialistic. Her example is teaching you what to do and what **not** to do in regard to money, material resources and sensual gratification. This parent is also a role model (positive or negative) for later love relationships. If your initial relationship is comfortable, stable and affectionate, your later partnerships are likely to be equally so. If you are still working through some issues with mother, you may attract a partner who reminds you of Mom (in terms of bullheadedness, materialism, self-indulgence, etc.) in order to resolve those issues. Your social interactions may revolve around the domestic area; you probably prefer a sense of safety with people and may value privacy.

One possibility is looking for a partner to give you the unconditional love and acceptance you always wanted and never got as a child—or trying to be the all-loving, all-protective partner (hoping to get it in return). Your partner could be warm, dependent, nurturing or empathic. Your relationships are an arena for balancing dependency and equality, for learning to **exchange** parental nurturing to achieve true partnership.

You probably enjoy food, nurturance, emotional ties and a sense of roots. You find comfort in family, feelings, food and emotional warmth. Security, for you, is both emotional and physical. Your possessions are a source of reassurance for you and you may have trouble throwing things away. (You could be a compulsive collector of whatever you enjoy). You might earn money through a family business, in your home, or with home, land, or heredity-related fields. You seek gratification through emotional ties.

VENUS IN 5TH HOUSE

You are likely to have creative, artistic talent, with an urge to pour out into the world in some fashion which will add beauty and grace. You probably enjoy excitement, drama, the lime-light and thrills. You may find comfort in attention, approval and applause. You find security in loving and being loved, in admiration and respect. You may have a very sensual approach to sexuality. You are naturally receptive, magnetic, attractive.

Your self-esteem could be connected to your possessions and bank account. You want to be proud of what you have. If what you own is seen as an extension of yourself, you may be ego-threatened when those possessions seem less than they ought to be. Alternately, you might tie your self-worth to your appearance and connect your self-esteem to how you look. Yet you can also simply enjoy a childlike spontaneity, zest, and enthusiastic outreach into life.

You could earn money through working with children, promotion, entertainment, sales or any form of persuading or swaying people emotionally. You are likely to feel somewhat torn between security needs and risk-taking instincts. You want to do something more, to take a chance on enlarging your scope and gaining greater return, yet you also want to play it safe, protect what you have and ensure enduring safety.

Your love relationships bring in issues of pride, power, passion and self-esteem. You probably want social interactions which are dynamic, entertaining, lively and expressive. If you are out of touch with your Venusian side, you may attract lovers (and/or children) who express those qualities excessively. They may be beautiful, easygoing, comfortable, and sensual. They may also be materialistic, boring, indulgent and hedonistic. Ideally, you and those you love share much mutual affection and truly enjoy one another.

VENUS IN 6TH HOUSE

You are likely to seek security in your work, preferring regularity and predictability. You also want to enjoy what you do; you work for pleasure as well as for material rewards. You may appreciate efficiency, productivity and obtaining tangible results. You could find comfort in being competent, capable and dedicated. Security, for you, comes from doing your best, especially in work and health. Your possessions are practical and may be work-oriented. You could earn money through organizing, maintaining, or repairing bodies, minds, machines, businesses, or systems on any level. Any field is possible if it involves details, analysis, or a concentrated focus. You may work on relationships (e.g., counseling), do artistic work, sensual work (e.g., massage), or financial work. For personal satisfaction, your job should provide comfort, pleasure and security.

If carried to an extreme, the desire for ease can lead to wanting work without any effort, a job which is always pleasurable. It is possible to be too passive and lazy to be effective. The socially desirable jobs are usually only attained with considerable effort. Charm can sometimes persuade others to do one's job but it is rarely effective for long. If the Venus desires are projected, co-workers may be too hedonistic, hung up on physical beauty or sensual indulgences.

In terms of health, the orientation is toward comfort. You are not prone to disciplined pursuits. You might overindulge, especially in sweet things, particularly when frustrated in a job or using sugar as a substitute for love. Illness could also be an unconscious escape from having to work hard—or an unconscious route to being pampered and indulged. You are likely to prefer the easy way in regard to health care and may be quite concerned with its effect on your appearance. Yet you enjoy feeling good and can steadily and reliably pursue a program once you've made a habit of it.

Your social interactions are often work-related, or involve overtones of repairing or improving the situation. You might turn partnership into a career (working with people or being or having a professional spouse). Some business executives can still afford to support a spouse who cares for the home and family or works at entertaining business associates rather than at a separate job outside the home. You could also work with people (in personnel or as an administrator); marry someone who is willing to work for you (often a workaholic); work with a partner in a family business, work **on** a partner (attracting people who need some improvement); or turn relating into your job (maintaining a critical, judgmental, flaw-finding attitude). Your partner may be hardworking, humble, pragmatic, critical, nitpicking or restrained. Your relationships are an arena for you to develop and constructively channel your efficiency urges, critical judgment, service needs and analytical abilities.

VENUS IN 7TH HOUSE

You are attracted to beauty and comfort in relationships. You want to enjoy people and interactions. You probably find pleasure in relating, harmony, grace and form. You may make money through art, partnerships, or aesthetics. You tend to appreciate balance and have an instinctive sense of give-and-take. Your social interactions can be quite pleasurable and graceful when you allow your natural diplomacy to flower. You are likely to have a strong visual sense with potential talent for work or hobbies involving color, design, form, photography, painting, architecture, etc.

If these relaxed themes are overdone, you might feel that relationships should always be easy and pleasurable without any personal effort. You might expect beauty all the time. This can include being drawn only to people who are physically attractive, or having the fairy tale idea that love means one shouldn't ever argue, fight, disagree, etc. You may have trouble facing negativity in partnerships, perhaps expecting, "If I am charming, sweet and nice, the other person ought to be as well."

You may look for security in relationships and could even marry for financial reasons. You want someone with whom you can feel comfortable. Your partner could be pretty (handsome), passive, charming, graceful, artistic, or smoothly cooperative. You expect to take turns and seek fair play and evenhandedness in your interpersonal exchanges. Sensual connections are quite important. Money may be a focus. If the urge for gratification is carried to an extreme, power struggles over finances or possessions are possible. Either party may view the other as a possession to be "owned" rather than a person to be cherished. You are capable of much affection in relationships and apt to have a teamwork orientation. Creating a rewarding balance in your partnerships is apt to be a priority.

VENUS IN 8TH HOUSE

You want intensity, passion and an in-depth commitment. You may find comfort in shared pleasures, possessions, sensuality and sexuality. You find security in power, control and mastery. Your social interactions are likely to stir up strong emotional issues; superficiality bores you. Digging beneath the surface gratifies you.

Your possessions are tied to those of others; learning to share equally is an important issue. You might feel "I should be provided for materially; you are here to serve my pleasures and desires" or you might attract people who expect that of you. Power struggles over resources (who owns what, who enjoys what, who does what to whom) could be an issue until you reach an inner balance between self-indulgence and self-mastery and an external balance which preserves the rights of both partners. You could earn money through or with other people, or through sources such as inheritance, government grants, royalties or return on investments.

You want to enjoy a passionate bond with a mate, yet also have a need to go within to probe your own inner depths. You are learning to balance intimacy instincts with your inward tendencies. If you are only conscious of your urge toward purification, regeneration, and transcendence to the point of denying your own darker side, you might attract a partner who is self-willed, probing, powerful, manipulative, hermit-like, intense, or overly passionate. Generally, however, you want your closest relationship to be pleasant as well as intense, gratifying as well as confrontational. You and a mate may literally or figuratively make beautiful music together, deeply motivating each other.

VENUS IN 9TH HOUSE

You are likely to enjoy adventures, broadened horizons and philosophical explorations. You can find pleasure in education, religion, spiritual quests, travel and fun. Your security rests in the capacity to expand your visions, your knowledge, or your circle of experience. You may love knowledge, books and learning. Ethics, morals, teaching and studying could be sources of intense personal enjoyment.

Beauty, pleasure, sensuality, or love may be an ultimate ideal for you. You might idolize art, money, sensual indulgence or a romantic partner. If comfort and security are your ultimate goal, you may visualize and actualize a stable, easygoing existence. Excessive materialism is a possibility if faith is placed in things. You could earn money through the mind, travel, religious or spiritual paths or anything involving promotion, broad influence, or big dreams. Perhaps beauty is seen as the source of life's meaning—and sought through art, concepts, travel or people. Hedonism may be adopted as the ultimate lifestyle. You may be torn between valuing the truth but wanting social interactions to be attractive and pleasant which may sometimes lead to using tact or "polite lies" rather than honesty. Your ideal world puts love and affection on a pedestal.

If your search for the ideal is tied to partnership, you might look forever for the perfect partner or the perfect relationship, never being satisfied. Or, you could try a variety of relationships, each time disappointed when an idol reveals his/her feet of clay. It is also possible to literally marry God, to choose a religious vocation. Another possibility is getting involved with someone who believes s/he is perfect, or trying to play the all-wise, all-knowing, all-perfect individual with a partner. Some people will flirt with many possible partners, thus keeping their options open in case that "ideal love" does someday appear.

Another alternative is to be attracted to foreigners or people who have an exotic perspective which gives you a chance to metaphorically look "over the next hill." The most satisfying option is to share beliefs, goals, and ideals with a partner, permitting joint travels, studies, religious or spiritual quests or shared humor, optimism, fun and faith. Your partner may be witty, confident, rash, nature-loving, sporty, philosophical, moralistic or perfectionistic. Your social interactions are probably lively, with much movement, intellectual stimulation and good humor.

VENUS IN 10TH HOUSE

You are looking for ease and comfort in the structured world of natural and cultural laws and limits. Dealing effectively with that world calls for realism about what is possible and what is necessary. You may want your career to provide beauty or pleasure, not wanting to work hard, but you might have to compromise on your desires. You want achievement that is stable and secure and are likely to seek some degree of control over the physical, sensual world—over things. If you are realistic, you can find comfort in duties, thrift, rules, structure and safety.

You may look to money and possessions for reassurance and security. Your possessions are apt to be practical and sensible, and may further your professional ambitions. You probably enjoy responsibility, accomplishments and tangible results. (Occasionally, beauty and charm may be used to control the world: "If I am sweet enough, people will do things for me.") Your career could involve beauty, pleasure, finances, or sensual gratification. You could earn money in business, with or through a father figure, in a bureaucracy, or through steadily working your way up the ladder of success

You have the potential of a comfortable, accepting relationship with the conditional love parent (usually father or authority figure). There may be much affection between you. It is also possible that the parent may be overly materialistic, self-indulgent, passive or lazy. This parent is a role model (positive or negative) for later partnerships. Unresolved issues with Dad (or authority figure parent) will be faced again with partners. These issues are most likely to involve money, security, affection, comfort and pleasure. Your partner might be dictatorial, a workaholic, expect you to carry the load, or be responsible, dedicated and realistic. Your social interactions tend toward the conventional and are often work-related. You appreciate responsibility, fidelity, dedication and competence in your partner(s). You're willing to exert effort for love.

VENUS IN 11TH HOUSE

You are seeking pleasure through knowledge, astrology, progressive ideas, friends, groups, technology, the new, or your own uniqueness. Comfortable relationships are likely with friends: mutual support and pleasure. Associations may be easygoing and fairly stable. You can be a diplomatic, tension-easing center within your social milieu. If you deny your Venusian side, you might draw in only physically attractive friends, or be involved with organizations which promote artistic pursuits. You might choose friends who seem stable and secure but end up resenting their stolidity, stubbornness, passivity, or indulgence. You may want each interpersonal exchange to be a thing of beauty and a joy forever. Yet, you can be very tolerant and accepting of your own individuality and that of others.

You usually enjoy the new, the different, the unusual and the individualistic. You can find pleasure in change, innovation and communal efforts. Security, for you, lies in the mind, the future and your friends. Equality, in your eyes, should be a fact of life; each one of us is unique and as irreplaceable as every other person.

You may earn money through an unusual career, have nonstandard hours, or working conditions, or labor in a very different manner. Perhaps your possessions are unpredictable, unconventional or unusual. You are likely to experience inner tension between your desire for stability and security and your urge to change and innovate. You may swing between playing it safe with money and taking chances; between staying in a vocational rut and trying something new. With integration, you can enjoy both sides without pitting them against each other.

Your social interactions are likely to be wide, but casual. You can probably relate to many people but are close to only a few. You appreciate variety and intellectual stimulation and want your partner(s) to be unique, independent, cool, humanitarian, weird or bright. People may start out as friends and become partners, or remain friends even after you have been partners. You are capable of much objectivity and detachment in relationships.

VENUS IN 12TH HOUSE

You probably pursue Neptunian pleasures which may include meditating, dreaming, drinking, drugs, artistic endeavors, healing and helping others, psychic experiences or the emotional intensity of mystical, spiritual or religious fervors, etc. Overindulgence could be a danger in any of these activities. Moderation is important. You can gain gratification through art, assisting the downtrodden and imaginative activities. You may find comfort in fantasy, visions and ideals. You may idealize beauty and security. Your sense of safety is tied to faith in the goodness of the universe.

Some kind of artistic expression is a healthy outlet for your need to be inspired and swept away by grace. If beauty is overidealized, you may have difficulty facing your own or the world's flaws and sordid side. Despite the futility of the effort, you could try to avoid all conflict, striving for a perpetually pleasant and easy atmosphere and running away from the imperfections of life through alcohol, sleep, daydreaming, drugs, etc.

You might idealize nature and beauty. "What a wondrous world that gives us such sunsets, such sensations, such loveliness." You may be drawn toward possessions that are infinitely lovely, or fanciful. If the material world is turned into "god," people can worship mammon and constantly indulge themselves materially and financially. Laziness is possible, or unrealistic fantasies about great windfalls ("when my ship comes in"). Yet you are capable of earning money through work involving the arts, helping/healing activities, fluids including drugs and chemicals and the ocean, or anything involving the infinitely large (e.g., astronomy), the infinitely small (microbiology), or the perception of patterns.

Since Venus is a key to partnership, another alternative for this combination involves idealizing love and/or a partner. This can be a very romantic placement, "in love with love," seeking that perfect, ideal experience. There is a need for privacy; feelings tend to be soft and tender. Some individuals will search forever for Prince or Princess Charming (who does not exist). Others will suffer painful disillusionment as they find that the individual they idolized is human and fallible after all. Or, worse, the tendency to project one's ideal and to not see the real person can leave one vulnerable to con artists. Some romantic idealists will place their faith in love (or a partner) and be crushed when they feel they have lost it. (The "perfect" partner dies young before we can discover his/her human flaws.) Some will unconsciously seek to play "God" themselves, attracting victims whom they try to save: alcoholics, psychotics, drug addicts, chronic invalids or other human casualties who need to be rescued. Co-dependent associations do not work in equalitarian associations.

What can work is shared faith and inspiration. Partners may meditate together, share artistic creations, be fellow healers or otherwise seek something Higher in life without expecting the partner to **be all** or **do all** in the relationship. Thus, you and your partners may be artistic, attractive, idealistic, savior types, gentle, compassionate or empathic.

Venus in Aspect: *Pleasure Principles*

The nature of the planets involved in any aspect is the most important factor. For any pair of planets, please read **all three** aspect delineations: conjunction, cooperating (sextile ✳, trine △), and challenging (square ☐, opposition ♂, quincunx ⊼). The conjunction is the basic, most fundamental aspect and its themes carry through with other aspects. The cooperating and challenging analyses will offer additional choices regarding of constructive and nonconstructive ways of handling the basic issues.

Remember that the life issues represented by cooperating aspects (or conjunctions) may still require some attention. We might overdo certain themes, or succumb to projection, repression or displacement in trying to balance our many, different drives. It is also quite possible that you could have integrated some of the conflicts (shown by challenging aspects) which were present at birth and are now manifesting potentials more reflective of the delineations in the cooperating or conjunction sections.

Other factors will complicate the picture. The potential inherent in any given placement might be overridden by other configurations in the chart. As you read the interpretations for the various pieces of your chart, bear in mind that certain pieces will suppress others. As always, repeated themes, which recur again and again, are the most likely to manifest in your psyche and in your life.

VENUS CONJUNCT MARS

You can be quite sensual, passionate and pleasure-oriented. You could enjoy acquiring things and may seek immediate gratification. Or you might be highly artistic, especially drawn toward forms of beauty which include action such as dancing, playing a musical instrument or gymnastics. You might define yourself through possessions, money, class or status—or identify with partnership. You are learning to blend personal will and desires with interpersonal needs and the art of compromise.

If you are unable to combine personal and interpersonal drives, you could need approval and yet rebel against it. You might feel confused about compromise, boundaries, assertiveness and compliance. Perhaps you act appeasing and smile when angry—or attract anger from others. You might feel torn between passion (lust) and affection (love) or not perceive them as aspects of each other. You may seek affiliation, yet sometimes feel trapped by it.

You can be quite magnetic and may be naturally attractive to the opposite sex. You may unconsciously put out sexual vibes. You can be quite charming, sensitive, tasteful and pleasant. You may believe in love at first sight and could respond rapidly in terms of sex.

You have a marked capacity for enjoying life, and—if you choose to—bringing pleasure to others as well.

VENUS COOPERATING MARS (✶ △)

You have an instinctive capacity for compromise. You can make room in relationships for your needs, wants and desires, as well as those of the other person. You know how to pursue what you want without stepping on someone else's toes, and how to please others without totally denying your own personal power.

Sexual charisma is a strong potential. You may have a natural capacity to love and be loved, to attract the opposite sex. Your instincts are likely to be good in terms of interpersonal attraction; you put out sexy vibes.

You can blend action and reaction, pushiness and passivity. You know when to initiate and when to wait. You are likely to have a good sense of balance between being assertive and being receptive. You can be direct, forthright, energetic and strong, but also tactful, polite, laid-back and gentle. You have a sense of when to express each side in life.

You may have a strong feeling for beauty and could be very involved with aesthetics in your life, whether through personal hobbies or in more serious pursuits. You can express beauty in motion and might love dancing or other physical activity which includes grace and rhythm.

VENUS CHALLENGING MARS (□ ☌ ⊼)

You are working on the balance between assertion and accommodation. You may sometimes be too compliant, needing approval, avoiding anger or putting yourself last. At other times you might be too aggressive, demanding, wanting what you want. The challenge is to know when to compromise and when to protect your own needs.

You may feel torn between gratifying yourself versus satisfying the desires of the people you care about. Personal independence could vie with the desire for relatedness. Life is big enough for both freedom and closeness. You need a sense of space along with affectionate connections to others.

Initially you may have trouble blending sensuality and sexuality, affection and passion. With practice, you can combine them or make room for both at different times, in different ways in life. Your physical needs may be strong. You might seek immediate gratification.

Sexual charisma is possible. You may be easily and sharply attracted by and attractive to the opposite sex. Issues of anger, assertion and independence may challenge your relationships with women while issues of affection, tact, resources, possessions or money could challenge your relationships with men. Your goal is to know when to do your own thing and when to compromise with others.

You can be quite magnetic, charming, tasteful and ardent.

VENUS CONJUNCT JUPITER

You are likely to indulge in pleasure in a **big** way. You could love enthusiastically; be generous with time, money, energy and affection; and seek comfort, ease, hospitality and good times.

You might revere money, success, abundance or resources. Material goods might be overvalued or you might slip into being smug, complacent, wasteful, lazy or gullible (seeing only positives). Yet you are often "lucky," instinctively taking advantage of opportunities.

You could idealize and overvalue romance, loving easily and expecting to be loved back. You might want more than is possible in relationships, yet you can also be fair, tolerant, accepting, and try to love (or appreciate) something in everyone.

You may come across as attractive, popular, friendly, permissive, generous, poised, lavish, or benevolent. You might also incline toward overindulgence (of yourself and/or others), extravagance, and excesses.

You may enjoy travel, education, religion, ritual or a search for meaning in life. You are working on the balance between personal relating needs and personal pleasure versus the quest for infinite understanding and ultimate values. You may feel torn between the sensual and the spiritual until you are able to blend them.

You are likely to be naturally friendly, kindhearted, sociable, generous, easygoing and attracted toward the best in people, circumstances and life.

VENUS COOPERATING JUPITER (✶ △)

You are probably friendly, popular and sociable. Optimistic, you have a knack for accentuating the positive—in yourself, in others and in life. Your values are likely to encourage relationships. You gain pleasure in seeking the best, the brightest and the most in life.

You are attracted by the finer things in life, and are apt to want material goodies. You might even be overindulgent, extravagant, exaggerative, or expect everything in life to come too easily. Due to your faith and visualizing potential, you could be fortunate in the financial or material realm. Your income might be enhanced through education, travel, religion, ideals, or anything involving broadened horizons. Because you know what you enjoy, what you want, and how and when to recognize and to capitalize on opportunities, you can appear quite lucky.

You need a partner who shares your values. Whether you focus on honesty and sincerity, on spiritual principles, on education, on travel or on some other form of truth seeking, your love relationship must support your quest for meaning in life. This can sometimes lead to you expecting too much from a partner, to a partner looking to you to be more than human, or to multiple associations ("perhaps the next one will be better"). A shared foundation of trust, appreciation and goals works the best.

Your focus on the best could be a handicap when difficulties must be acknowledged and addressed with patience. Generally, however, you can make the most of your potentials, and turn liabilities into assets.

VENUS CHALLENGING JUPITER (□ ⚼ ⚻)

Your ideals may sometimes be at odds with love needs or financial necessities. You are learning to ground your visions in the real world. If you become too invested in pursuing the "good things" in life or the "right crowd" (turning money or success into "God"), you may end up losing material or social rewards in order to discover a wider perspective (find a bigger God). This combination can indicate potential extravagance, exaggeration and even ostentation. When handled constructively, you can consistently increase your assets and instinctively expand on life's positive possibilities.

Expectations are an issue where love relationships are concerned. You may sacrifice the potential of a person or an association because of an insatiable seeking of more and better. You might keep standards so high, no one could measure up. You might feel commitment deprives you of freedom and be a flirt. You might get involved in guru/student associations, or idolize someone, placing them on a pedestal. The challenge is to relate to another human being with perspective, each of you encouraging the best in each other, without demanding inhuman perfection.

Spiritual needs may seem at odds with material demands. This could manifest as tension around money (e.g., do you try to amass more material wealth or spend resources on the pursuit of knowledge, education, philosophy, etc.). Your stable, rooted side may pull against your urge to travel, to adventure, to explore and seek answers in wider vistas in the world. A full life requires some of each.

You can be quite pleasant, generous and forgiving.

VENUS CONJUNCT SATURN

You are likely to be practical about beauty, love and/or material resources. You can be quite grounded and sensible, able to appreciate logic, common sense and necessities.

You may seek control of your emotions, passions or pleasures. If this is carried too far, sexual repression is possible, or blocks in expressing love. You may feel it is necessary to discipline or restrict your love or desire for comfort. Duty might overwhelm pleasure. Perhaps you feel one must earn love, or you experience deprivation, rejection, separation, or withheld affection. You may be cautious in relationships, fearful of being hurt, dominated, rejected or used, or you may unconsciously be drawn to people who are controlling, withholding or authoritarian in love. You may be looking for a "father figure" for a mate, or afraid of getting involved with someone like your father. Perhaps you consistently "test" people's love for you. Yet you are likely to value commitment, stability and protection (and might exchange love for security). You may be attracted by older people when young, and younger people when old. You seek integrity in love and loved ones.

You function best when you work in fields involving beauty (e.g., the arts), pleasure or relationships. You could put aesthetics to commercial use. You might work in art, counseling, personnel, or as a business consultant. You are apt to seek control of your resources and may feel you have to work hard for what you earn. You may have difficulty in relaxing and enjoying the fruits of your labor. You might be quite thrifty (or feel that your resources are limited).

You can be quite responsible, reliable, loyal, polite, realistic, committed and dutiful.

VENUS COOPERATING SATURN (✳ △)

You are likely to have good basic common sense and practicality. You may be naturally skilled in business or in handling finances, with a knack for knowing when to pull back and be cautious. You might have a flair for aesthetics, able to put art to commercial use.

Love and work can be complementary in your life. You take relationships seriously. You instinctively understand the balance needed between outer world achievements and loving contact with others. You know how to make room for emotions as well as pragmatism, affection as well as common sense, ease as well as effort.

Partners or other people in general may contribute to your career and worldly success. You may receive financial assistance, emotional support, practical ideas. A mentor could enhance your vocational prospects. Similarly, your sense of responsibility and willingness to work will enhance your relationships. You can be quite dedicated, faithful and helpful to a partner. You are able to be practical about people. You may contribute materially to others. Your vocation may enhance your love relations and vice versa.

Planning ahead could be one of your strengths. You probably have a respect for time and experience and are likely to do better at work and at love with maturity. You might be a late bloomer, but can certainly be successful in both the material world and in the world of love and attachments. You are apt to be reliable, sensible, dutiful and capable.

VENUS CHALLENGING SATURN (□ ☍ ⚼)

You are working on the balance between love and work. If you allow one to overwhelm the other, you may feel that worldly success takes you away from personal attachments, or that close associations handicap you in attaining your ambitions. You might feel torn in deciding how much time and energy to devote to a partnership versus a career. Both are essential for you to experience life fully; you cannot sacrifice one for the other.

You must also balance your parental, power-oriented side with your equalitarian instincts. Know when to take charge and when to yield and be a team player. If the desire for safety and control is carried too far, you might take on too much responsibility or authority in love relationships. You might also hold back because of insecurity, be afraid to trust, or fear hurt, rejection or dominance from others. You may push away your gentle, vulnerable side, seeing it as weakness. (Men are inclined to project this softness onto the women in their lives.) With effort and realism, you can create a working environment that supports your interpersonal needs, and emotional attachments that enhance your outer success.

You may also be dealing with tension between ease and effort. Your passive and your hardworking sides could be at odds with one another. The challenge is to choose appropriate times and situations for a nose-to-the-grindstone approach and equally appropriate times and situations to relax and kick back. Duty and pleasure both have a place in life.

Monetary challenges are possible. One extreme involves feeling that you must control everything about your financial situation, not trusting the world or others to give to you materially. You may believe you have to work very hard to make a living, or struggle to maintain anything that you have, but you may achieve great success through personal effort. The other extreme involves feeling that your earning capacity is limited, inhibited or blocked in some fashion. Perhaps the reality (or perceived reality) of your finances is frustrating. By expecting the worst (an unconscious script of poverty, deprivation or financial oppression), you may set yourself up for more problems. This pattern indicates that monetary pragmatism is essential. Building resources slowly and steadily (no big gambles) is advisable. Face facts about your finances, avoiding the extremes of too much (or too little) responsibility, power and control over the material realm. You are neither totally at the mercy of the universe, nor totally in charge financially. The more grounded and sensible you are, the better you will do.

You can be quite practical, helpful, responsible and dedicated. You could be a real "salt of the earth" type.

VENUS CONJUNCT URANUS

Your individuality is apt to predominate in the areas of the arts, resources, and/or relationships. Any aesthetic abilities are likely to be unique and inventive. You may be drawn to the avant garde or progressive in terms of beauty. Your taste will be unconventional, unusual, apart from the norm. You could be interested in photography, computers, video, scientific or political art. You may contribute a new perspective to the world of beauty.

Your income may relate to the unconventional (unusual hours, a different shift, part-time work, self-employment or other nonstandard or esoteric approaches), or you could work in fields involving technology, the cutting edge of change, astrology, groups, networking, or anything off the beaten path.

An attraction to the different and the unusual is likely in terms of love relationships as well. This combination can be drawn to marriages between people of different religions, races, backgrounds. Sudden attractions are possible; "falling in love" seems natural. If the desire for freedom, uniqueness, and the need for change are not satisfied, relationships may remain unstable. Commitment may be a challenge (as if you have one foot out the door). You might pull away from a partner when feeling confined, or unconsciously choose people you can't have — married, living a long distance away, unavailable, etc.

You may swing between the conventional and unconventional in relationships, between wanting closeness and security and wanting freedom and separation, You might turn friends into lovers and lovers into friends. You can be quite tolerant, open, cooperative and equalitarian.

You need a constructive source of emotional excitement, experimentation, and challenge. You may come up with creative solutions to relationship problems. You thrive on freedom, and intellectual stimulation with other people.

VENUS COOPERATING URANUS (✶ △)

Your handling of money, pleasure and love relationships can be enhanced through your individuality, inventiveness and originality. You may be able to relate to anyone and everyone, with a knack for bringing out the inner essence of each person.

When dealing with aesthetic matters, your unusual perspective and fresh, original eye can be helpful. You could have a flair for the avant garde, progressive or futuristic in artistic endeavors.

You have the capacity to blend freedom needs with the desire for affection and attachment. (You may also be subject to sudden attractions.) You can love with an open hand, be committed without trying to own or be owned. Your approach to romantic attachments is apt to be one of tolerance, openness and encouraging uniqueness. You are able to both love and let go.

Your attraction to the unusual could lead to unconventional associations. Partnerships might be different; partners might be out of the ordinary, or your style of relating could be nonstandard. Sometimes you could want most what seems out of your reach, or be attracted by the unavailable (married, unwilling to commit, etc.). Being a friend as well as a lover works best.

Your instincts can help you to balance security needs with your desire for change, variety and the new. You can bring together risk-taking and safety-seeking, by choosing when to take chances and when to solidify your gains. Astrology, new age principles, networking, friends, groups, technology or anything unusual might contribute to your income as well as being a source of pleasure.

A friendly, accepting attitude comes naturally to you.

VENUS CHALLENGING URANUS (□ ☍ ⊼)

You are dealing with an inner conflict between independence and attachment. Until integrated, this can indicate instability in relationships, with difficulty in maintaining long-term commitments. Once balance is achieved, you are likely to love with openness, tolerance, acceptance and space. A committed partnership with you should highlight individuality and freedom.

If you aim for totally conventional relationships, you are apt to feel confined, trapped or hemmed in. You might enact the rebel role. You need some essence of the atypical in your love life and might be willing to experiment sexually. If you deny your own desire for separation, you may attract people who are married, unwilling to commit, geographically distant, or otherwise not readily available. You might attract erratic, unpredictable partners. You need an element of independence within the solidity of an emotional tie.

Surprises are also possible in the area of finances. You may make sudden decisions or choices which affect your monetary stability. Your desire for variety and change could vie with your quest for safety and the status quo. You could feel torn between playing it safe versus taking chances monetarily. By working unusual hours, or in an unconventional field, or in a nonstandard manner, you can help satisfy your inner drive for uniqueness. By balancing security and risk-taking needs, you can make optimum choices in most circumstances.

This combination can indicate difficulty reconciling lovers and friends, but has the potential to turn lovers into friends and friends into lovers. By combining the best of both, you are committed and caring to friends, and open and tolerant with loved ones.

VENUS CONJUNCT NEPTUNE
Beauty is a strong, central thread in your nature. With a marked feeling for aesthetics, you may have talent for a number of different artistic realms. You are naturally drawn toward grace, harmony, ease, beauty and pleasure. (At times, you may seek the "easy way," falling into passivity or laziness.) You may want to improve the world through art or counseling.

You may make money through art, through helping/healing professions (medicine, therapy, nutrition, etc.), through liquids (chemistry, oil, drugs, etc.) or through use of your creative imagination. You have a high level of empathy and feeling for others. Misdirected, your idealism and romantic attitudes could lead you to see only the best in others, or to get too involved with a rescuing role. Then you could be victimized financially (and on other levels). Denial is a common defense for you—not admitting to what you see as ugly or unpleasant. You can use spaciness, confusion or fantasy to avoid intimacy. Don't set yourself up to be taken advantage of or hurt!

You may be in love with love. It is easy for you to believe in a beautiful dream, particularly where loved ones are concerned. You could fall for an illusion and wake up later disappointed, disillusioned (and possibly disadvantaged). You can easily succumb to savior/victim (or co-dependent) associations. Your quest for the ideal love ("love can cure anything") could lead you to invest someone with all sorts of imagined virtues. You yearn for a spiritual (unattainable) union, an idealized equality. Your desire to cure, to heal, to assist could attract you to doormats, addicts, or people with serious problems. You may seek pleasure through being swallowed, subsumed, rescued (or rescuing) or a form of symbiosis. Beware of how easily you can sacrifice/martyr yourself in relationships. The more you channel your idealism and aesthetic needs into outer world production or inner meditation, the less they will spill over into your relationships.

You can be quite artistic, romantic, creative, sensitive, ethereal, graceful, tender, yielding and loving. You can imagine a more ideal existence and are willing to ask "what if" and "why not."

VENUS COOPERATING NEPTUNE (✶ △)
Love, beauty, grace, harmony and charm are highlighted in your nature. Artistic talent is quite likely. You have a flair for beauty which might manifest in many different forms. You are drawn to aesthetics, to what is lovely in life.

With a preference for ease and "niceness," you might sometimes succumb to seeking the "easy" route. Laziness, passivity, little white lies, and trying to avoid unpleasantness are possible. You could focus on what is pretty, and deny (or run away from) life's less attractive facets. You have talent for making life more beautiful, but must realize that not everything in life is lovely.

You are likely to accent the positive in your love relationships. You tend to focus on the Higher Self (best potential) within the people you care about, and willingly contribute to enhancing their abilities. At times, you could take rose-colored glasses too far and be susceptible to disappointment (people aren't perfect) or being taken advantage of by those you idolize. Generally, you can be quite romantic and idealistic. You want to create the perfect love.

You can be quite compassionate and sensitive. If overdone, this could lead you to entanglement in savior/victim associations. Meditation, spiritual studies, artistic endeavors, mysticism and involvement with nature offer helpful avenues for your yearning, seeking, searching side that needs inspiration.

VENUS CHALLENGING NEPTUNE (□ ☍ ⚼)

Your inner desire for the beautiful dream may challenge your handling of finances and/or love relationships. You must find a constructive channel for your inspired, compassionate side—without succumbing to the lure of escapism (e.g., through drugs or alcohol) or trying to be all things to all people.

Idealization is apt to be a factor in love relationships. You might seek the perfect love (and be disappointed in fallible human beings), try to play the all-loving rescuer/savior to a partner (unconsciously attracting victims of various sorts), or believe you have found heaven on earth—only to wake up later disillusioned and possibly victimized by someone you put on a pedestal. Seeking the best together with a partner—through meditation, spiritual paths, artistic activities or nature worship—can help to maintain a fulfilling relationship.

Handling money realistically might also be a problem. You may be susceptible to seeing what you want to see, rather than what is there. You could "space out" when it comes to balancing the checkbook. You might be a "sucker" for a sob story. You might overvalue material goods (or deny them any importance). You could make money through beauty, art, relationships, counseling, other people, etc., but must balance the quest for infinite perfection with some practical assessments of material world necessities.

You could have real artistic talent, sensitivity, natural compassion and the ability to uplift and inspire others.

VENUS CONJUNCT PLUTO

You are likely to face intense issues involving sensuality, sexuality and finances in your life. You have the potential to be quite magnetic, alluring, seductive and sensuous.

The struggle between self-indulgence and self-control will probably affect your life. You may experience sexual or sensual extremes: swinging between pleasure and pain, or between feast and famine around food, alcohol, sexuality, money or other material resources and pleasures. Life may have an all-or-nothing, seesaw flavor. Moderation is a challenge.

Financial issues are probable. You may feel torn between earning your own living versus depending on others monetarily. Power struggles with loved ones are possible (over money, sex, etc.). You may collect, accumulate, share, covet, envy and/or keep score in regard to money, possessions, sex and power. You are likely to be concerned with consuming and consummation.

You may be quite sensitive to power issues in relationships. You could use love to transform (yourself and/or others). You could vacillate between intense relationships and intense aloneness, between a desire to control and a desire to yield. You can withhold yourself and withdraw from others (both for healthy, inner processing and as a form of punishment to a partner). You might get involved in manipulative, triangular or obsessive relationships. Favors or gifts might take on the flavor of bribes or threats. You may know what you do **not** want before you know what you do want.

You can be incredibly committed, loyal and tenacious. You would willingly face the darkest depths for those you love. You are a natural sensualist and need to enjoy the material world in constructive ways.

VENUS COOPERATING PLUTO (✶ △)

You are likely to have a strong sensual streak and may be quite skilled at dealing with the material and financial world. Your instincts about money could be excellent and you may have real talent for the business world (especially dealing with resources or finances). You can assist others through your grasp of material principles, and may well inherit or receive monetary rewards from others.

Your desire nature tends to be strong, and you could intensely enjoy sexual and sensual experiences. You may be more focused on eating, drinking, making love, making money, or other physical outlets, but the central core highlights the material realm. Although overindulgence is possible, in general you are likely to have a good balance between self-indulgence and self-control.

Intensity is important to you in love relationships. Superficialities tend to bore you. Depth attracts you; probing beneath the surface comes naturally. You could be like a therapist in relating to others, digging into the psyche, and operating as a catalyst for transformation. Power issues may sometimes emerge, and knowing how and when to cooperate is essential. (Competing with a partner is rarely a good idea.) You are capable of great loyalty, commitment and dedication.

You may enjoy investigating hidden matters, whether in other people's psyches, through occult studies, detective work, mysteries, insurance investigations, historical analysis, research, etc. You find pleasure in understanding root causes and fundamental motives.

VENUS CHALLENGING PLUTO (□ ♂ ⊼)

You are naturally drawn toward intense emotional issues involving other people and the handling of the sensual, sexual and financial world. Your perseverance and dedication can be helpful in working to a positive resolution of thorny issues.

You may feel torn between self-indulgence and self-control. Perhaps you flip between "feast" and "famine" around food, alcohol, spending/saving, sex/celibacy, etc. You may have trouble being moderate in your approach to sensual pleasures. Practice and discipline can help you learn to enjoy the material world in appropriate ways without being ruled by it.

You might also be facing the struggle between earning your own way versus depending on someone else financially, or the question of how much support to give to a loved one. "Yours, mine and ours" could be significant questions in terms of money and possessions. Power struggles over the checkbook, over inheritances, over financial decisions, are quite possible until you and your mate learn to give, receive and share comfortably in this realm.

When love relationships are uncomfortable, you may be tempted to manipulate, intimidate or withdraw—or you could find these weapons directed against you. It is important to face the dark side of your nature, and of your partner's nature. You are challenged to deal with natural human emotions, including jealousy, fear, resentment, anger, etc., in a constructive way. Learn how to let go of negativity. Develop the capacity to forgive (especially yourself), not assigning too much credit or too much blame to yourself or others. Practice turning liabilities into assets, and finding constructive channels for negative emotions.

You have incredible endurance, loyalty, and a dogged determination to get to the bottom of things, to do what is necessary.

CHAPTER SEVEN

MARS
ASSERTION AND ACTION
IN YOUR HOROSCOPE

Mars in Signs: *Assertive Action*

MARS IN ARIES

You probably need to be physically active and tend to be naturally assertive. You may be direct, forceful, and competitive. Self-expression is important to you. Doing your own thing could be essential. If free self-expression is too blocked by other parts of your nature, there is a risk of repression (which can lead to illness), projection (which can lead to meeting aggression in others), or displacement (which can lead to fighting team members). It is important to find areas where you can be spontaneous. You may have a flair for starting things or for mechanical skills. You may be good at facing obstacles and at confrontation but might have to control rashness or impatience. You function best with lots of freedom, variety and a chance to pioneer. You are probably restless, willful and have a high degree of initiative, sexual drive and physical energy. You may be impulsive in sexual matters. Your identity is tied to independence and spontaneity.

MARS IN TAURUS

You are likely to be naturally sensual and to appreciate the physical gratifications of life. Your determination and endurance are probably strong. You can assert yourself steadily and stubbornly. Being grounded is important; you need tangible results. Your energy goes toward consolidation or physical beauty. You are happiest when you can control the situation and achieve material success in your own, particularly personal way. Your identity is tied to pleasure, possessions and comfort. (Too much material focus can lead to possessiveness or sloth or to overdrive.) Your sexual drive and physical energy can be quite enduring and influenced by a deep appreciation and savoring of the physical senses.

MARS IN GEMINI

You are naturally curious and probably have a restless mind and tongue. You can assert yourself flexibly, cleverly, with multiple talents. Verbal expression and learning are important to you, along with having variety and being on the move. Your energy flows easily into mental pursuits and/or skill with your hands. You generally direct yourself toward learning more, developing new skills and making additional connections between people and/or concepts. You can be quite versatile and adaptable, but are easily distracted as the focus of your desires can change quickly and often ("once is enough"). Your identity may be tied to your thinking and communication or to your skill with your hands. Your sexual drive and physical energy are affected by what you see, by your thinking (new ideas), and by conversations.

MARS IN CANCER

You are naturally emotional, but pulled between expressing feelings and holding them in. When security needs inhibit a normal expression of irritation that you can't do what you want to, it may eventually come out explosively as a temper outburst. The desire to nurture others or to protect yourself can lead to such holding back. You want emotional security, so you may assert yourself indirectly, shyly, sensitively, or carefully. You function best in a protective atmosphere. Your identity is tied to your home, family and feelings. Connecting with your roots helps you to clarify your desires. Generally, you pursue your wants tenaciously and intuitively, with an instinct for self-preservation. Moodiness and self-protection can inhibit your self-assertion, yet you may be fearless on behalf of those you care about. Your sexual drive and physical energy may be lessened by unconscious fears, vulnerabilities, and dependencies, but they are likely to be strengthened by feeling cherished and protected.

MARS IN LEO

You are naturally dramatic and can "make a statement" in your actions. Attention, the limelight and admiration are essential to your being. You can assert yourself warmly, majestically, radiantly, or arrogantly. Your normal inclination is toward zest, fun, enthusiasm, creativity and generosity. You can be quite exciting with a strong sense of pride and an urge for recognition. You are likely to be quite vital and alive, with a creative flair. Your identity is tied to being special and to increasing self-esteem. You probably have an instinctive urge to express yourself which can sometimes lead to being pushy or pompous, but you can also be quite magnetic. Your sexual drive and physical energy thrive in an atmosphere of attention; compliments are especially stimulating for you.

MARS IN VIRGO

You are naturally analytical, painstaking and thorough. Efficient functioning is important to you—both in your work and in your body (health). Your basic inclination is toward practicality, thrift, dedication and an approach which tries to "find the flaw and fix it." Your identity is tied to competence and doing things **right**. Cleanliness may be important to you. You assert yourself analytically, modestly, helpfully, and sometimes with criticism. Too much nitpicking, self-criticism or focus on details may inhibit your ability to act. You can put a lot of energy into working, being productive, repairing or improving people, things or situations. You tend to strive to do everything "just right" and may be quite demanding (of self and/or others). Your sexual drive and physical energy are influenced by your sense of effectiveness and competence. (Too much focus on performance could lead to inhibition.) You can be quite dedicated, thorough and productive.

MARS IN LIBRA

You are naturally people-oriented and learn through relating to others. You can be quite cooperative and also highly competitive. You are working on the balance between personal and interpersonal needs. Your natural inclination is toward beauty, grace, and fair play unless you feel personally threatened. When feeling secure, you may assert yourself cooperatively, charmingly or sociably. Your initiative and drive are directed toward balancing opposites and indecision is possible if you overdo the need to weigh and balance everything. Your identity is tied to interactions with others. Your physical energy and sexual drive are strongly influenced by your partner and by aesthetic considerations.

MARS IN SCORPIO

When confident of your own power, you are naturally intense, driving and confrontational. You can be quite sexy, passionate and incisive. You are apt to experience strong desires and compulsions and to thrive on challenges. Achieving your desire may require transforming and transmuting some intense emotions. You may be susceptible to vengefulness, resentment, an urge to control others, or a lack of trust in others. At times, your desire for control, secrecy or your concern with the balance of power in relationships, could inhibit decisiveness and free expression. But you are capable of great endurance and followthrough. Depth understanding is vital to you. Your natural inclination is go to the end, to never give up. Your identity will be strengthened through self-mastery, self-discipline, self-control. You can be the sexpot or the hermit as you struggle to balance personal power and will with that of another person. You have all-or-nothing tendencies. Your sexual drive is grounded in an urge to share the deepest recesses of your psyche, to experience profound emotions and to make an irresistible intimate bond.

MARS IN SAGITTARIUS

You are naturally optimistic, confident, extraverted and humorous. Freedom and expanded horizons are essential to you. Your spontaneous inclination is toward athletics, philosophy, education, adventure, exploration or anything seeking **more** in life. Your identity is tied to your beliefs and values. You are likely to assert yourself idealistically, bluntly, extravagantly, generously, or pompously. Your wants are guided by your faith which determines your goals and your morality. You act most decisively when pursuing a vision for the future, or a personal aspiration. Your sexual drive and physical energy are fed by adventurous activities. You thrive on excitement, risks, movement and exploration.

MARS IN CAPRICORN

If you have claimed your share of the world's power, you are likely to be responsible, productive and conscientious. (If you think that the world has all the power, you may feel anxious and blocked). Being realistic is important to you. When you know your own strength, you tend to assert yourself seriously, cautiously, with authority and discipline. You can be decisive but you can also plan ahead, blending confident action with patience. You are working on the balance between self-will and the limits of the world. Don't push too hard **or** give up too soon. Your energy flows well into achievement and worldly success. Attaining material goals feeds your basic energy. Your sexual drive tends to be controlled, and you may sometimes inhibit it for fear of criticism, hurt, rejection, or being vulnerable to others. You can be quite practical about desires. You tend to go after what you want in a conventional, deliberate manner.

MARS IN AQUARIUS

You are naturally independent, unconventional and unique. Being an individual is essential for you. Your spontaneous inclination is toward tolerance, openness, and a willingness to fight for equal opportunity. Your identity is tied to progress, the future and the new. You may assert yourself in innovative ways. You have a strong need for free expression and broad perspectives, and can be eccentric, creative and even revolutionary. Your passion may sometimes be sidetracked into a detached or scientific perspective. Your physical energy and sexual drive are fed by variety, mental stimulation, freedom, experimentation, and the possibility of something new. You need openness and free flow in your life.

MARS IN PISCES

You are naturally sensitive, compassionate and vulnerable. You may express yourself through art, especially with some form of beauty in action such as dancing or playing a musical instrument. Alternately, you may be drawn to healing or helping activities, fighting for causes, or escaping reality. You are balancing self-assertion and self-sacrifice; action and intuition.

You may assert yourself with kindness, idealism, or empathy but there is also a risk of inflating your own will as your supreme value. With faith in a Higher Power and a sense of the oneness of all life, your will and initiative would be softened by compassion. Your physical energy and sexual drive may be influenced by your dreams, moods and emotions. You might feel vulnerable, or unclear about who you are, susceptible to the feelings of those around you. Intuition, inspiration, a spiritual urge, or a need to save, rescue and heal are apt to motivate you.

Mars in Houses: *Doing Your Thing*

MARS IN 1ST HOUSE

(The following interpretation is applicable to individuals who freely express their Mars nature. It is possible to block these natural inclinations, but this will usually lead to low energy or even serious illness. Society tends to discourage Martian expression in women. Individuals having trouble expressing these themes can become more physically active, build muscles, take assertiveness training or other steps to build their confidence and courage.)

You are likely to have a strong sense of personal freedom, independence, and often a "loner" tendency. You may be quite strong-willed and could exhibit marked courage (on many levels). You tend to be open, spontaneous and direct.

Your physical energy is probably high; you may bounce back easily from illness (or setbacks in general). Your natural impatience can lead you to sometimes act without thinking. You may rush "head first" into life (and can sometimes have the head injuries to prove it). Accidents are a potential if you carry rashness to an extreme. Immediacy and urgency are built into your nature. When the desire strikes, you feel you **must** act. Spontaneity is very good, but sometimes needs to be tempered with a bit of caution.

Innate self-confidence makes you willing to take risks, to naturally rise to any challenges. Competition often spurs your best efforts. You may have a talent for handling crises, with rapid response your forte. You may be drawn to sports or other physically active outlets. Your high level of energy (and sharpness) needs a constructive physical outlet. You can be quite assertive, with a firm sense of what you want. (If overdone, there may be impulsiveness, self-centeredness or combativeness.) With natural pioneering spirit, you initiate easily.

Your sense of identity is very personal: "I am me"—not based on other role models, but uniquely you. Although you can get angry quickly, you are also likely to get over it quickly. The more you do what you want, the more you grasp your essential nature. "I do my own thing" could be your motto.

MARS IN 2ND HOUSE

You are likely to actively pursue beauty and/or sensuality. Your identity is tied to the material world, and to pleasure. You may push for physical gratification and material rewards. You naturally initiate pleasurable sensations and enjoyable experiences. Self-indulgence is possible—in terms of eating, drinking, sex, spending, or any sensual pleasures. You might express beauty through physical action: dancing, diving, skating, etc.

You are likely to be deliberate, determined and persistent. Your energy is enduring; you can start things but also follow through. With a powerful will, you tend to resist the influence of others. You want personal control over matters of comfort, pleasure, beauty and finances. You are likely to resist depending on anyone else monetarily. Despite your ability to be deliberate, your impatience might sometimes manifest as impulsive spending. (Immediate gratification appeals.) With confidence in your own ability, you are willing to be courageous (and take risks) in terms of finances and pleasure. The conquest always appeals to Mars so the initial challenge of acquiring something often means more than hanging on to it! You can turn the financial realm into a battlefield—a place to prove your mettle. Beware of excessive competition here, or using money as a weapon against others.

Your sense of self is comfortable; generally, you like who you are. You are probably slow to anger, but can be a bulldozer once your ire is aroused. Although you are easygoing about your independence, you can be quite immovable; no one pushes you around. Your motto might be: "I enjoy myself."

MARS IN 3RD HOUSE

You are identified with the mental realm, with your capacity to think and communicate. You are likely to have a quick mind, and may have a quick tongue as well. This can result in impulsive speech (foot-in-mouth on occasion), but also indicates skill at debating and extemporaneous speaking. You can use words as weapons and may be biting, ironic, sarcastic at times. You are competitive mentally, and susceptible to arguments. You may turn simple conversations into combat arenas! You tend to express your anger verbally (or rationalize it away). You can also use anger, aggression or action in order to communicate.

You are an independent thinker and do your own thing in speech as well. Your courage is particularly marked in the realm of the mind. You can be quite assertive (even demanding) in your verbal expression. With a talent for quickly grasping essentials, you can initiate ideas, concepts and the gathering of information. You learn well by **doing** (direct experience) and may prefer to learn on your own. Because your wits are quick, you may be irritated at having to wait for others to catch up to your thinking and processing. Your insatiable thirst for new experiences ("I've done that once. Now what?") can lead to skimming lightly and then moving on.

Your energy flow is probably restless; you might even be prone to nervous tics or twitches. Your concentration may be scattered, as you try to observe everything, and pick up knowledge from many sources. You are flexible, adaptable, multi-talented and may have good coordination and hand skills.

Sometimes a third-house Mars indicates an only child, but more often there is a sibling (or other relative or neighbor) who serves as a role model—positive or negative—for your personal behavior. With the assertive/aggressive quality of Mars, sibling rivalry is common. You may imitate a sibling with whom you have a positive identification. Or you may fight with a sibling (or other nearby associate) in order to develop your own sense of courage, independence and personal power. You may experience relatives as quarrelsome, argumentative, aggressive, etc., until you can defend your own rights and feel strong within yourself. (Physical violence from relatives is an extreme form of this.)

You could have good coordination and skill at a variety of physical as well as mental games. Mechanical ability and talents with crafts are also possible. Your curiosity is insatiable; your mind hungers constantly for more stimulation.

You have skill at cutting to the heart of a matter under discussion.

MARS IN 4TH HOUSE

You are likely to be identified (positively or negatively) with your mother or a mother figure. In some way, the nurturing parent is a role model for handling aggression and assertion: teaching what to do, or what **not** to do. Perhaps she was assertive and independent and taught you the value of courage and personal power. Perhaps she was aggressive (even violent) and you had to fight to defend your own rights, developing strength in a painful way. Your sense of self is tied to your home (or homeland) and may be strongly influenced by your mother figure. That early relationship has a profound impact on your self-confidence, assertiveness, handling of anger, and capacity to define your identity.

This placement suggests that both you and your nurturing parent are dealing with a "freedom/closeness dilemma" in terms of the home. On the one hand, you are identified with the home, really wanting close emotional ties and a safe domestic connection. On the other hand, you easily feel trapped and tied down there. Thus, you may be restless, run away from home before adulthood, move often, or satisfy your need for change by remodeling the house and/or moving the furniture. (Mars needs action.) You might travel to get away, or simply arrange the home so that your need to be alone and do your own thing is satisfied.

You may push and pull in relationships, as you want both independence and attachments. You could have moods swings as well. You may get angry with the people closest to you (and they at you), but you also may hold it in. You are capable of caring very deeply. You can be courageous in emotional contexts, in confronting feelings. You are willing to assert yourself in emotional matters, especially where home and family are concerned. Your energy flows easily into empathy, compassion and a need for security.

MARS IN 5TH HOUSE

Personal magnetism is likely. You probably have a strong instinct for drama, especially the dramatic action (or gesture) and may have an attraction to acting, teaching, etc. (whatever puts you onstage in some fashion). You want love, attention, admiration for just being who you are. Pride, ego, confidence, enthusiasm and energy may be quite high. You can be exciting, vibrant, generous (and perhaps arrogant). Your courage is joyful, powerful and dynamic. You might initiate easily in sales, promotional activities, humor, entertainment, recreation, or anything involving emotional persuasion—where your connection to your inner child allows you to touch that in others. Your sense of self is apt to be larger than life, needing a stage or screen on which to gain admiration, attention or love. You may push for power, the limelight, creativity and self-expansion.

Your independence is expressed through creativity or dramatic acts which bring attention and applause. You may be quite blunt, direct, forthright and confrontational with loved ones and children, or when creatively active (art as a forum for freedom). You are likely to encourage independence in those you love, because you want room to do your own thing as well. (This placement tends toward a single child as that ties one down less.) You may get easily irritated by lovers or children, but it tends to blow over quickly as well. If you have children, one child is very likely to remind you of yourself. If you like yourself, all will be well, but if the child lives out some parts of yourself which you dislike, problems are likely until you come to terms with your own inner conflicts.

If you deny your own Martian side, your children or lovers are apt to carry Martian themes to excess: they may be self-centered, demanding, quarrelsome, excessively independent, or (in extremes) violent. One form of projection involves being consistently attracted to free souls (people unwilling to commit in love relationships)—where consciously you want to love and be loved, but unconsciously your desire for freedom leads you to choose unavailable people. With integration, you and those you love share excitement, honesty and a mutual respect for each other's individuality and need for space.

Your willpower is intense, emotional and could draw you toward leadership roles. Your energy flows easily into speculation, thrill-seeking and ego-expressive roles. (You might be rash in terms of investments, ego expansion or love affairs.) Your sexuality rises to a molten peak almost instantly; your passions are quickly aroused. You feed your vitality through self-expressive acts which build your self-esteem and pride in yourself.

MARS IN 6TH HOUSE

Your identity is tied to a need to function efficiently. It is almost as if, "to be is to work." This can be an extremely productive, dedicated, hardworking combination. You may naturally analyze, discriminate, improve, and produce. If carried to an extreme, you might be susceptible to performance anxiety, constantly nit-picking and feeling you should do things more perfectly. This attitude involves essentially turning yourself into a job, so you have to do everything right and are constantly looking for errors and trying to correct them.

You might also identify too strongly with your job: "I am what I do, and I am nothing unless I am working and being productive." Learning to relax and enjoy yourself might be difficult, but you could be an employer's dream: quiet, efficient, dedicated and practical. Your courage may be expressed through exacting efforts, dedicated analysis and unceasing discrimination. As long as inner motivation is present, (you choose to do what you are doing), you face hard work unflinchingly and do what is necessary. Your will is focused and concentrated; you are very organized. Your energy is directed very capably; you will get the job done well. You may get angry with colleagues or co-workers, especially if you feel tasks are not being done "up to snuff." Your standards are exacting. You push hard on the job, dedicated to competence and productivity.

An alternate extreme is the person who says "I will only work when I want, where I want, and how I want." The self-will of Mars is carried to the extreme of "If I cannot do it my way, I won't do it at all!" This can be the individual who is constantly quitting or getting fired from jobs. S/he may feel that colleagues are quarrelsome, aggressive or selfish. Satisfaction and success are more likely if the willful and independent Martian energy is channeled into appropriate fields of work. These could include jobs involving physical activity (forest ranger, sports, etc.), assertion or aggression (military, police), or anything independent, varied, self-expressive, competitive, or challenging with minimal repetition and routine (freelance sales, entrepreneurial businesses, etc.).

You may also assert yourself in matters of health. You can be very direct and forthright in pursuing good health, and might sometimes be aggressive in promoting nutritional or other health concepts. If your energy is not channelled into accomplishment, or you lack the desired freedom and variety in your work, you could have health problems. Repressed frustration can lead to minor cuts, burns, accidents (energy unconsciously turned against the self), fevers or even major surgery. An active pursuit of good health (with focus on exercise, diet, etc.) is in your best interest. You can be a pioneer in this area, as well as in your chosen vocational field.

MARS IN 7TH HOUSE

You are learning about who you are through relating to other people. Your courage is expressed through confronting relationship issues (and you may sometimes jump head first into an emotional bond). Your sense of self is tied to partnership and you are learning to balance separation and sharing; assertion and accommodation. You need relationships with a certain amount of space and freedom. Your partnerships do best if each person has room to do his/her own thing. You tend to be identified with a partner yet your independence is aroused in relationships; you could swing between giving in too much and demanding too much from a partner.

You may sometimes feel like "my power is in the hands of other people." This can result in being too accommodating (and being taken advantage of by others as you consistently try to please and appease). It could lead to attacking others ("the best defense is a good offense") in an attempt to protect yourself. It could lead to withdrawing from relationships, convinced that you will only be savaged if you participate.

Your will may never seem totally separate from that of others (especially partners); you are learning to separate personal desires from interpersonal needs. You can assert yourself with others, but may be torn between too much and too little. Three positive forms of balance include: compromise (negotiation, meeting in the middle between your needs and a partner's needs); healthy competition (going one-on-one with rules and regulations so no one gets hurt, but in a manner which builds strengths within each of you) and helping people (reclaiming your own power and using it to assist others).

You could get angry with partners or may choose partners who get angry with you, but you are learning to share power with each other in a positive manner. You push hard in relationships (or feel pushed) because you are learning to balance your needs and desires with those of another person. If you are out of touch with your own Martian side, you are likely to attract it in excess through other people: too independent (classic "free souls" unwilling to commit), too self-centered, too aggressive, too focused on personal will. A compromise means sharing time and space, but also ensuring room for each person's "on my own" time. You can initiate well in a teamwork situation; shared efforts come naturally. Your energy can also flow easily into artistic projects.

MARS IN 8TH HOUSE

You are intense, passionate, strong willed and concerned with control. Your sense of self may be focused on purification, elimination, transformation and/or mastery. Your courage is expressed through confrontation, facing the depths and shadows in your own psyche (and others') and pushing to the limits in life. You tend to drive hard in life, determined to get to the bottom of things, accepting no excuses, relentless, unflinching, taking issues "to the death."

Your will is powerful. If you are still working to develop the capacity to compromise, you may fall into power struggles, or intimidation or manipulation games with other people. Money or sexuality could become battlegrounds with other people (especially your mate—the individual sharing an intimate bond with you). Although you want to do it your way in terms of finances, possessions and pleasures, relationships are more satisfying when both partners have learned to compromise. (Running away is not an ultimate solution).

Your energy flows naturally into sex, intimacy, intense sharing and control. You know what you want, and may sometimes believe what you want is best for everyone. You can be a sexual initiator; you have an urge to take charge of shared resources and pleasures—to leap into the breech. Impulsively jumping in can create difficulties on occasion. Don't push too hard at someone else's limits. Let your desire feed the fires of theirs. Give them room to respond, for the spark of passion to become a flame.

Your independence vies with your need for an intimate, passionate connection with another human being. As much as you want a passionate connection, a part of you feels the hermit's urge to withdraw and shut everyone out. To share a meaningful bond with another will require some adjustments by both of you. You can get angry to the depths of your being, and may brood about it; resentment could be an issue. You must learn to forgive (yourself as well as others) lest negative emotions build up to the point of being poisonous to the body. Your strength and endurance are immense; you have a phenomenal capacity for passion. The more you master yourself (through insight and dealing with the dark side without excessive self-denial), the more excitement feeds your intimate exchanges.

MARS IN 9TH HOUSE

You are adventurous, confident, extraverted, fun-loving and optimistic. Your courage is high; you go for big dreams and large schemes. Your sense of self is connected to and expressed through knowledge, philosophy, religion, travel, long-range goals, ethics or anything that extends the horizons of life. Your independence is extreme; you need the freedom to seek personal truth and personal meaning in life. You assert yourself in matters involving beliefs and values; be wary of aggressively pushing your world view on others (religious wars). You can get quite angry about moral principles and could be self-righteous if this is overdone. You tend to push hard where beliefs, values, faith, trust and/or ideals are concerned.

Astrological research found this placement associated with sports champions and military leaders. Theoretically, such people have made personal skills, action, assertion, aggression, courage, competition, or physical activity into ultimate values. (Naturally, this could be carried to the extreme of producing aggressive, self-centered, pushy people.) A mental form of this principle is represented by zealots or "missionary types" who are convinced that they, personally, possess the one and only truth about life and its meaning. Their way is the **only** way. A variation is found in some gurus who offer themselves as "enlightened beings," already arrived at perfection, human representatives of God.

It is also possible to have high personal idealism without insisting that others conform to your standards. You may just expect and demand a lot of yourself. And, if perfectionism is carried too far, we can find the person who says "I ought to be perfect. Since I'm not, I'm nothing." People can make themselves miserable, living chronically dissatisfied because they didn't do more, or better, or faster, etc. A high "ideal image" of what one would like to be need not be a problem if we recognize that life is a journey **toward** perfection, that most of us will not get there in this lifetime, and that it is OK to enjoy the journey.

Your pursuit of knowledge is likely to be active and personal, and you could be willing to fight for your beliefs, values and ideas. Your will is vigorous and expansive; you can be extravagant, rash and overly impulsive. Your energy is high, but could burn out as you easily overextend yourself. You have a keen sense of humor which can be helpful as you initiate adventures, seek Truth, travel, or just continue your restless quest for your personal goals.

MARS IN 10TH HOUSE

Your identity is tied to career, responsibility, control, work, achievement and the conditional love parent. You probably feel a **need** to work. If you are not producing, you may feel "useless." You are likely to have a strong drive to succeed, to achieve, to control the world around you.

You are apt to have confronted the issue of personal will versus the limits of personal will through an early authority figure; often a father. Sooner or later, we have to learn that there are limits; some things we can't do and some we have to do if we are going to survive in this material world. This learning could come through arguments or fights with authority figures (usually beginning with the conditional love parent); through taking on too much at work and eventually being overwhelmed (physically or emotionally); through butting heads against any of society's laws or conventions and receiving the consequences. You may get angry at authority figures (or "The Establishment") and rules, and must learn to balance self-will with the limits of what is possible in physical reality. At times, the need to "outdo" or "win out" over dear old Dad remains many years after the parent is dead and buried. You may be unconscious of feeling that you are really responsible and will be guilty if you do not force the world to be the way you think it ought to be, or you may feel that you are only safe when your "will is Law." (Zip Dobyns calls any of these extremes "overdrive.")

Alternately, it is possible to be a "self-blocker." Individuals who feel that the world has all the power may give up without even trying. Such individuals express their need for control, stability, and predictability by overcontrolling themselves. They give up before even beginning, telling themselves, "Why should I attempt it? I know I'd just fail anyway. Or, society would block me." They have the predictability and safety of knowing exactly what will happen—nothing. (There is a possible combination of the "my will should be law" and the "self-blocking" action which can be expressed as "If I can't do it my way, I won't play.")

Between these two extremes is the compromise position of people who work hard and achieve much, without trying to run the whole world. With this approach, you are likely to put much energy and enthusiasm into your career. You may find vocational challenges and competition exciting. You are responsible, realistic, hardworking (and may be self-critical). Your courage expresses through ambition, achievement drives and a need to be on top. You are enterprising and effective. You "prove yourself" through your work, status and outer world accomplishments.

You may express independence through your vocation; you want to work for yourself or on your own terms (and may refuse to work otherwise). An entrepreneurial spirit is likely. You initiate well in business or any forum involved with tangible results for productive efforts. Your energy is enduring; you can both initiate and follow through, be creative and practical.

MARS IN 11TH HOUSE

Your identity is tied to individuality, technology, friends, social causes, change, innovation and/or a progressive spirit. You may be a super pioneer, full of original, inventive ideas. You could be independent, freewheeling, rebellious and individualistic. If you carry these urges to extremes, you might be aggressively different (even weird and strange). Your courage is often expressed mentally; you are on the side of the new. Your energy flows easily into groups, friendships, new-age knowledge, technology or anything on the cutting edge of change. You sense of self is tied to liberty, uniqueness, and the future. Your independence is quite strong; you resist being tied down, pinned down or labelled.

Your will is intense; you fight against limits of any kind—on you, on ideas, on anybody's options. You assert yourself in groups, causes, social action and intellectual exploration. You may get angry when free flow or the new is blocked; you will fight for progress. You might be involved in battles for equality, or for any variety of humanitarian causes (including astrology). You probably push communal ideals, progress, opportunity for all and intellectual openness and tolerance. You initiate ideas, concepts, changes, alternatives and options. You could have high-level mechanical skills and the potential for creative inventions.

Your boredom threshold is very low. With a restless, eager urge for more intellectual stimulation, you can move on very easily (from people, situations, etc.) Sometimes picking a fight (consciously or unconsciously) can be a way to escape a friendship or tie which has become too confining or stifling. If the Martian energy is not fully integrated, you may experience fights with friends, self-centered or combative people in organizations or lots of anger around political issues. The more you direct your personal energy and desire into supporting equal opportunities, free flow of information and support of the new, the more satisfactory relationships and associations are likely to become. You need action, excitement and passion in your friendships and transpersonal activities.

MARS IN 12TH HOUSE

You are blending personal will and assertive action with the infinite in some form, seeking oneness with the whole or perfect love and beauty. This challenging mixture can be experienced as feeling that you have infinite power, the right to do as you please. This could be physical power. Astrological research found Mars in the twelfth house in the charts of highly successful athletes and military men and surgeons. The power could express in self-confidence by being willing to cut and destroy in order to heal. If the physical energy takes an artistic bent, it will often express as grace in motion, e.g., water ballet, synchronized swimming, gymnastics, dancing, skiing, etc. The danger of identifying personal will with the Infinite is a grandiosity of feeling that only one's own desires matter or that what we want is automatically the best for everyone.

The opposite extreme is seen in individuals who seem incapable of the mildest form of self-assertion. They seem to be saying unconsciously, "If I can't do something perfect, I won't do anything." Or perhaps, "When I can do the great, marvelous thing that will save the world, I will do something." Such people sit on their energy. They feel everyone else has more right to act, to be, to do, than they do. They usually end up as victims in some way, whether physically ill, subject to multiple surgeries, or occasionally retreating into psychosis. They constantly sacrifice themselves on behalf of others. Their internalized (and disowned) aggression is making them ill. Such a blocked person may benefit from identifying with some cause which they see as ideal. They can then fight for the cause (even if unwilling to fight for themselves), to bring up Martian energy and deal with it constructively.

Absolutes can be a real danger. People may take things too far. When assertion or aggression is turned into an ultimate value and given too much importance, we see the athlete who believes that "winning is everything;" the surgeon performing unnecessary surgeries, the military leader who idealizes aggression and glorifies war, etc. When one's capacity for self-defense and self-expression is too blocked, we get the classic victim, astrology's traditional association with the twelfth house. Your challenge is to integrate personal will and assertion with the recognition of a Higher Power in life and the rights of all life.

You can be gentle, compassionate, idealistic, artistic and/or escapist—or you can make courage, action, assertion and personal will into ultimate values. Your sense of self is tied to a quest for infinite love and beauty, but you can express it through helping, healing, aesthetic channels, through fighting for a cause, or through running away. Your will is connected to a universal source; you could have infinite energy at your fingertips or feel lost in the immensity of the cosmos. Your energy flows easily into artistic, idealistic or victim channels.

You can assert yourself in arenas of art, mysticism, spirituality or idealism. You may get angry when your ideals are threatened and you may fight for what you believe, or you may retreat into escapist behavior.

You need a strong, inner sense of faith in something bigger than your own will and power, a feeling of union and a connection to the Highest in life which can feed your self-confidence or overwhelm you. You can be active in terms of visions, dreams, and products of your imagination. You can also act on your inner wisdom, sometimes instinctively doing the right thing without knowing why.

Mars in Aspect: *Immediate Instincts*

The nature of the planets involved in any aspect is the most important factor. For any pair of planets, please read **all three** aspect delineations: conjunction, cooperating (sextile ✳, trine △), and challenging (square □, opposition ♂, quincunx ⊼). The conjunction is the basic, most fundamental aspect and its themes carry through with other aspects. The cooperating and challenging analyses will offer additional choices regarding of constructive and nonconstructive ways of handling the basic issues.

Remember that the life issues represented by cooperating aspects (or conjunctions) may still require some attention. We might overdo certain themes, or succumb to projection, repression or displacement in trying to balance our many, different drives. It is also quite possible that you could have integrated some of the conflicts (shown by challenging aspects) which were present at birth and are now manifesting potentials more reflective of the delineations in the cooperating or conjunction sections.

Other factors will complicate the picture. The potential inherent in any given placement might be overridden by other configurations in the chart. As you read the interpretations for the various pieces of your chart, bear in mind that certain pieces will suppress others. As always, repeated themes, which recur again and again, are the most likely to manifest in your psyche and in your life.

MARS CONJUNCT JUPITER

You are likely to exhibit dash, flair and daring. You can be quite energetic, confident and optimistic. You are probably drawn to excitement and have a natural inclination to enjoy life.

Your headstrong tendencies could lead you into grandiose or overly expansive activities. You could be extravagant, outspoken, exaggerative, or overextended. You are likely to be direct and forthright, and may sometimes carry bluntness too far (ruthless honesty). You can be quick to anger (and usually quick to forgive) and susceptible to ethical or moral outrage. You might overdo self-righteousness. You tend to have a firm, personal sense of the truth and could be a missionary, guru, or proselytizing type—trying to push your world view onto other people. At times, you might come across as abrasive, angry, theatrical, or arrogant.

The strong physical theme highlighted in this combination may incline you toward sports, martial arts, or other forms of athletic prowess. Another option is a large sexual appetite. Or, you may be impatient. A constructive competitive outlet (games, sports, business, politics) is advisable for your challenging nature. The restlessness within you could equally lead toward travel or other forms of exploring and adventuring. You probably have natural elan and are instinctively assertive.

You can think quickly, but may leap to conclusions or oversimplify. You are likely to be active in seeking personal answers or a sense of meaning in life, or you could be a risk-taker, involved in gambling or speculating on some level. You tend to do things that will lead to growth and enlarged perspectives. You can increase your opportunities through personal action and self-expression.

Your sense of humor is likely to be lively. You can be quite exuberant! Your intentions are generally good. You usually act on your personal beliefs, ethics, and values.

MARS COOPERATING JUPITER (✶ △)

Your ideals inspire your personal action, and you'll have lots of energy for what you believe in. You can be quite exuberant, humorous, confident, and expressive. You could be active on behalf of your beliefs, the law, justice, travel, education, ethics, spirituality, or anything expansive and broadening. You are willing to fight for your faith, and must be wary of overdoing the "true believer" or "missionary zealot" role. Your faith must fit your personal experience, but it won't be a fit for everyone.

Your vitality is likely to be high, and your restless spirit might find an outlet in sports or idealistic pursuits. Your self-confidence is good, and you are willing to take risks. Enthusiastic and optimistic, you tend to envision the best and assume you can make it happen. On occasion, you may veer into rash or foolhardy behavior. Generally, you tend to be on the go, expressive, ardent and extraverted.

You are probably direct, forthright and sincere. You may detest evasion and dishonesty, and could sometimes overdo candor (read—"foot in mouth"). Manipulation is not your style; what people see is what they get as far as you are concerned.

You are eager to learn and your driving thirst for something more could sometimes pull you in many directions. You might end up overextended, trying to take on too much too quickly. Your search for your personal goals is apt to be life-long.

You can be quite dynamic, exciting, energetic and philosophical. You are likely to have promotional and persuasive skills, and a real knack for helping people to laugh.

MARS CHALLENGING JUPITER (□ ☍ ⊼)

A high degree of energy is suggested, but restlessness is likely. You may slip into impatience or impulsivity, sometimes acting against your better judgment. You thrive in an atmosphere of mental stimulation, adventures, exploration, expansion and risk-taking.

Your search for an adrenaline rush could lead to gambling, speculation, or trying to do too much, too fast. Although you have a great deal of energy and talent, you must sometimes learn moderation. It is easy for you to overextend yourself.

Faith may be a challenge in your life. Too much trust in your own abilities can lead to arrogance, extravagance, self-indulgence, or biting off more than you can chew. Too little faith can lead to a fear to act, a tendency to demand perfection before you extend yourself. Excessively high standards can keep you dissatisfied and discontented. You must balance intellectual understanding and physical action. Avoid the extremes of rash, foolhardy behavior or endless rationalizations and intellectualization. Keep clear priorities and reachable goals!

Issues around beliefs, values, ideals, ethics and morality are significant in your life. Although you are apt to have strong feelings about spiritual principles, avoid falling prey to religious wars! A proselytizing attitude won't win friends. Be direct about what you value, but don't aggressively push your beliefs onto others by trying to be a guru. Tolerance is an important virtue.

You have a flair for excitement which you can share with others. Your humor, liveliness, honesty and perspective can enrich people's lives.

MARS CONJUNCT SATURN

You can accomplish a great deal and have executive capacity. You can be efficient, practical, ambitious, and pragmatic. With marked self-discipline, you may work your way to the top. You can be quite painstaking and productively organized.

You will personally confront authority issues. This might include conflicts with your own father. You tend to either fight authority, feel blocked by it, or seek control and dominance yourself. You may fear your own (or other people's) force, control, anger, violence or abuse. Father is apt to be a role model (positive or negative) for the handling of freedom, self-expression, assertion (or aggression), personal desires and the definitions of accomplishment and success. You tend to both identity with and battle against dad, the law, the government, and career demands. You are learning to make peace between self-will and the limits set by the world, between what you want and societal responsibilities and duties.

If you overrate the power of the world and underrate your own abilities, you might inhibit your actions (or anger), feeling frustrated or blocked. The repression of anger can lead to feeling sullen and bitter. Fear could cover anger (and vice versa). You might experience sexual blocks (fearing dominance, criticism, being controlled, or losing control). You (or a partner) might withhold sex (choose to be ascetic) or use sex for power. With less fear of the world but still some lack of personal confidence, you might be inhibited, serious, sober and shy, viewing life as a challenge, pitting yourself against the world. You may believe that one must earn everything in life, and that it isn't easy. You could criticize and devalue yourself. Fear of making a mistake or not measuring up could block you from acting, or tempt you into endless procrastination.

The opposite extreme is to be compulsively active, busy and driven. You might slip into workaholism, feeling "if you want it done right, do it yourself." You might measure your worth only in what you can **do** (performance). You could be overly responsible (carrying the world on your back), seeking safety through controlling everything. You might fight only when certain of winning.

By constructively combining practicality and confidence, you can act for yourself as well as productively in the world. You can work hard but not obsessively, gaining great personal satisfaction from your accomplishments, yet recognizing your inner individuality. You can enjoy **being** as well as **doing**. You can express yourself and your independence, while still meeting worldly demands.

MARS COOPERATING SATURN (✶ △)

You are capable of achieving a great deal. You can harness drive and discipline, promoting yourself successfully in the world. Your ambition is backed up by hard work and competence.

Your sense of timing is apt to be good. You know when to push ahead, and when to be cautious (or when to fight and when to run). You are able to meet your personal needs while working within societal rules and regulations. You can please authorities as well as yourself!

Even when young, you may have instinctively understood how to work within a structure. You could handle your father (or father figure) better than many people. Whether or not his example was positive, you learned self-discipline, dedication, pragmatism, responsibility and courage from interactions with your father. You learned to constructively deal with authorities, and might have benefitted from a mentor in your career. You are likely to grow stronger as you grow older.

Blessed with both initiative and follow-through, you are able to begin as well as end projects. Your leadership instincts could be valuable in politics, the business world, law or law enforcement. Your practicality may attract you toward engineering or similarly grounded interests. You naturally expect to test assumptions, ideas and possibilities against reality. You keep what works!

You can be quite productive, sensible, hardworking, ambitious and success-oriented. You are self-motivated and eager to produce results.

MARS CHALLENGING SATURN (□ ☌ ⚼)

Once you get out of your own way, you can accomplish a tremendous amount. You are working on the tension between personal desires and societal demands. This inner conflict has roots in your childhood, especially in your relationship with your father (or father figure).

You probably challenged authorities, or felt that they blocked, criticized and frustrated you. You may have experienced your father as abusive, angry, frustrated (frustrating), impossible to please, or insensitive to your individuality. He might have been incapable, inadequate or incompetent. Somehow, his early example is apt to have fed a sense of fear, failure, mistrust, or inadequacy in you. Since children internalize parental images, you could still be criticizing yourself and feeling less competent than you are, or more at odds with rules, regulations and responsibilities. The basic issue in this combination is a struggle between self-will and the limits of self-will. We learn by consequences what we can do, what we can't do, and what we have to do if we want to survive in a society with other people. We have to maintain some confidence in personal rights and power but also recognize that we can't do everything.

You may seek to establish a sense of self through what you **do**, how you perform. One extreme is giving up, feeling blocked and just not trying ("it won't be good enough," or "they'll just stop me anyway"). The opposite extreme is taking on excessive demands, feeling you **have** to do everything in order to compensate for inner self-deprecation, or because that is the only way you feel safe, or to keep your conscience off your back. You need tangible results and measurable success, but you also need to practice loving yourself and appreciating your essence and your being, apart from what you can accomplish.

While you are working on raising your level of self-appreciation, your timing may sometimes be off. You might act too quickly on some projects (rashly) and hold back on others (not trusting yourself). The more you develop an inner sense of your worth, the more you can act in the moment, taking advantage of realistic opportunities, making the most of your assets.

MARS CONJUNCT URANUS

Thrill-seeking could come naturally to you. Intense excitement, novel sensations, and freedom are the breath of life for you. You can be quite creative, courageous, risk-taking and independent. "I'll do anything once" is a possible motto.

You might make sudden physical movements (or act on impulse). If done carelessly, accidents are possible. Your energy could come out in sporadic bursts, unpredictable, uneven and erratic. You might be fitfully assertive or suddenly aggressive. A quick temper is possible. You can be an adrenaline junkie, constantly testing your nerves and addicted to daredevil activities. (You might love fast cars, flying, racing or thrill sports.) Your reflexes are probably quick. If you don't want negative forms of excitement in your life, seek out positive forms (e.g., roller coasters, flying, adventuring, etc.).

Personal freedom is essential to you. You detest restriction or other people's authority. You can be a runaway: "If I don't like it, I'll leave." You may be quite eccentric or unusual. You might fight for social causes or for angry causes. You are likely to identify with your friends and with groups which are original, inventive, or revolutionary. You are quite independent and love liberty, but can take these to extremes by being rash, reckless, foolhardy, abrupt, antisocial or contradictory. You are likely to confront issues and debate. Individuality and being unlike anyone else is essential to you. You may pioneer and be a ground-breaker.

Psychic impressions might go directly into action (without going through your conscious awareness). You could have flashes of insight, "right-on" impulses, or suddenly understand new ways to do things. You can be quite progressive, individualistic, unique and quick. You thrive on excitement, the new, the different, and activities accentuating freedom.

MARS COOPERATING URANUS (✳ △)

You are apt to be innovative, inventive, and personally involved in a quest for freedom. You may be drawn by the future, attracted by the unusual or oriented toward the new. You thrive on excitement and are naturally mobile.

A free spirit, you will tend to resist being penned in, hemmed in, or tied down. You need variety and intellectual stimulation in your life. If you feel too confined, you may rebel or carry the revolutionary role too far. Trying to break loose or break free physically, or acting on impulse could lead to accidents if not balanced by some caution. You encourage individuality and uniqueness in others as well as in yourself. You may have friends who are very different from one another.

You tend to be tolerant in regard to sexuality. You are probably open-minded and might be experimental yourself. Often, however, the "anything is OK" philosophy is more a mental attitude than an actual physical expression. You could experience sudden attractions ("falling in love/lust"). If the desire for freedom or new experiences is overdone, you may only want what you cannot have, enjoying the chase but not the conquest. Generally, the accent is on friendship in love relations.

You are willing to take risks, to live life on the edge. You enjoy thrills and the adrenaline rush. Creative problem solving is right up your alley. You may have intellectual and/or intuitive flashes of brilliance (even genius) on occasion. You may have an instinctive grasp of how things function (or how they might function better) which expresses as mechanical or technological skills. Your attitudes are fresh and innovative; you are open to myriad possibilities in life.

MARS CHALLENGING URANUS (□ ☌ ⚹)

Freedom is a watchword and you may detest confinement of any sort. If this attitude is too extreme, you could be a chronic rebel or revolutionary, consistently battling the old and fighting for the new. You might set yourself up for accidents by acting too quickly, or on impulse, or from anger and frustration at feeling hemmed in. You need openness and free flow in your life; look for constructive ways to express your innovative, inventive spirit.

Thrill-seeking could be a way of life. Risk and the lure of an adrenaline rush could draw you on. Whether you look to flying, racing, amusement parks, social causes or other activities for your sense of excitement, the challenge is to keep your involvement constructive, rather than finding negative excitement (accidents, arguments, fights, etc.).

Restlessness is natural for you, so regular movement is important. This could be physical activity or lots of change and variety in your occupation and/or interests. If your hyper side has opportunities to expend energy, tension will not build up to a disruptive point.

You thrive in an atmosphere of alternatives and possibilities. You may be skilled at brainstorming or otherwise generating new alternatives and potentials. Lack of equality or fair play might anger you. Social causes or pursuing justice could provide an outlet for your fighting spirit. Look for ways to use your mechanical, technological and inventive skills to improve the world.

You are willing to challenge yourself, others and the world to foster new ideas, choices and options.

MARS CONJUNCT NEPTUNE

You can be inspired, compassionate and mystical. You may express grace in action or beauty in motion (through your own appearance or dancing, diving, skating, skiing, etc.). You could be charismatic and magnetic.

Your identity is tied to the quest for infinite love and beauty. You need a sense of mission or service. If you allow your transcendent focus to overwhelm your personal needs, you could feel weak, paralyzed, victimized, martyred, or unable to cope. Your energy might be diffused. You could be too sensitive, picking up other's emotions and/or illnesses or susceptible to allergies, drug problems, and infections. You may be reluctant to fight for yourself, to defend your own rights. You could deny your anger or your sexuality, or turn personal drives (including sexuality) into an addiction. You might rationalize, or take covert rather than direct action. You could chase rainbows, or run in circles, misdirecting your activity. Spirituality could be misdefined as self-denial.

If you overpersonalize your mission, you may believe you have a right to whatever you want. You could idolize freedom, self-expression or doing your own thing. This can be a guru configuration, identified as an embodiment of God.

You are working on the balance between self-assertion and self-sacrifice, between action and submission, between personal wants and humanity's needs, between idealized fantasies and the world as it is. The challenge is to achieve a sense of flowing, mystical union with something infinitely ecstatic, compassionate or inspirational, without losing a sense of yourself. Spiritual or artistic activities which are self-expressive allow you to feed your inner essence while still contributing more grace, harmony, healing and love to the world.

MARS COOPERATING NEPTUNE (✶ △)

You are able to combine compassion and passion in life, inspiring others while still meeting your own needs. Artistic creativity is quite likely and you may have talent in any of the performing or other arts. Grace in action is also possible which could incline you toward dancing, diving, skating, skiing or other forms of beauty in motion. You might engage in mystical pursuits, healing, service, philanthropic activities or a field involving liquids (e.g., chemistry, oceanography, oil, drugs).

Imaginative and somewhat plastic, you can adapt to circumstances, putting on different masks for each milieu. You may act on intuition, instinctively doing the right thing without knowing why.

A sense of mission or spiritual dedication can feed your energy and vitalize you. You are apt to express yourself through idealistic, helping channels. If you overidentify with the universe, you may lack ego boundaries and lose your sense of self in the cosmos. An alternative is extending the ego to the infinite and believing you have a right to do exactly as you please. A balance between personal desires and rescuing instincts allows you to protect your own rights while still serving and assisting others.

Your may spiritualize sexuality, idealizing and highly valuing it. Or, you might sexualize spirituality, imbuing it with a core of magnetic, seductive allure. You are likely to have natural charisma, dramatic flair and creative inspiration.

MARS CHALLENGING NEPTUNE (□ ♂ ⊼)

Beauty and spiritual or helping activities offer your best sources of support, but you must balance a personal focus with a diffused awareness of universal needs. Cosmic images and urges might vie with desires which are uniquely your own.

If your idealistic urge to save and succor is allowed to take over, you could end up drained, exhausted and martyred. Others might take advantage of your desire to help. Self-sacrifice is not a healthy choice. The opposite extreme is feeling a "divine right" to whatever you want. Real life involves compromises—but not at the expense of one person's essence.

If you view life through rose-colored glasses, you will be disappointed and disillusioned when people fail to be live up to your utopian standards. Imagination may affect your sexual attractions; be wary of seeing what you want to see rather than what is there; savior/victim entanglements may complicate your sexual satisfaction. You need a sense of inspiration and merging with something higher, but spiritual or aesthetic paths are safer than looking for ultimate perfection in other people or in yourself.

Emotional sensitivity may correlate with physical sensitivity for you, so be cautious in dealing with drugs (including prescription), alcohol, and chemicals. You might be susceptible to allergies. Channeling your sensitivity into healing, medical, nutritional or other compassionate activities can be helpful.

You may be intuitive, almost absorbing things from the ether. Perhaps you are clairvoyant, clairaudient or otherwise pick up psychic impressions. You may sometimes act **only** on intuition, or act **against** your intuition. The goal is to use your common sense and logic as well as psychic insights.

You need to blend your graceful, spiritual side with your active, assertive side. One excellent route is beauty in motion: skating, skiing, diving, swimming, dancing, or other forms of graceful physical activity. You may also be motivated to fight for causes, especially on behalf of the underdog. You can engage in active meditation, tantric yoga, or other spiritual paths which involve a physical, expressive component.

MARS CONJUNCT PLUTO

This combination pits personal power and rights against the power and rights of others who are close to us, forcing us to learn to share power or risk the alternatives of a lifetime of perpetual power struggles versus a life of surrender or retreat. If you have claimed your power, you may exhibit tremendous strength of will (and body). You can focus intensely and concentrate on your ambitions. You have good stamina and organizational skills. You can be magnetic, seductive, sexual, powerful, compelling and passionate. You can contend successfully against difficult odds.

Less positively, if you elevate your rights over those of others, your temper and passions may be wild. You could be ruthless and relentless, even violent or explosive in extremes. Hidden anger or passive-aggressive forms of anger are possible. You are apt to feel anger equals pain, get angry when feeling pain, and feel pained when angry. Highly competitive, you may be a poor loser. Sports, games, business, politics and causes offer constructive outlets for your forceful nature. Although you are capable of being belligerent, intrusive, punitive or threatening, you can also bargain and be a talented strategist. You thrive on challenges and tend to achieve your objectives no matter what the cost (to self or others).

If you have not yet claimed your own power, you might attract others who use and abuse power against you. Withdrawal may appeal. Yet your challenge is to be forceful (but not demand total control), to neither deny nor abuse your strong drive and will.

At times, you may confuse aggression and sex. You could be attracted by danger, fear attraction, or confuse fear and attraction. You might associate sex with death or loss of identity. You may be susceptible to jealousy and possessiveness. You can be quite secretive, manipulative, repressed, private, obsessed and brooding. Game-playing in relationships comes easily. You may feel torn between pursuing and holding back, between freedom and bondage, between being alone or together. You could swing between extreme self-indulgence and self-discipline (or even self-punishment).

Your attitude tends to be "do or die; fight to the finish." You probably strive to break your own records. You can be quite fervent, dynamic, uncompromising and courageous.

MARS COOPERATING PLUTO (✳ △)

A harmony aspect suggests that you can stand firmly for your own rights but also respect the rights of others. Since a competitive nature is likely to be present, you can be a crusader for constructive causes. You are willing to intensely confront the dark side, to fight for light, for transformation and transcendence. You can be quite courageous and are able to persevere as well as initiate. Your spirit may be indomitable.

There is a drive for power within your soul that can be highly effective in business, medicine, sports and any competitive milieu. You need to strive, to drive, to aim for the top. If you do not direct your dominating, forceful side into politics, business, games or other constructive outlets, there is a danger of power struggles when cooperation would be more effective. It is important to keep the competition for the opposing team, not for members of one's own team.

Sex and money are potential battlegrounds if your emotional intensity is not directed into socially-approved areas. You may argue, fight and debate with mates over spending, saving, desires and personal pleasures. Look for win/win solutions in your close relationships. Always "winning" (having power) over those you love is a losing proposition in the long run.

You may be attracted to hidden matters, eager to probe beneath the surface into the occult, history, investigations, research, therapy, oceanography, chemistry, etc. You have an instinct for ferreting out people's subterranean motives and hidden agendas. Sensitive to buried issues, you can help bring up anger and resentment, clear it up, release it, and forgive and forget.

You have a strong sensual streak, and need a profound, intimate connection with a mate. When you are focused on sharing, there is no one more committed, loyal, and brave. You will face the darkest of demons for the ones you love. One of your strengths is the capacity to help transform negatives into positives. You have the courage to face challenges and the insight to turn liabilities into assets.

MARS CHALLENGING PLUTO (□ ☍ ⊼)
Emotional intensity is a core theme in your nature, but there is a push/pull between your desire to express what you feel and your urge to hold back and hold in. Consequently, feelings (especially anger) may sometimes build up to an explosive point. If resentments are not cleared on a regular basis, you can be like a walking bomb: cruel and even abusive or meeting those emotions through other people in your life. Yet your inner urge is to face the dark, destructive side of life (in yourself and others) and learn to control it and eventually transform it. You are facing the challenge of turning negatives into positives.

Your passions can be wild and strong on all levels, including sexually. Yet a part of you fears the loss of control associated with sex. So you might vary between repression (self-denial) and forcefully seeking what you want. A mate relationship can be a very valuable tool in your personal development, helping you to gain self-control and self-mastery, to learn how to give, receive and share pleasures and power with another.

You are apt to be highly competitive and probably hate to lose. Some would say that winning at any cost is your goal. Fighting with people on the same team is not helpful, but you need an outlet for your feisty nature. Competitive sports, games or business can offer constructive outlets to you. Your power drive could also be put to use in politics or fighting for justice and social causes.

You are a survivor par excellence and can surmount almost anything. You can transform yourself on the deepest levels of your psyche, should you so choose. You can also be a catalyst in the transformation of others.

CHAPTER EIGHT

JUPITER
BELIEFS AND BENEFITS
IN YOUR HOROSCOPE

Jupiter in Signs: *Values and Vistas*

As one of the outer planets, Jupiter spends a fair amount of time in each sign (about one year). Thus, the themes which are indicated are shared by people your age. The house placement of Jupiter will have more to say about where you look for ultimate value and how you handle beliefs, education, religion, and expectations. Your cultural background is also highly important in shaping your belief system.

JUPITER IN ARIES

You tend to value action, assertion and self-expression. Your beliefs are based on personal experience and you may (on occasion) aggressively urge others to accept your faith. You may idealize doing your own thing, pioneering, independence. Your ethics/morals highlight courage and personal willpower. You tend to believe in yourself, to put your faith in personal initiative and self-reliance. But if you can only believe in yourself, problems can arise from overconfidence initially and from anxiety later as life presents challenges too big for any single individual. Too narrow and dogmatic a faith can also lead to disillusionment. But realistic self-confidence can support leadership skills and you can grow through confidently doing your own thing.

JUPITER IN TAURUS

You may value money, possessions, physical gratification or beauty. You are likely to have a deep appreciation of sensual pleasures. Your beliefs probably center around practicality and the material world, whether you devote a major part of your income to books, seminars and a search for knowledge or to collecting art objects. You might put too much importance on possessions or gratification. You probably trust the safe, secure and familiar. You may idealize enjoyment, finances, ownership, or strengthen your faith and trust in life through contact with nature and simple pleasures. Growth can come through being steady and reliable.

JUPITER IN GEMINI

You tend to value the intellect, information, learning and communication. Your beliefs are pursued with mental exploration and versatility. Your vision of something Higher tends to be rational and logical as you probably trust and base your ethics/morals on intelligence and reasoning power. You are also likely to value adaptability and objectivity. You seek life's meaning through wide-ranging interests and may idealize variety, communication, cleverness or fluency. You may grow through communication, learning and developing many different skills.

JUPITER IN CANCER

You tend to value the home, family, feelings or emotional safety. Your beliefs are likely to be influenced by your family background and center around emotional attachments. Your ethics/morals highlight compassion, caring and commitment. You understand humanity's need for security, but your faith may sometimes be shaken by fears or self-protective urges. Your trust may rely too much on the kin group, as you look to them for empathy or emotional support. You may idealize motherhood, the home, the land, or your nation. Yet you also have the capacity to leave your home to seek a bigger dream, and you might choose to make a home in a country other than the land of your birth. You can grow and expand through nurturing opportunities, through helping others to find security.

JUPITER IN LEO

You tend to value excitement, drama, zest and creativity. Your faith, your enthusiasm, your talent at promotion, and your capacity to be generous may stem from your self-confidence. You may be quite warm and supportive of others with your natural understanding of people's need for recognition. Your ethics/morals probably encourage risk-taking, generosity and self-esteem. You may idealize love, children, ambition, power or charisma. Your faith is likely to be strong, but you might slip into egotism or arrogance ("divine right") on occasion. Or, alternately, if you have put all of your faith in your own power, you may be dismayed when life presents a challenge too big for a single ego. But usually, your natural flair and showmanship will attract admiring followers. You grow through doing more than you have before, being exuberant, enthusiastic, and willing to live life fully.

JUPITER IN VIRGO

You tend to value work, productivity, efficiency and/or health. Your beliefs are probably connected to your job and sense of dedication. Your ethics/morals may highlight the puritan virtues. You may idealize purity, cleanliness, precision. You are learning to blend idealistic visions with practical reality, learning to avoid being chronically dissatisfied, overly judgmental, perfectionistic, or giving up too soon. A positive blend allows you to visualize the best and take concrete steps to manifest it. You tend to put your trust in hard work and self-discipline. You are probably ever ready to improve yourself. You are likely to grow through dedicated service and competent helpfulness.

JUPITER IN LIBRA

You tend to value relationships, balance and grace. Your beliefs are probably influenced by other people. Your ethics/morals may highlight sharing, cooperation, harmony, or competition and fair play. You may idealize love, partners(hip), fair play, or beauty. You might need to guard against expecting too much in your relationships. You tend to put your faith into equality, broad-mindedness and impartiality. Opportunities for growth could arise through art, sharing, teamwork or supporting others. You may grow through relationships and further expanding your objectivity and capacity to see both sides of an issue.

JUPITER IN SCORPIO

You tend to value intensity, concentration, thoroughness. You may believe that something more always lies beneath the surface. A lack of faith (in yourself or in a Higher Power) could lead to putting too much faith in other people. Faith in others can, in turn, result in dependency on them, in disappointment when they turn out to be human, or in fear of their power, leading to secrecy and an attempt to control relationships. With a realistic faith, you can value relationships enough to seek understanding and mutual good. Your ethics/morals can be built on shared beliefs and values. Opportunities may come to you through your capacity to shrewdly assess people and situations and through your resourcefulness. You are capable of facing the dark side of human nature and can handle power insightfully. Intense emotional experiences can help you to further develop faith and trust in something Higher. You may idealize sexuality, secrecy, depth insights or transformations. You are likely to grow through transmuting negatives into positives, understanding the inner essence of life and working through compulsions or obsessions.

JUPITER IN SAGITTARIUS

You tend to value big dreams, schemes and expanded horizons. You may believe in education, religion, spiritual paths, travel, philosophy, or simply in the freedom to pursue your ideals wherever they take you. Your ethics/morals may highlight faith, optimism, and generosity. You may idealize gurus, honesty, humor or trust. You grow through trusting in your faith and following your visions (long-range goals). Too much faith can lead to overextension, foolhardy risks, too rapid expansion, or arrogance, any of which will usually bring a letdown. But your natural optimism and trust in a Higher Power should help you to understand life's spiritual/religious levels. Opportunities for exploring—both within and in the outer world—will enhance your development.

JUPITER IN CAPRICORN

You tend to value success, the Establishment, hard work and responsibility. You probably believe in paying your dues, that there is no "free lunch." Your ethics/morals may highlight expertise, effort and endurance. You may idealize power, control, "making it" or practicality. You may have an innate aura of authority so that people trust you. Your growth opportunities are likely to come with effort and steady, disciplined progress. You tend to trust in reality, experience, and tradition. However, when too much faith is put in the material world, it can lead to pessimism and fear which could inhibit your success. You are balancing ideals and reality. Too much idealism is fuzzy-headed and incompetent. Too much realism is depressed and anxious. A reasonable blend allows you to be competently confident, to ground your visions, to make your dreams come true.

JUPITER IN AQUARIUS
You tend to value the unusual, unconventional or progressive. You may believe the future will be better, or place your faith in humanity and democratic principles. Your ethics and morals may highlight fair play and justice for all. You could idealize the intellect, the different, the new, the "cutting edge" or detachment. You are likely to trust knowledge, humanity and the principle of freedom (tolerance which permits free expression to everyone). Your faith is likely to be unique to you, unorthodox, or unusual. Your opportunities for growth may involve the intellect, experimentation, or humanitarian principles and social causes. The scientific attitude comes naturally to you. You can sometimes be overly detached (looking at the broad perspective), but are usually tolerant toward others.

JUPITER IN PISCES
You tend to value compassion, empathy, the mystical, and the beautiful. You might believe in a beautiful dream, a utopian ideal. Your ethics/morals could highlight healing, assistance or inspiration. You may idealize art, grace, nature or mysticism. You can improve yourself or grow through a generosity of spirit—through living your ideals. If your utopian side is overdone, you might succumb to escapism or unclear, romanticized attitudes. You tune into the universe through sympathy with the underdog, or anyone who is suffering. Compassion and sensitivity stimulate your sense of faith, bringing you grace. You have a naturally mystical bent, understanding the importance of devotion to an ideal and faith in a Higher Power.

Jupiter in Houses: *Optimism and Overdoing*

JUPITER IN 1ST HOUSE

You believe in/value personal action, self-expression and freedom. You tend to trust (put your faith in) yourself and doing your own thing. You probably have high standards for your personal action. You may demand more than is reasonable of yourself, feel you are already perfect, or consistently strive to improve yourself. The drive to do more, better, higher, faster, etc., is central in your being. You may want to expand your self-expression on the physical, emotional, mental, or spiritual level (and could be prone to gaining weight physically unless you stay active). Knowledge is important to you, but your eagerness can sometimes lead to exaggeration or overgeneralizing. You want to understand yourself and may theorize about freedom or the meaning of identity and action. Naturally buoyant, generous, gregarious and witty, you can be a bit "larger than life." Others tend to trust you and find you persuasive.

Your world view is very personal and you are apt to resist the dogmas of others. You need to find your own truth, but if you become too certain that you have "the" answer, you might aggressively push your views on others (acting as missionary or stirring up minor religious wars). You could be fierce and demanding in your moral and ethical stands or you could make your own desires your ultimate value. A natural teacher and preacher, you are also an instinctive student of life, seeking more and more answers, meaning and adventures from life.

JUPITER IN 2ND HOUSE

You are likely to believe in and value comfort, security, pleasure and possessions. If the focus on gratification is carried too far, you may be overly indulgent (with food, alcohol, or other appetites) or place too much importance on money and material goods. You probably want to expand your material base and you can bring in a lot of money, but you can also spend easily. With the confidence that you can always get more, you may be quite generous. You can generalize about what you earn and own in life, and may leap to unwarranted conclusions. Financial opportunities come your way through optimism, positive visualization and social networks. Your persuasive, motivating skills can be a tool for monetary gain. You are likely to both learn and teach in the realm of money, possessions, aesthetics and/or pleasure.

Your world view tends to be based on contentment. You may trust (put your faith in) stability, material security and gratifying experiences. You want to believe in happy endings. Your ethics and moral principles are likely to be easygoing and accepting. You want to understand the sense world, finances and beauty. Pleasure is an important goal in your life.

JUPITER IN 3RD HOUSE
You probably believe in the mind and communication and tend to place your faith in talking things over. You may put your trust in gathering all possible information about an issue. A perpetual student and natural teacher and writer, you want to understand and share ideas, concepts and abstractions. You may theorize about thought, language or communication. You are eager to learn about anything and everything. You constantly expand and enlarge your quest for information; you can never know too much in your opinion! With an impetus toward the overview, you may sometimes be too simplistic or too ready to see a whole where none exists. You could be somewhat physically restless with an urge to travel. New horizons can expand your base of knowledge (although you are sometimes content to travel only in the mind). Your eager enthusiasm might make you **too** articulate at times. Remember that conversation is a two-way street. You are likely to continue developing your intellectual skills lifelong, in light of their importance to you.

Your world view is mental, based on knowledge and understanding. You tend to trust logic over emotion. Your ethics and moral principles are objective and may be influenced by your relatives. You are prone to generalizing and assuming you understand the people around you; be a bit cautious about jumping to conclusions about neighbors, siblings or other relatives. With friendly, gregarious impulses, you can talk to almost anyone about anything. You are also likely to have an excellent sense of humor and be able to laugh at many things.

JUPITER IN 4TH HOUSE
You tend to believe in and value warmth, compassion, family and caring. You may trust (put your faith in) blood ties, roots,

security and protection. And yet your innate wanderlust could have lured you from home early in life and you might travel widely and even live in other countries. You may idealize the nurturing principle, putting family (or mother figure) up on a pedestal of perfection, and then feel disappointed when they are only human and reveal their flaws. Your family may have emphasized cultural experience, intellectual stimulation, or the free flow of ideas and sociability. Perhaps your family was proud of its social status, educational achievements or heredity. Expectations were probably an issue in your early conditioning; you may have felt motivated to greatness or burdened by hopes you believed were too high to meet. You could generalize about and assume that you understood your home and family, but need to be careful in regard to leaping to conclusions. Hopefully, you can also find humor in domestic issues and family interactions.

Your world view emphasizes sensitivity, protection and preservation. You may seek understanding of dependency and nurturance needs. Your ethics and moral principles are strongly impacted (pro or con) by your nurturing parent. You are likely to do a lot of learning (and teaching) about emotional ties, mothering instincts and closeness. You may theorize about feelings, emotional needs and heredity. You probably want the best in your home environment and eagerly promote your ideals there. You may wish to expand or enlarge your home (literally) or your family perspectives (through travel or broadening influences).

JUPITER IN 5TH HOUSE

You probably believe in and value excitement, creativity (of which children are one form) and doing more than you have done before. Your drive for the adrenaline rush may sometimes lead to rash or heedless behavior (an "I can do anything" style of confidence). You need to pour out into the world, doing more than you have done before and achieving recognition for it. You may trust (put faith into) love, joy, power, attention, sex or magnetism. You are apt to constantly seek to expand and enlarge your capacity for attention, admiration and approval. (This could range from lots of love affairs to lots of children to lots of gambling, etc.) You have a naturally buoyant spirit, with a zest and enthusiasm for life, the limelight, entertainment and risk-taking. Your humor is likely to be dramatic (sometimes exaggerated) and you can be a skilled entertainer. You may have instinctive charisma with flair for social rituals and persuasion.

Your world view is dramatic, confident and expansive. You need positive attention (praise and ego support) for your philosophy of life. You may be quite a persuasive idealist. You want to understand children, love relationships, pride, shame and power. You may teach as well as learn about speculation, ego-expansion and the ability to have an emotional impact on people through stage, screen, sales, love, etc. You may generalize or assume you have full information about creativity, loved ones, pride or ego needs; do not jump too quickly to conclusions. Expectations are probably an issue in love relationships. You may demand more than is possible from yourself, lovers or children—or idealize the people you care about, believing they can do no wrong. Ethics and moral principles are based the universal human need for love and pride, the human right to be recognized and appreciated even when we fall short of our aspirations. Families which share intellectual, religious, philosophical or idealistic beliefs and goals can continue to grow together and can bring out the best in each other.

JUPITER IN 6TH HOUSE

You tend to believe in and value work, productivity and efficiency. You may trust (put your faith in) maintaining healthy functioning on the job and in your body. Your idealism is focused on the workaday world. This might manifest as a quest for the "perfect" job which produces a job-hopper who keeps on hoping the "next" position will have the ideal pay, duties, position, colleagues, etc. Another option is trying to do your work perfectly—expecting to know everything and never make a mistake. This can produce chronic frustration (while continuing to work) or the attitude "If I can't do it perfectly, I won't do it at all." Another choice is to idealize the work ethic and believe that everything can be taken care of simply by working hard. This can lead to burnout or overextension—taking on more and more in the mistaken idea that you can do anything. Because you want to constantly enlarge and expand your scope of effectiveness, you may generalize about your vocational duties and assume you know everything; beware of jumping to conclusions or missing finer points in your tendency to emphasize the **big** picture. The most satisfying way to combine work and ideals is to choose a job which helps to create a more ideal world. This could be in any service profession, healing, education, inspiration, motivation, the broadening of people's horizons or bringing visions down to earth.

Your world view is probably practical, pragmatic and sensible. You want to understand your job and your health. You may learn and could teach about health, hygiene, analysis or service. You may enjoy theorizing about efficiency, reality, health, and healing methods. Your ethics/moral principles are exacting and you could be perfectionistic. You are looking for the best in your practical experiences.

JUPITER IN 7TH HOUSE

You probably believe in and value relationships, give-and-take exchanges, and justice. You tend to trust (put your faith in) fair play, balance and equality. You are apt to generalize about and make assumptions regarding other people; be wary of leaping to conclusions socially or giving others too much credit. You may overextend yourself, promising more than you can deliver to others. You probably enjoy theorizing about relationships, balance and harmony. You may seek an understanding of aesthetics and of partners. Your humor might emerge in interpersonal relations; you can learn much about people and teach as well. You are seeking a sense of inspiration and idealism in relationships, so expectations are an issue. You may want more than is humanly possible from your partners, the relationship or yourself. Too high expectations can lead to reluctance to commit to just one person. Someone more ideal might show up, or different people may each offer one of the collection of ideals you are seeking. The union of ideals and partnership is best handled by finding someone who shares your faith and goals. Then you can continue the quest for meaning together whether you look to religion, spirituality, metaphysics, education, travel, etc., but neither needs to look to the other to "be everything" for him/her.

Your world view is likely to promote grace, harmony, pleasure and sharing. Your ethics/moral principles highlight a passion for justice, harmony and taking turns. You are naturally sociable, and may acquire wisdom through interpersonal exchanges.

JUPITER IN 8TH HOUSE

You believe in and value intimacy, intensity and going "to the wall." You tend to trust (put your faith in) mates, joint possessions, or self-mastery. You may want to expand or enlarge your drive for intimacy but there is some danger that you will expect more than is reasonable from a mate (or pick a mate who expects too much from you). You are looking for an inspirational experience—to be "swept away" and might give too much significance to a lover, to sex or to shared resources. Beware of turning money, sexuality or another person into "god"—something you cannot live without. Co-created ecstasy is important, but neither individual should feel s/he needs the other to exist. You are learning (and teaching others) about sharing possessions and pleasures equally with another person. Your quest for knowledge may take you into hidden (Shadow) areas of the psyche. You can generalize and assume you already understand deep, emotional details; beware of overlooking important issues. You might enjoy theorizing about psychic insight, death, occult studies or hidden matters.

Your world view is complex, many-layered and stirs deep emotions. You probably seek to understand sex, emotional bonding and power. Your ethics and moral principles may arouse intense emotions; you might even be fanatical at times. Your humor can be biting; your wit is sharp and acerbic. You may need to learn "when is enough and how to let go." You may be pulled between the future and the past. But you want the best in interpersonal relations and can pursue wisdom, moving toward self-knowledge and self-mastery.

JUPITER IN 9TH HOUSE

You may believe in and value education, knowledge, travel, spirituality or anything that means **more** in life. You tend to trust (put your faith into) expansion and extended horizons. You could easily feel "more is better" and slip into excesses. A sense of "God is on my side" is possible which can lead to arrogance. Your world view is wide; your perspective is broad. You are drawn toward travel, or involvement with different cultures and perspectives. A constant student and a natural teacher, you are eager to tease information from any person and every experience. Your quest is oriented toward wisdom. You may occasionally slip into pomposity or self-righteousness (particularly around ideals), but humor can be your saving grace. You are likely to be quite glib and articulate.

Seeking understanding of the meaning and purpose of life is important to you. Your ethics and moral principles are high; you may be overly idealistic or want more than is humanly possible. You have a buoyant, resilient spirit with natural optimism. If you exaggerate your faith or enlarge your confidence too much, you could be rash, rushing in "where angels fear to tread." You are prone to making generalizations, assuming you understand things, and may leap to conclusions on occasion. You want the best, the brightest, the fastest and the highest in life and will be a perpetual seeker of whatever you set up as your ultimate value and goal.

JUPITER IN 10TH HOUSE

You tend to believe in and value structure, predictability and authority. You may trust (put your faith in) the rules and regularities of life. Your world view could be conventional, sensible, realistic and may incline toward materialism. Success and "making it" in society's terms may be quite important to you and you are apt to make fortunate contacts which could assist your rise to the top. Orthodox answers may be the ones you trust or you might idealize power and authority. Your father (figure) was an important influence on your beliefs, values and moral principles. Whether he set a positive example of aspirations backed by hard work, or a negative example of wanting more than is possible or expecting things too easily, you had an opportunity to learn about blending reality and ideals. You may enjoy theorizing about authority figures, power, karma, reality and responsibility. You can both learn and teach about ambition and achievement. To avoid being too serious about life, it is important to maintain your humor in situations of control, mastery and career pressures.

You are apt to have high expectations for your vocation. This could lead to expanded accomplishments or to grandiose ambitions that expect more recognition that is realistically possible. You seek understanding of the laws of life. You could be inclined to generalize about your duties or assume you understand all your responsibilities and obligations, but you are less likely than most people to reach hasty conclusions. You need a sense of activity and movement in your career. You might travel, deal with foreign countries, or be involved with large-scale issues, dissemination of knowledge or networking activities. You can be an inspired leader.

JUPITER IN 11TH HOUSE
You tend to believe in and value individuality, uniqueness and independence. You may trust (put your faith in) progress, the future and freedom. Your world view is open, tolerant and allows many different perspectives. You seek understanding of all people, humanitarian principles and how to keep one's options truly open. You can probably relate to just about anyone in the world. A natural motivator, you might be the spark plug in groups, generating enthusiastic activity and the confidence to keep on going. You may expect a lot from friends and your social networks (and they of you), but you are also likely to encourage the best in one another. Your humor can emerge in group situations or with friends or causes.

You probably want to expand and enlarge your seeking of freedom from restrictions; beware of demanding **too much** independence or rebelling against structure of any sort. Much restlessness is likely. You may enjoy theorizing about modern technology or anything new, different or changing. You might tend to generalize about the future, social causes or tolerance, yet could be intolerant by jumping to conclusions, or you could be intolerant of intolerance and dogmatism. Your ethics/moral principles are individualistic and may be rebellious. You are probably eager to learn about anything on the cutting edge of change and can teach enthusiastically about progress and anything new.

JUPITER IN 12TH HOUSE
You may believe in and value compassion, empathy, sensitivity and idealism. You might trust (put your faith in) a Higher Power or a quest for the Absolute. Your world view is probably perfectionistic, believing in the best and the beautiful. You could idealize faith and confidence. Your personal quest for the truth is apt to be paramount. Beware of turning a fragment of life into a "god" and giving it overwhelming importance. Ex-

cesses are a real possibility ("If this is good, then more is even better.") Grandiosity may occur on a cosmic scale. Some Nazi leaders had this placement of Jupiter. The Nazis showed the danger of a committed belief in principles which are destructive toward others and life as a whole. The Nazi ruthless pursuit of one idea of the "truth" produced the death camps. Keep a firm distinction between inspiration which has some grounding and blind "blue sky" optimism. You need an understanding of faith, unity and the capacity to transcend. Your ethics/moral principles can be idealistic, confused, illusory, absolutist, or beautiful.

If you have a firm faith in yourself **and** in a Higher Power, you are likely to have strong confidence and the ability to face anything in life. If you lack faith, you may feel anxious, overwhelmed, or inclined toward escapism. Meditation, inspirational materials, art, nature, and healing activities can feed your faith and trust in the Universe. Temporary internal retreats feed your inner spirit, refresh your psyche, and enable you to come forth again. Some kind of religious or spiritual activity may be essential for you.

You have a strong urge to learn about imagination, fantasy, dreams, visions and ideals. You can also teach mystical and transcendent concepts to others. You need to expand and enlarge your quest for the Absolute (without going to ruthless extremes which are possible when an individual is convinced s/he already is the Absolute, knows what should be, and has the right to enforce personal goals and values on others). Because you seek to understand the **big** picture, you might indulge your penchant for abstractions so far that you end up confused. You could overgeneralize about compassionate situations, ultimate truth, moral principles, or the needs of the underdog; don't condescend. You are intuitively drawn to think and theorize about selflessness, healing and ultimate answers. Your challenge is to make sure that you don't just get lost in your visions, but work to bring worthwhile dreams into action and to manifest them in the world.

Outer Planets Aspects

Because the outer planets take many years to circle the zodiac, they can hold aspects to one another for long periods of time.

Thus, millions of people may share the same aspect between Jupiter, Saturn, Uranus, Neptune or Pluto. Such aspects point to generational themes and are less individually significant than aspects involving the inner "planets" (Sun, Moon, Mercury, Venus and Mars). A Saturn/Uranus conjunction, for example, highlights a large number of people dealing with the polarization between old and new, conservative and liberal, caution and risk, or stability and change.

Although aspects between outer planets signify issues which are faced by a whole group of people, each person will confront these issues in his/her unique fashion. Some people grow and transcend through their generational issues; others experience difficulties. And people can change over time in how they handle these generational issues.

The different houses occupied by such aspecting planets will give some clues about how individuals may approach shared themes in diverse ways. Someone who has a Saturn/ Uranus conjunction in the 2nd house is likely to feel torn between a stable, "bring home the bacon" approach to earning a living, versus a desire for creativity, excitement and variety (which can end up unstable, erratic and unpredictable). Someone who has a Saturn/Uranus conjunction in the 7th is apt to feel torn between choosing a safe, stable (but perhaps a bit boring) partner versus choosing an exciting, risk-taking, changeable (but perhaps a bit undependable) partner.

If the outer planets which are aspecting one another also aspect inner planets in an individual's horoscope, the personal involvement in this generational issue is likely to be even more intense.

Jupiter in Aspects: *Seeking and Searching*

The nature of the planets involved in any aspect is the most important factor. For any pair of planets, please read **all three** aspect delineations: conjunction, cooperating (sextile ✶, trine △), and challenging (square □, opposition ☍, quincunx ⚻). The conjunction is the basic, most fundamental aspect and its themes carry through with other aspects. The cooperating and challenging analyses will offer additional choices regarding of constructive and nonconstructive ways of handling the basic issues.

Remember that the life issues represented by cooperating aspects (or conjunctions) may still require some attention. We might overdo certain themes, or succumb to projection, repression or displacement in trying to balance our many, different drives. It is also quite possible that you could have integrated some of the conflicts (shown by challenging aspects) which were present at birth and are now manifesting potentials more reflective of the delineations in the cooperating or conjunction sections.

Other factors will complicate the picture. The potential inherent in any given placement might be overridden by other configurations in the chart. As you read the interpretations for the various pieces of your chart, bear in mind that certain pieces will suppress others. As always, repeated themes, which recur again and again, are the most likely to manifest in your psyche and in your life.

JUPITER CONJUNCT SATURN

You can be quite impartial, just, parental and trustworthy. You may be quite concerned with the moral issues of society. This combination is said to signify the "great teacher" since it shows the potential for knowledge (Jupiter) of the **law** (Saturn) which leads to good judgment as well as wisdom.

To actualize your highest potential, you must integrate a number of polarities. You are working on the balance between expansion and contraction; liberality and conservatism; optimism and pessimism; trust and mistrust; ease and effort; risk and safety; future and past; ideal and real; faith and fear. With polarities, the challenge is to avoid seesawing swings between opposite extremes; or living out one side while someone else overdoes the other. Synthesis—combining the best of both—is essential.

Your career might involve education, travel, writing, philosophy, religion, law, or anything including ideas, ideals and large perspectives. You might idealize the work ethic, seek the perfect job (and be chronically dissatisfied), work to make a better world, or try to do your work perfectly. You could also deal with business on a large scale and have a knack for patient, careful growth. You are likely to attend to underpinnings, strategy, goals and rules. You learn from your experience, test, practice and pay attention to life's lessons.

Your father (or father figure) had a strong impact on on your beliefs, values and world view. You might have idealized him (sometimes in absentia), or he could have been religious, idealistic, perfectionistic, impossible to please. In some form, he affected your moral, ethical and religious principles. Whether you followed his example, or went in the exact opposite direction, his influence was significant. Be sure that your present faith is one that serves you well, and not a reaction to past history.

Alert for opportunities, you can be the practical idealist who makes dreams real. You know how to structure and solidify long-term goals. You are able to visualize and to manifest results. You can be persevering, industrious, resilient, honorable, and successful. You may enjoy a protective, parental attitude. You probably have solid charm, being generous in a practical form. The teacher or preacher role comes naturally to you.

(This conjunction occurs about every 20 years.)

JUPITER COOPERATING SATURN (✶ △)

You have a fine instinct for synthesizing polarities. You seek to ground visions, to manifest dreams in practical events, and to turn them into reality. You can blend confidence and caution, expansion and contraction, ease and effort.

Your capacity to visualize and extrapolate toward a better future can enhance your career and professional accomplishments. Your education, world view, philosophy, extraversion, wit or intellect can contribute to your worldly attainments. Because you plan ahead to make the most of opportunities, you appear more fortunate than the average mortal. Your sense of timing is probably good.

You can put enthusiasm into your career and are likely to be successful on the material plane. Your natural understanding of and respect for rules, regulations and the limits of the physical world help you to operate within that world to reach your desired goals. You are willing to work hard to reach your aspirations.

Your philosophy, religion or world view is likely to be solidly grounded in experience. You are drawn to beliefs that function in the physical world, that are constructively pragmatic (positive and practical). You want to blend the material with the ideal; the sensible with the inspirational.

You may be motivated to bring together the letter of the law with its spirit. Issues of moral probity, honesty, ethics and justice could be very important to you.

You are likely to put knowledge to use, to consistently seek a purpose. You probably make systematic progress and believe "where there's a will, there's a way." You can be quite impartial, parental, trustworthy, protective, ethical, and goal-oriented.

JUPITER CHALLENGING SATURN (□ ℰ ⊼)

You can accomplish a great deal, but may feel pulled in different directions. At times, you might plunge into new projects and challenges before completing and consolidating old ones. Or, you might hold back from what you truly **can** do, because your standards are too demanding or perfectionistic ("If I can't do it perfectly, I won't do it at all"). Establish clear priorities about what matters most to you so you can allocate your energies appropriately. Break your goals down into bite-sized steps so that you do not feel overwhelmed, but can labor incrementally toward a larger vision.

You are working on the combination of expansion and contraction. Fluctuation is possible, if you swing from one extreme to the other. With attention and focus, you can choose when to reach out and begin new possibilities and when to ground and solidify what you already have. Making the best of both means you can be successful, more consistent, resilient and productive.

You may also experience some tension in regard to beliefs, values, moral principles and religious or spiritual views. Conflict with a father (or father figure) over world views, philosophy, ethics or ideals is possible. You must make peace between your visionary, optimistic, idealistic side and your pragmatic, cautious, realistic side. Don't let faith battle fear, but do be sure your sense of meaning and understanding of life's purpose is grounded in experience and practicalities.

Because you are willing to learn from experience, you can become a practical idealist, a competent mystic, someone who makes dreams comes true!

JUPITER CONJUNCT URANUS

The mind is very important to you. Indeed, you may idealize knowledge and wisdom, insatiably seeking to acquire more of both. You are likely to think quickly, but may sometimes jump to conclusions or oversimplify. You are an idea person and might think in metaphors, symbols or archetypes. You intuitively make connections and can use information creatively.

You are drawn to the future and tend to be hopeful and optimistic about what lies ahead. Instinctively progressive, you are likely to believe in the common man/woman and democratic ideals. You tend to be concerned with fairness, groups, principles. You may espouse the right to be different. You could be honest, blunt, exaggerative, haphazard, or farsighted. You probably put your faith in freedom and individuality and may be attracted to causes. You thrive on excitement.

You detest confinement of any sort and most likely seek to break free of any restraints. You can be eccentric, eclectic, individualistic, restless, and unorthodox. On occasion, you could be rash, reckless, tense, careless or defiant. You may live by your principles, especially when in opposition to others or when challenging the establishment. You may have many friends, unusual friends, or be constantly on the move. You might travel on impulse, or simply enjoy other cultures. You could put your faith in computers, astrology, technology, the law, advocacy, or anything on the cutting edge of change and growth.

You can practice creative originality on a large scale. You see the large picture, understanding patterns and context. You probably aspire to wisdom and enlightenment, and could sometimes be prophetic. You may also experience sudden changes in your philosophy or opinions (as you gather new information). You are likely to seek your own individual truth or religion and can be a reformer.

(This conjunction occurs about every 13-14 years.)

JUPITER COOPERATING URANUS (✶ △)

You are likely to be independent, progressive and bright. With a restless, free spirit, you tend to seek variety and plenty of mental stimulation. At times, you can be rash, careless, impatient, or challenging. A life full of ideas, ideals or travel might appeal. You may exhibit originality on a large scale (perhaps even genius).

Your mind is apt to work quickly, but you could jump to conclusions or fall into oversimplifying. You have talent for seeing the big picture, understanding patterns and contexts. Your thinking may include metaphors, symbols or archetypes; you work well with theories and ideas. Apt to emphasize principles and your individualistic form of the truth, you may play out the role of rebel or reformer.

Optimistic, you tend to trust in the future, and may have little patience for people who are not willing to try to do more. Your belief system probably emphasizes freedom, equality, the intellect and a broad perspective on life. Honesty is apt to be very important to you, perhaps to the point of bluntness.

With a transpersonal focus, you could deal in issues affecting many people. You care about humanity and justice, but could seem less personal on the one-to-one level because you are focusing on broader issues. You may be drawn to the advocacy role, concerned with fair play and social justice.

You could have talent for astrology, computers, politics, broadcasting, education, technology, foreign relations or anything new and exciting. You seek stimulation, knowledge, and unusual perspectives. You may exhibit inspired wisdom.

JUPITER CHALLENGING URANUS (□ ♂ ⊼)
Enthusiastic and independent, you thrive in a stimulating atmosphere. Drawn toward variety, you could be ever on the go. Travel or new experiences of all sorts can help satisfy your restlessness. Your mind is apt to be quick and active, but you may jump to conclusions, oversimplify, overgeneralize or be impatient with other people's thinking processes. You have a talent for ideas, theories and broad perspectives.

Your natural inclination is to challenge religion, philosophy, ethics, spirituality or world views. You probably seek to innovate in terms of belief systems and may adopt a rebellious or reforming stance. You might change your opinions suddenly, or abruptly reverse your beliefs. Your desire for "absolute truth" could seduce you into a dogmatic stance, or a continual dissatisfaction with your faith. If you avoid the extremes of the "know-it-all" role or the "religion-of-the-month" club, your creativity can help you to constantly update your sense of meaning, purpose and spirituality. Your values must be true to your inner individuality.

Independence is the breath of life to you, and change has a great deal of appeal. Your desire for the new could lead you to scatter your forces, overextend, or be too impatient (demanding rapid rewards). Because you easily see the big picture, you could overlook significant details. Yet theorizing, visualizing and working toward dreams of the future are among your strengths.

Your passion for justice and truth could involve you with the law, politics, moral principles or questions of fair play. You might carry honesty to the extreme of a lack of tact on occasion. You are likely to be articulate, resourceful, bright and far-sighted.

JUPITER CONJUNCT NEPTUNE

You may have a special yearning for the unseen, the mystical, the pure and the visionary. You might be drawn to spiritual activities, concerned with wider truths, or idealistic images. You are seeking the ecstasy of merging with the sublime in life.

You could be quite optimistic and may tend to see only the best. You might gamble, speculate or take excessive risks because you trust too much in "happily ever after." You could be too gullible, escapist, naive, suggestible, altruistic, or superstitious, preferring to believe only in goodness. You might live in an ivory tower, or be lost, aimless, disoriented because you are often moved to take in too much. Mutable and flexible, you may have a talent for foreign languages, an ear for accents, or an eye for images and imagery. You are likely to be strongly drawn by grace, beauty and art. You could become scattered, trying to do and understand everything. You want to experience the sublime, but must practice staying grounded as even the sublime has earthly foundations. Keeping clear priorities is vital; a value hierarchy will help you make choices and be less likely to overextend yourself.

You could put your faith in education, freedom, philosophy, travel, religion, escapism, beauty or dreams. You might idealize sacrifice or martyrdom. You could easily try to do too much for other people. You can be quite empathic and inspired. You are willing to work for the good of all (without personal gain).

Castles in the air come naturally to you. You probably have a rich fantasy life and may be a real or armchair traveler.

You tend to think in terms of the big picture, the broad overview, and could get carried away with generalizations or assumptions. Sometimes you believe that what **should** be true **is** true.

You are capable of a strong faith, a dedicated spiritual search. You can touch the cosmos through devotion, rapture and a quest for ultimate perfection.

(This conjunction occurs about every 13 years.)

JUPITER COOPERATING NEPTUNE (✶ △)

Both your heart and mind unite to seek the highest in life, or at least your concept of the highest. If you are strongly grounded, your goals may lie anywhere, but the conscious and the unconscious values are supporting each other. If you are highly involved in the transpersonal side of life, your idealistic and compassionate nature is likely to draw you toward religious, mystical, philanthropic or healing activities. Because you want to believe in the best, you can be susceptible to wearing rose-colored glasses. You might see what you want (rather than what is) and could be taken advantage of by others, or be too lost in fantasies and imagination to face life's necessities. You might consistently want more than is possible, because your ideal images rest far above your mundane life.

Your talents lie in imagining something better than what currently exists. You can use affirmations, visualization techniques and other imaging skills to help make dreams come true and hence can offer the world an elevated vision through art, literature, film, or the healing professions. (Don't forget to back up your dreams with hard work and common sense.) Your intuition could contribute to success in education, the law, writing, philosophy, social work, broadcasting or other fields which deal with large issues or many people. An involvement with grace, beauty and art can be very refreshing for you, replenishing your energy and confidence.

You could have a transcendent impulse, naturally merging with others, or drawn to experience union with a Higher Power. Your mutable nature can also contribute to skill with languages, accents, music, or a flexible interest in everything. This same urge to absorb it all can cause you to be overextended, scattered and confused. Assign clear priorities in your life; no one can do (or know) everything.

One of your strengths is harmony between your intellectual faith (what you believe and conceptualize in words) and your emotional faith (what you feel in your gut). Your mind and soul work together toward your version of ecstasy.

JUPITER CHALLENGING NEPTUNE (□ ⚹ ⊼)

Ideals and expectations are a core issue in your life. Perhaps your head is at odds with your heart: intellectual understanding at war with intuitive "knowing" or emotional yearnings. Perhaps you feel torn between truth (bluntness) and compassion (tact). Perhaps you hold your ideals too high ("perfect or not at all") or have sold out to expedience. Perhaps you feel frustrated because your visions of what **could** be are so lofty that you feel they are all unattainable. Or perhaps you are just not sure what you believe in, trust, and value in life. Your challenge is to create a firm sense of faith in yourself (without the extremes of self-righteousness or self-sacrifice) as well as a trust in a Higher Power that will take over once you have done your bit.

Idealized images can lead you astray. Because you want to believe that "everything's coming up roses," you could be rash, gullible or victimized in matters of speculation (gambling) or the legal system. You might be too sentimental or inclined to go overboard with altruism. A motivation to make the world a better, more beautiful place is excellent, but don't assume the "golden age" is already here or requires only visualization. Skepticism and hard work have their places too.

Your inner drive to save, to rescue, to help and to make better can lead to victimization or martyrdom if overdone. You might make promises you cannot keep (meaning well at the time) because you take on too much and get overextended. By keeping clear priorities and focusing on what is most important, you can get things done (even if you always want to do more than you can). Accepting that life is a **process** and that we never make it to perfection can also be helpful. See yourself as an evolving, transcending soul, reaching toward perfection, but not forgetting to enjoy the journey!

JUPITER CONJUNCT PLUTO

You have the capacity to combine breadth and depth, seeking fundamental motives and drives in life, as well as illumination and inspiration from above. You are likely to search for a broad perspective as well as an intense understanding of the root causes of human behavior and experience.

You might put your faith in self-control, or best express idealism when you have power and control. You could over-value material success, mastery or possessions. You might seek power through politics, religion, crime, manipulation or education. You may deal in explosive ideas (persuasion, propaganda) or be a leader in spiritual matters. You could be a powerful and effective teacher, a teacher of mysteries, or an inspired researcher. Your beliefs may be uncompromising, dogmatic, devious or you might blame and resent religion. Another choice is an intense search for understanding, a deep focus on goals, values and ideas, a life philosophy which is rooted in an intense, inner investigation and testing.

You are facing several polarities in your life and might confront extremes of good and evil. You may feel that you can undergo almost anything—pushing and testing the limits—and come out a survivor. You need to balance between the future and the past; freedom and attachments; generosity and possessiveness; bursting out and holding in; losing and maintaining control; profligacy and conservation; exposure and secrecy; and bluntness and deviousness.

Your personal life could center around a desire to grow and you are likely to both teach and learn (transform and be transformed) in relationships, particularly in regard to sex and sharing resources/pleasures. You might seek the ideal mate or union and yearn for impossible perfection. You could overdo both self-indulgence and self-discipline. You might put too much faith in, or exaggerate the importance of, sex or shared possessions. You may have extreme ideas about resources. You may be sexually exploited, deal in sex for profit, or make money through other people's money, sexuality, assets or ideas. You are learning wisdom in the handling of shared pleasures and possessions.

You are capable of great courage, energy, endurance and resourcefulness. You face intense, emotional issues and can move people deeply.

(This conjunction occurs about every 13 years.)

JUPITER COOPERATING PLUTO (✶ △)

Emotional reactions are likely to be a source of learning for you and those about you. Intimate associations operate like a mirror to your soul (and can put you in touch with the cosmos); a mate will probably act out issues significant for your personal growth. You may explore the teachings of many ages, seeking to deepen your understanding of life. Capable of persuading others, you can teach (formally or informally) with zest and fervor. You are likely to search intently for insights and for a sense of meaning and purpose in life.

The belief system you follow (religious, spiritual, etc.) can enhance and strengthen your close, emotional attachments to a partner. Your capacity to visualize the best and inspire the ideal visions of others can contribute to a real soul connection. Your faith and confidence may encourage others to seek the heights, and reach their highest potential. If this quest for an absolute is carried too far, perfectionism could cripple relationships, or a "perfect or not at all" attitude might prevail. With shared values, you and a mate can appreciate the best in one another and constantly transcend the past, evolving toward more and more self-mastery.

Because you appreciate the intellect as well as emotions, and confident expansion as well as careful, controlled discipline, you can create a constructive blend between thoughts and feelings, rationality and intuitive perceptions. Your sensitivity to innuendoes, nuances and nonverbal cues adds to your logical understanding and grasp of any situation. You can also be quite persuasive in your communications.

You can be a powerful advocate for what you believe in. You are likely to be strong, ambitious, brave, enduring and intense.

JUPITER CHALLENGING PLUTO (□ ☍ ⚻)

You are likely to face intense emotional issues around relationships and beliefs. Part of you is naturally exuberant, enthusiastic, expressive and extraverted. Another part inclines toward self-control, self-mastery, holding in, and holding back. You may blow hot and cold, letting it all hang out on occasion and being very reticent (even secretive) at other times. By blending these polarities, you can appropriately choose discretion or bluntness, expression or discipline based on circumstances.

Idealistic urges may affect your relationship with a mate. This could manifest as a quest for the "perfect" (larger-than-life) partner (who doesn't exist). Being unwilling to settle for less than the absolute best can be an unconscious method of maintaining freedom from attachments. Another possibility is getting involved with someone on a student/guru basis (where one seems to offer ultimate wisdom, meaning and truth to the other). You may expect more than is humanly possibly in relationships (or attract other people who have perfectionistic demands). Ethical, religious, philosophical or moral conflicts with a mate are possible. Seeking a partner who shares your world view and your quest for something more in life is apt to work the best.

Stress around money, possessions, pleasures or sexuality is possible. If your values are at odds with your mate, power struggles, intimidation, manipulation or jockeying for control might occur. Clarity and perspective in your expectations regarding giving, receiving and sharing the material, sensual and sexual world will help to build a constructive exchange with your intimates.

You can be quite resourceful, courageous and persuasive. You know how to have an emotional impact on people.

CHAPTER NINE

SATURN
REALITY AND RESPONSIBILITY
IN YOUR HOROSCOPE

Saturn in Signs: *Rules and Regularities*

Saturn takes about 29½ years to travel the zodiac circuit, so spends about 2½ years in each sign. Thus, you share certain themes with people around your age. How you handle these issues, however, will depend on you (and your whole horoscope—including the house placement of Saturn). The challenge with any Saturn placement is to be appropriately realistic. People often take on either too little or too much responsibility in the areas connected to their Saturn's house and sign placements. Practice doing what is possible, neither giving up (fearing failure), nor trying to control and handle everything, but working pragmatically within the limits of the world. Saturn represents the "rules of the game," and the consequences of how we have handled the rules in the past. Fear is not helpful, but Saturn does point to areas of life where we have something to learn, so it calls for attention and respect.

SATURN IN ARIES

A father or father figure is likely to have played a significant role in your early life, setting an example of what to do or of what not to do. He may have been over-controlling or unreliable, but he was a key to your learning how to handle power. In response, you may structure your self-expression and try to control life, or you may inhibit yourself for fear of doing something wrong and failing or falling short. A variation on self-doubt and projection of power into the world is a continuation of the child's role into adulthood. "The world has all the power and the responsibility." Alternately, it is possible to feel that your personal will should be the Law, that you have the right and power to do whatever you want. With a proper compromise that calls for voluntarily living within the Law and handling your share of the responsibility, you can be disciplined, dedicated, and successful in what you do. You are oriented toward doing your own thing professionally and might run your own business, be an entrepreneur, or choose a field full of action, competition, spontaneity, freedom, risks, or self-expression. You can be identified with your career, dedicated to achievement, and focused on personally changing the world.

SATURN IN TAURUS

You could be very responsible or quite insecure in regard to possessions, sensuality and comfort. If you assume that almost all power is in the world, you may feel anxious and afraid to spend money, or you may remain dependent on others to support you. If you assume that you have the power to handle the material world, you are likely to be successful and responsible. If you were raised in a cultural setting that emphasized Puritan ethics, you might be highly successful but still limit your indulgences and save rather than spend. It is possible to work hard but have trouble relaxing and enjoying the fruits of your labors. It is also possible to turn indulgence into a "career," to overdo sensuality, luxury, indolence, and to need to learn self-discipline. The challenge is to balance ease and effort within your psyche. Your career might involve beauty, money, pleasures or you might just want stability and regularity. Your security is tied to loyalty and reliability, but you may sometimes succumb to inertia or too much stubbornness. You can be quite productive and may put diligence into furthering your appreciation of art, nature or sensual pleasures and material resources.

SATURN IN GEMINI

You may seek to learn and communicate in a structured fashion or you may focus on learning practical skills which will produce tangible results. You could be talented in working with your hands. You might have to work through some self-doubt about your mental ability, whether due to limited education in your early life or to excessive self-criticism. Once you prove to yourself that you have a good mind, it can be a fine asset. Your mind is likely to be very thorough and disciplined, but skeptical attitudes might inhibit your capacity to perceive many different concepts and potentials. Facts are important to you; you want to think in a rational, organized manner. Your career could involve communication, paperwork, travel, transportation, the media, variety, or a multiplicity of duties.

SATURN IN CANCER

You are likely to feel very responsible toward your home and family and might feel insecure or overburdened at times. It is often fears of dependency and vulnerabililty which lead to attempts to stay in control, including the tendency to constantly play parent in life. Alternately, it is possible to "control through helplessness," through maintaining the child's role into adulthood. As the nurturing parent, whether with family, friends, or the needs of the planet, you can be quite helpful. If you find yourself over-controlling your emotions, look for hidden insecurities and try to find ways you can allow your feelings to express, perhaps in a sheltered situation such as a psychotherapy group. Your career might involve a family business, the land, the public, women, food, shelter, commodities or anything relating to emotional security.

SATURN IN LEO

Power is an important issue in this combination of king who makes the law and executive who carries out laws which are bigger than personal will. You may swing between feeling that you have a right to control your world and feeling that you should inhibit your own desires. If caution wins, you may structure and control your risks and thrill-seeking, holding back rather than taking a chance. You may seek security by channeling your creative, self-expressive side into material achievements and ambitions. In such cases, you are learning to trust rather than fear your legitimate desires, to avoid harsh self-criticism that can destroy your self-esteem. It is also important to avoid extreme egocentrism, to achieve a balance between self-discipline and self-promotion. You are likely to be quite responsible where children are concerned and might take your duties too seriously. A fear of falling short as a parent can even block the ability to have children. Or your career could involve children, with other possibilities including promotion, entertainment, sales, speculation, or creativity. You need a sense of pride in what you do and work best when gaining recognition for your creative efforts.

SATURN IN VIRGO

You tend to be either very dedicated and hardworking, or to avoid responsibility for fear of making a mistake. If you are too self-critical, it can interfere with your capacity to work well. You want to do everything right in regard to your job and health, and could do more than your share, not trusting others to do things correctly. But if you feel that your work is not worthy of your skills, illness can be a danger since it frees one from the work without feeling guilty. You can be quite discriminating, dutiful, service-oriented and painstaking. You are likely to be good with details and very conscientious, working consistently to hone your skills. Your career might involve nutrition, health, repairs, efficiency or anything careful and analytical. You need tangible results and function best when you have measurable output and productivity as well as some control over the job to keep it up to your high standards.

SATURN IN LIBRA

Power tends to be an issue in your partnerships, sometimes a lesson. You may want balance and fair play yet tend to feel very responsible for things working out. You may choose a strong, competent partner so both need to compromise, to share the power. Fairness, tact, and impartiality may be important and require attention. You could try to organize your relationships, or you or a mate might play parent when you should be peers. If you are unsure of your strength and self-worth, you might fear commitment with its danger of being hurt, criticized or rejected. Such fears can inhibit your capacity to make an intimate connection. Mutual trust is essential in any partnership. You are willing to be practical and work on relationships. Once a commitment is made, you want to be faithful; you honor your promises and agreements. Your career could involve the visual arts, personnel work, counseling, consulting, or any kind of teamwork.

SATURN IN SCORPIO

You may put serious effort and dedication into intimacy, shared resources, and power issues. Emotional mastery is desired, so you may seek to understand your own unconscious and to control your own passions. If your need for self-control is too strong, it might inhibit intimate connections which call for sharing power and passions. Any partnership is in jeopardy if either partner tries to dominate and intimidate the other in terms of money, possessions, sexuality etc., or if there is a lack of trust in each other. Relationships are an important part of your nature, so don't give up the effort to share life, but you might also be learning when is enough and how to let go of past hurts and/or resentments. You have excellent organizational skills and can be very successful in work which involves detail, patience and persistence. Your career might involve investment, taxes, or any other handling of joint resources, law, sexuality, depth psychology, the occult, research or digging thoroughly into anything. You may be quite skilled at renovations, reforms and totally transforming (or revitalizing) something (bringing the "dead" to life).

SATURN IN SAGITTARIUS

You may put effort and dedication into your philosophy, religion, or search for meaning. You gain security through a clear formulation of goals. You are apt to be serious about ethics/moral principles, yet you might carry out responsibilities with a sense of humor. Your beliefs may be quite firm (even rigid on occasion). Your need for tangible evidence may make you a skeptic in some areas, wanting proof before you are willing to believe. You may feel torn between contraction and expansion, pessimism and optimism or realism and idealism; a compromise works best. Your career might involve travel, the law, education, spiritual quests, writing, publishing, broadcasting, or anything that expands human horizons.

SATURN IN CAPRICORN

You are capable of being quite serious, responsible, dedicated, hardworking and competent. In fact, you might sometimes overdo criticism and inhibit your own potential achievements. You are likely to seek a position of authority in society but you might hold back if you feel that the world is too powerful for you or you might sometimes overdo a need to control. If you overrate the power of the world, including authority figures, you could be vulnerable to their or society's opinions. You tend toward conservatism, caution and traditionalism. You are likely to be reliable and may try to do too much yourself because of your strong sense of responsibility or because of a lack of trust in other people's willingness to contribute properly. You have a talent for planning ahead and can be quite organized and successful.You have executive ability and naturally would work your way to the top of your field. Your career could involve power, authority, structures, bureaucracies, business, government at any level, or anything requiring practicality.

SATURN IN AQUARIUS

You have the potential to combine traditional values with new age insights, to bring democratic, humanitarian principles into form in a hierarchal, bureaucratic world. However you might overdo trying to structure and organize your sense of individuality, and this could sometimes inhibit your originality and uniqueness. You can be responsible and dedicated in an unusual way. You may be quite committed to social change or progressive principles. You are apt to be logical and rational, with a talent for science. Your career might involve friends, groups, networking, computers or anything on the "cutting edge." You may have talent for organizing people or ideas. You may achieve through groups (teamwork). Too much focus on your drive for individuality and uniqueness could hinder your worldly achievements, but too much concern with what is "proper" could block your independence and inventive spirit. Keep a balance between the old and new, the structured and the free.

SATURN IN PISCES

You may look for structure with your imagination, and may be trying to bring a utopian ideal into manifestation. You could sometimes be too critical of fantasies or imagery, but can also be very practical about visions. Don't let your desire for tangible evidence keep you from experiencing faith in something ultimate and beautiful. Or, alternately, don't let your idealistic images hinder you from taking on essential duties and responsibilities. Your visualization capacities can enrich your ambitions and worldly attainments. With integration, you can be practical about healing and compassion, and can dissolve limits or blocks through faith, love and empathy. Your career might involve mysticism, transcendence, inspiration, the infinitely large or the very small, water, fluids, drugs or chemicals. You will feel the greatest satisfaction if your achievements contribute to making a more ideal world.

Saturn in Houses:
Authority and Achievement

SATURN IN 1ST HOUSE
You tend to structure yourself and may overcontrol your self-expression. You are directly confronting the limits of life (including the "rules of the game") and could either live in "overdrive," trying to make the world conform to your will, or you could hold yourself back through self-criticism or self-doubt. Responsibility is a core issue in your being and you may take on too much or too little. Your identity is tied to work and productivity and you probably "need" to work—defining yourself through productivity and accomplishment. However, you could also insist on working how, when, and where you choose, on your own terms. You are susceptible to guilt regarding your desires and what you want in life. You may strive to master literal physical limitations, or simply face the challenge of overcoming inhibitions and outer barriers to success and achievement. Measured discipline is important for you. You are naturally restrained, cautious, pragmatic and self-controlled. You are learning to accept yourself as you are, rather than pressuring yourself in terms of how you think you "should" be.

Your father (figure) is a role model (positive or negative) for your handling of assertion, anger and your sense of identity. You are likely to be similar to him—or the direct opposite. You probably perceive authorities (including father) as assertive (perhaps aggressive and dominating), active, courageous, direct or self-centered. You tend to get direct and immediate feedback ("instant karma") on the consequences of your actions.

You will be more satisfied if your career is self-directed and it may involve assertion or movement. Your duties may demand much energy, activity, initiative or courage from you. You are learning to balance self-will and the limits to self-will (societal constraints, outer world demands, etc.). You may feel torn between self-blocking and overdrive until you reach the middle position of energetic achievement. You can be quite realistic about who you and what you can do. Success is likely if you put high energy and confidence into doing what you want while staying within the limits of possibility in this world. Inner-motivated work **within** the rules can take you to the top.

SATURN IN 2ND HOUSE

You tend to structure your gratification and may overcontrol your pleasures in life. You are apt to feel quite responsible for finances and personal possessions. Initially you may feel limited monetarily or materially and need to overcome a "poverty consciousness." You may be insecure about your resources. You might be susceptible to guilt regarding indulgence, beauty or pleasure (feeling you must work hard to "earn" every penny or pleasure). You may experience karmic tension around finances, possessions, or your capacity for physical indulgence. If other parts of your nature tend toward overindulgence, you may be learning to be self-supporting and self-disciplined in handling the material world. You tend to take ownership seriously. As you gain in maturity, competence and inner strength, you could choose a vocation in the area of possessions, pleasures or money and become a professional there. You could achieve and accomplish in very practical, tangible ways. You build up your assets best through slow, steady, concentrated effort.

Your father (figure) is a role model (positive or negative) for the handling of pleasure and possessions. You tend to perceive authorities (including Dad) as easygoing, hedonistic, materialistic, self-indulgent, stubborn, or contented. Your father (figure) was teaching what to do (or what **not** to do) in terms of finances, physical pleasures and possessions.

Your career needs to involve beauty, comfort, pleasure, ease or tangible assets. You may work primarily for financial reasons or you may feel that you should be able to enjoy your work. You can apply regular, steady, dedicated effort to making a living and may need, at times, to remind yourself to relax and indulge at bit. You can be quite realistic about what you earn and what you enjoy, and are apt to be more comfortable if you have some savings tucked away.

SATURN IN 3RD HOUSE
You are likely to structure your thinking and communication and may sometimes overcontrol your speech or gathering of information. You might speak tersely, choosing your words carefully. You may initially feel limited mentally and need to avoid being too critical of your intellectual skills. Self-doubt may be connected to educational deprivation in your early life, to criticism by authority figures, or to comparing your mental ability to that of relatives, especially siblings, to your own detriment. You may have to prove to yourself that you have a good mind. You may be learning to take things more lightly. You tend to feel responsible for communicating very clearly and thinking logically. You could have quite a strong, focused, productive and practical mind. You are apt to learn best through experience. You can be quite realistic about what you know and how you share information.

Your handling of control and power will be faced in your early environment and people relationships. Karmic tension may affect your capacity to communicate, your thoughts, or your relationships with relatives. You may perceive a relative as critical, performance-oriented, hardworking, dominating, etc. You may attempt to control a relative, or experience a relative (aunt, uncle, cousin, sibling, etc.) as an authority figure in your life. A father (figure) is a role model (positive or negative) for handling the world of the mind. That individual could be bright, communicative, open and equalitarian. He could also be scattered, feckless, superficial, flippant or talkative. He is teaching you, well or poorly, about versatility, flexibility, or equality; when to be responsible and when to be a spectator.

Your career could involve working with your mind, tongue, or hands. Your duties are apt to be many, varied and changeable.

SATURN IN 4TH HOUSE

You may structure your feelings and could overcontrol your nurturing instincts or your vulnerability and dependency needs. You may feel quite responsible for your home, family, roots and emotional security. Your early home focused on the need to blend conditional and unconditional love. As a result, you may feel uncomfortable with being dependent (or inadequate in your ability to nurture) and may feel guilty about your home, family or domestic needs. Your karmic challenge is to blend compassion and pragmatism, caring and the bottom line, to be able to take turns giving emotional support and being supported by those you love.

This placement suggests a mother/father blend. It can mean that father played a more nurturing (traditional mothering) role—warm, emotionally supportive or passive/dependent. It might mean a father who was home more often then usual (found with farm families, a home business, work in construction, etc.) or a father whose presence dominated the home environment. Another possibility is that mother played a more powerful role—working in the world, acting strong, responsible, etc. Alternately, mother and father may have had overlapping roles, neither locked into traditional behaviors, or one parent may have played both roles (authority and nurturer) due to death, divorce, etc. Sometimes this placement indicates having to parent your own parent—where even as a child you felt you had to be strong, capable, and deal with reality in order to take care of an inadequate parent. You are learning to be sensible about your nurturing capacity and your need for emotional support.

Your career might involve caretaking, assistance, home and family, land, real estate, food, commodities or meeting people's basic needs. You might work in the home, or from your home (or follow a parent's footsteps vocationally). Your work might involve emotional nuances.

SATURN IN 5TH HOUSE

You are likely to seek structure in your expression of love and admiration. You can be too hard on yourself and may limit your creativity or self-expression. Beware of "hiding your light under a bushel" (creative blocks) or criticizing yourself to the point of low self-esteem. Fear or anxiety could stop you from taking chances; measured risks are advisable for you. You may feel a sense of karmic obligation to children and/or lovers and could be overly responsible toward loved ones (or fear doing anything lest you make a mistake). You are susceptible to guilt regarding love, power, sex, drama or speculation. Don't let anxiety about performance get in your way of enjoying life and love. An opposite expression of a fifth house Saturn involves too much confidence and overdrive, a combination of king and executive who makes personal will into law for others. "Steamroller" determination can achieve great success in the world, but sooner or later the personal will to power is likely to meet the limits inherent in social rules or natural law, and a fall from power is common.

Your father (figure) is a role model (positive or negative) for handling power, thrills, risk-taking, creativity, the limelight, and love. You may perceive authorities (including father) as exciting, dynamic, arrogant, bombastic, histrionic, dominating, generous or magnetic. The Establishment may seem powerful and demanding, or generous and magnanimous. You may "meet" your father again through lovers and/or children. Extremes can include the disciplinarian parent, the critical parent, the guilt-ridden parent, the person who avoids having children from a sense of personal inadequacy or because a career is more important or because they are still "waiting" until they can properly provide for a child, and the parent of children who need extra care, who require more effort in their raising. This is a good example of how the principles of astrology can manifest in a multitude of different details in the life, depending on individual understanding and choices. Properly handled, you can share work, responsibility and power with loved ones—with no single individual overdoing duty, judgment and control—but all contributing to mutual success and satisfaction.

Although you may inhibit your natural charisma when young, you are likely to flower with maturity and could incorporate your ability to shine and be significant in your vocation. Your career might involve power, excitement, thrills, creativity, a special loved one or fame. You will be motivated to manifest your creative zest in the world, perhaps through art, teaching, investment, entertainment, etc. Any vocation is possible which pours out into the world, hoping for a bigger return. You can be realistic about your need to be admired, noticed, and applauded.

SATURN IN 6TH HOUSE

You may seek structure in your work routines or follow quite regular health habits. You probably feel responsible for doing things well and not making mistakes. You may feel limited in your work or health and need to avoid focusing too much on what is "wrong" (rather than what is "right") and how to fix it or make it all better. Karmic issues for you revolve around efficient functioning in both your job and in your body. You are learning to be productive and effective without pushing yourself too hard and falling into a workaholic stance—or giving up and not trying because you feel inadequate or because you want to be in control and are reluctant to work for someone else. Regularity, practicality and realism are essential in what you do and for your physical well-being. If you demand too much of yourself, problems with your back, teeth, bones, knees or crystallization (stones, gout, arthritis) can indicate taking too much on your shoulders, trying to be indispensable. You might also get sick in order to take a "vacation" or because your work is frustrating but security needs or guilt keep you from quitting.

Your father (figure) is a role model (positive or negative) for your attitudes about competence and health. You may perceive authorities (including father) as hardworking, dedicated, demanding, nitpicking, fault-finding, humble or ill or inadequate in other ways. His example taught you what to do or what not to do in terms of service, fixing things up, dedication and effort.

Your career needs to include careful analysis, attention to detail, focus, concentration or quiet efficiency. You may be drawn to fields involving health, nutrition, repairs or any kind of improvement. Your duties are likely to be practical, sensible and to call for facing facts. You are susceptible to guilt regarding perceived faults and may be too critical of yourself, especially on the job. It is also possible for frustration with your work to be displaced into criticism in other areas of life. You are learning to be realistic about your capabilities and competence as well as learning what is possible and what is necessary in order to survive in a material world.

SATURN IN 7TH HOUSE

You are likely to seek structure in your associations with others. You may deal with power issues in relationships and must watch a tendency to take on excessive responsibility or to choose partners who try to dominate you. Feeling limited in relationships often signals a need to share the power so neither of you ends up being a controller or carrying all of the load. You may feel a sense of karmic obligation to partners and could be susceptible to guilt regarding other people. You are learning to share responsibility in peer relationships—neither carrying it all nor avoiding it.

Your father (figure) was a role model (positive or negative) for equality, balance, harmony, justice and interpersonal relations. He could have been cooperative, diplomatic, charming, competitive, a milquetoast, graceful or attractive. He might have had artistic ability or refined tastes. If his example was positive, he probably treated you as an equal. The two of you had a sense of teamwork and may have an ongoing relationship in your adult life. If your relationship with Dad was less positive, you are likely to face issues of authority, power, responsibility and competence in your partnerships. Beware of unconsciously choosing someone who elicits the same feelings as your father did. You are learning to be realistic about people, and about what is possible within a partnership. Extremes include avoiding relationships from fear of hurt, rejection or making a mistake; delaying relationships from anxiety; or choosing a "father figure" or someone who puts you in the parental role. The middle ground is for both people to "work" on the relationship, to be dedicated, practical and focused on building a firm foundation of mutual trust and support.

Your career may involve beauty, balance, harmony, grace or people. Your work could promote justice, fair play and equality. You might work with a partner as well as having a romantic association, or meet someone through your work. Or, interpersonal interactions could be a significant focus in your vocation. Appropriate choices include work as a counselor, consultant, lawyer, politician, in personnel management, etc. Your duties might be pleasant, aesthetic, sociable or highly competitive in fields such as litigation.

SATURN IN 8TH HOUSE

You may structure your intimate exchanges (including sexuality) with others and might over (or under-) control in personal or business associations. You may work hard at building an intimate bond, but can also take on too much and may worry excessively about shortcomings or flaws. You might feel limited by mates, shared resources, or intimacy demands and need to learn to give, receive and share easily with another. Slow and steady husbanding of shared possessions works the best. Close connections could arouse karmic anxiety and they offer you a chance to probe the depths of your psyche and your partner's. Performance anxiety and your own inner critic (judgmental side) could affect your passion, sexuality, intensity and capacity for transformation and transcendence. Safety might be sought in withdrawal or in overdoing self-control ("stiff upper lip"). Be willing to relax, accept, and find constructive outlets for your passion on all levels.

Your father (figure) was a role model (positive or negative) for the handling of power, emotional intensity and the dark side of life. You may perceive authorities (including father) as powerful, manipulative, controlling, intimidating, withdrawing or self-controlling. Issues of addiction or self-mastery could have been involved in your relationship with Dad—or simply strong emotional reactions. You are susceptible to guilt regarding the use and abuse of power and could attract mates who elicit feelings related to your experience of your father. You probably feel responsible for facing Shadow issues, and may unconsciously arrange confrontational relationships. Your drive is to eliminate what is no longer needed or healthy in interpersonal exchanges.

Your career could involve intensity, confrontation, shared resources, hidden issues or drives, death, the occult or strong emotions. Your duties may be demanding or emphasize penetration, elimination or control. You need to be fascinated, enthralled, and seduced by your vocation. You want to be totally absorbed in what you do.

SATURN IN 9TH HOUSE

You may structure your values, beliefs and world view and may overcontrol your faith. You may value order, predictability and thoroughness. Your belief system might be based on material reality (the scientist, the agnostic) or you could go through a "crisis of faith"—wondering if there is any meaning or higher purpose to life. If anxiety seems overwhelming, you may seek security through a firm, conservative religion or philosophical approach. You are likely to have a responsible attitude toward truth, ethics and inspiration. You may be susceptible to guilt regarding religion, spirituality or values. Moral or ethical issues could carry a karmic charge in your life. You could feel limited by your education, or by your belief system, and need to learn to trust what you gain through experience.

Your father (figure) is an important influence (pro or con) on your beliefs and values. He could be idolized and idealized (this is sometimes easier when he not present). He might have been religious, idealistic or perfectionistic. He could have been ethical, philosophical and broad-minded. You might perceive authorities (including Dad) as adventurous, optimistic, humorous, distant, overconfident, extravagant or grandiose.

Your career could involve travel, the dissemination of knowledge, education, philosophy, good times, sales, sports, nature or ethics. Your duties may include learning, fun, travel or expanded horizons in some form. You may believe in the work ethic, search for the perfect job, make your career your ultimate value (source of meaning and trust in life), labor for a better world or seek idealistic, motivational and inspirational work.

SATURN IN 10TH HOUSE

A desire for control, stability and predictability is highlighted. It is possible to feel responsible for the whole world, or at least for everything and everyone your life touches. Don't take too much on your own shoulders (lest back problems result). You may handle quite a few duties and feel pressure to do what is necessary in life. But since there are always more obligations which remain undone, you may be susceptible to guilt regarding your career and your responsibilities.

If, on the other hand, you feel that most of the power is outside you—in the world—you may often feel limited by authorities or regulations or your vocational demands. Be careful to separate realistic barriers from self-imposed blocks. You may sometimes give up and not try for fear of failure or not measuring up to your exacting standards or because you should be in control and aren't. You need to make tangible contributions to the world—to see measurable results for your efforts. You need to reach the role of competent expert.

Your father (figure) is a role model for the handling of power, work and responsibility. He could be a workaholic. He could overdo conditional love by being too critical—always focusing on flaws—in himself or in others. He might carry too much of the load in life, or hold himself back for fear of making mistakes. You could perceive authorities (including Dad) as critical, authoritarian, dominating, and controlling, or as guilt-ridden, blocked, and inadequate or as hardworking, achieving, practical and productive. You may feel a sense of karmic obligation to your father, or in your vocation—a sense of mission— a debt to pay to the world. An executive drive is likely; you can be conventionally ambitious and success is most likely to follow steady, patient effort.

Your career needs to involve tangible, measurable results, the ability to work your way to the top, and a sense of structure. Science, business, politics, a profession such as law or anything involving the material world and power could be a focus. You have talent for hard work, thoroughness, pragmatism and endurance. You can be realistic about paying your dues and doing what is necessary in order to achieve in life.

SATURN IN 11TH HOUSE

You may seek structure in your push toward the future and your humanitarian ideals; you might over (or under-) control your progressive instincts. You are learning to blend tolerant acceptance and critical judgment, to know when to follow the rules and when and how to break them if they are unjust and unrealistic. You may be called to distinguish between freedom and license. You probably feel responsible for intellectual exploration, openness to the new, and aiding progress. You could be susceptible to guilt regarding friends, causes or change. You might sometimes feel limited by your friends or groups if you have not learned to be an equal so you attract friends looking for a "father" and you end up being responsible for them. (You might also choose friends to take care of you and end up feeling dominated). You could also work for, or with, friends. Friendships which develop slowly over time and emphasize dependability and responsibility will work the best for you. Trust is vital.

You are learning to blend the power role and equal sharing; the conventional and unconventional; the old and the new. You may have a sense of karmic obligation connected to friendships, groups you associate with, or your humanitarian instincts and society in general. You are developing realism about freedom, the future, equality and tolerance. You want to make sense of (bring order to) multiple options and varied possibilities.

Your father (figure) was a role model (pro or con) for uniqueness, freedom, tolerance, openness and the unpredictable. You may perceive authorities (including father) as original, inventive, rebellious, chaotic, strange, different, detached or progressive. Father could be like a friend or erratic, distant and/or weird. He may be out involved with humanity rather than family.

Your career ought to be unusual or encompass nonstandard hours or duties. It could involve technology (computers, aviation, etc.), humanitarian principles (working for social causes, ecology, etc.), astrology, or other new age interests. Work in politics is possible, especially with elected officials in any level of the government. Freelance, entrepreneurial work is also appropriate. Your duties might be individualistic, idiosyncratic, different, or open-ended and varied. You might clarify your wild flashes or unique ideas and interests, putting them to pragmatic use in the world. You may gain executive power through groups or causes. You need to bring the future into form.

SATURN IN 12TH HOUSE

You may structure your sensitivities and impressions and must learn to positively blend your creative imagination and fantasy with realistic assessments (without retreating to escapism or critiquing your imagery to death). You can be practical about visions and have the capacity to make your dreams manifest. You can, at times, feel responsible for the universe and take the world on as a burden. You may feel a sense of karmic debt or obligation to humanity (especially the downtrodden). You can be susceptible to guilt regarding compassion, empathy and universal caring.

If you lack faith in a Higher Power, you may feel anxious or depressed, limited by fearful fantasies about possible dangers. But fears can also be realistic and valuable when they are based on common sense and when they impel you to take realistic precautions. You may face challenges around the issue of faith, unsure whether you can trust in the goodness of the universe. If you feel anxious or insecure, lacking faith and trust in the Infinite, you might be tempted to place your faith in your job, or in power in the physical world. But these are unable to provide the inner peace which comes with trust in the Absolute. Your challenge is to avoid the extremes of gullibility and cynicism, to find a firm connection to Higher Meaning within a practical context which implies that you are doing your share. Since the twelfth house is more connected to one's unconscious faith while the ninth house symbolizes conscious faith, it tends to be harder to attain faith here if it is weak or missing. Helpful actions can include meditation, reading inspirational literature, associating with people who have strong faith, and studying the evidence of psychic research.

Your father (figure) was a role model (positive or negative) for your handling of the beautiful dream. He may have been ill, missing, alcoholic (a victim). He might have been artistic or concerned with healing and helping people. He might be a saint, a sinner, a martyr. You may expect too much of Dad (or he of you). You may perceive authorities (including father) as weak, gentle, idealistic, escapist, assisting, compassionate, artistic, or sensitive. Father has a profound impact on your spirituality, your faith, your ability to connect to the Oneness of the universe.

Your career needs to involve ideals, artistry, healing, assistance, the infinitely boundless, the tiny or the imagination. It might involve such mundane fields as fluids, chemicals, the ocean, drugs, or the "glamor" industries such as films, advertising, public relations, etc.; fields which persuade people to do or buy something to make their lives more beautiful or ideal. You might put your emotional trust in power, responsibility, security or predictability. (Astrological research found scientists with this placement—who believe in materialism and see matter as the ultimate reality.) The work ethic could be an ultimate value. You might seek the "perfect" career, try to do your work without a mistake, or work for a better (or more beautiful) world. Your duties may involve artistic endeavors or service activities. You may work in an isolated setting, behind the scenes or with mysterious or mystical images and processes. Your primary need is to do your share in the effort to make a better world and then to give the rest of the job to the Infinite and to trust it.

Saturn in Aspect: *Reality and Restriction*

(Please see section on Outer Planet Aspects on page 220.)

The nature of the planets involved in any aspect is the most important factor. For any pair of planets, please read **all three** aspect delineations: conjunction, cooperating (sextile ✶, trine △), and challenging (square □, opposition ☍, quincunx ⚻). The conjunction is the basic, most fundamental aspect and its themes carry through with other aspects. The cooperating and challenging analyses will offer additional choices regarding of constructive and nonconstructive ways of handling the basic issues.

Remember that the life issues represented by cooperating aspects (or conjunctions) may still require some attention. We might overdo certain themes, or succumb to projection, repression or displacement in trying to balance our many, different drives. It is also quite possible that you could have integrated some of the conflicts (shown by challenging aspects) which were present at birth and are now manifesting potentials more reflective of the delineations in the cooperating or conjunction sections.

Other factors will complicate the picture. The potential inherent in any given placement might be overridden by other configurations in the chart. As you read the interpretations for the various pieces of your chart, bear in mind that certain pieces will suppress others. As always, repeated themes, which recur again and again, are the most likely to manifest in your psyche and in your life.

SATURN CONJUNCT URANUS

Within your psyche, several contradictory drives exist. Yet these inner polarities can contribute to a fuller, more effective life if you are able to create syntheses rather than conflicts by making room in your life for each of the different desires.

You are facing the push/pull between the conventional and the unconventional, the old and the new. Rigid adherence to what has been will be no more helpful than intransigent insistence on considering only the new. A blend will usually serve the best. You may also confront tension between restriction versus freedom, safety versus risk, slowness versus speed, and structure versus anarchy.

Your challenge is to create freedom within a structure (or freedom from excessive regulation). You might innovate or make changes in a disciplined manner. You could make order out of chaos (or chaos out of order). You might revise authority, rules or labels (or rebel against them). You may break rules, test rules or tradition (or limit freedom). You can both build up and break down.

Your relationship to dad (or authority figures) was an important influence on your capacity to be independent, original and objective. Perhaps father loved freedom, was inventive, was unconventional or unusual. He might have been erratic, unpredictable, aloof or eccentric. His example gave you a positive or negative role model for detachment, the free-ranging intellect, love of liberty and the ability to conceptualize choices.

You could be an innovative executive, an unusual teacher, a self-employed entrepreneur, or able to persist and endure under difficult, tense or unpredictable circumstances. You may focus on progressing slowly and regularly, or you might deal with sudden breaks and separations. You could be concerned with human laws, practical science, politics, voluntary organizations, or authority. You can be quite rational, logical, fact-oriented, scientifically-minded and interested in techniques. You are likely to take the intellect seriously and could have a dry sense of humor.

(This conjunction occurs about every 43-46 years.)

SATURN COOPERATING URANUS (✶ △)
You may be practical as well as intuitive. You can work hard to make changes, and may be innovative in your approach to creating structures. Logic and rationality are at your fingertips. You might be drawn to science, math, or similar pursuits as you naturally incline toward testing your knowledge against

experience and the real world. You may have technical expertise or technological interests.

You have the capacity to blend several polarizing factions: the old and the new; the traditional and the progressive; freedom and restriction; security and risk-taking. If these opposites battle within, you might rebel against authority, organization or rules (or fear change). But you have the capacity for synthesis, so you are likely to know the value of measured risks and to be able to put together inventiveness with common sense. Since you can handle both the mental and the physical realms, you can put ideas to work in the world.

Your individuality, independent spirit and inner perspective may enhance your career and professional success. Authorities or older people might contribute to you finding a unique niche. You could have the potential for politics, the law, science, or business. Detachment might be one of your strengths, with a capacity for objective observation and fact-finding.

You could have a dry wit, with a gift for perceiving the ironic or ridiculous. By innovating in a disciplined way, you can make steady, regular progress toward your ambitions.

SATURN CHALLENGING URANUS (□ ⚹ ⚻)

You are working on the balance between young and old, with challenges probably beginning with your relationship to your father (or father figure). In some way, your relationship to an early authority figure conflicted with your inner sense of uniqueness and individuality. Perhaps you felt that your father did not understand or accept who you really are. Perhaps he was erratic, unpredictable, undependable or cool, detached, aloof, or gone a lot. Perhaps he limited your freedom unreasonably. In some way, his standards may have made it difficult for you to be true to yourself.

If you internalize this conflict, you might continue to feel torn between following the rules and breaking them, between the old and the new, between control and openness, between the freedom to act on impulse and the discipline to finish things and do them well, or between change and the status quo. The resulting tension could lead to sudden breaks or separations in your life. You might find yourself simultaneously building up and breaking down. Contradictory impulses could lead to a sense of stress, defiance or intimidation. If you are able to reconcile these polarities, you can tear down what is no longer useful, and create new forms and structures. Your changes will be sensible, practical and well-planned. Traditions which foster creativity and new ideas will be supported.

You are likely to have talent for science, math, business, politics or anything involving logic, rationality and the testing of ideas against experience in the real world.

Your sense of humor could be subtle, with a nose for the ridiculous and ironic. You could be a disciplined revolutionary, a progressive executive, or a proponent of measured innovations.

SATURN CONJUNCT NEPTUNE

You can work with dreams, visions and fantasies to bring them into form in the physical world. Blessed with both practicality and imagination, you might choose a career connected to beauty, whether producing or promoting it in such fields as cosmetics, antiques, advertising, films, etc. You could also work with fluids such as oil, chemicals, drugs, the ocean. Other alternatives include any healing or helping job, any compassionate labor which makes the world a better place. You can channel inspiration into accomplishment.

Your relationship to your father (or father figure) had a strong impact on your unconscious sense of faith (trust or mistrust in the universe). He might have been idealistic, religious, philanthropic, artistic, or had high standards. He could have been absent, confused, a victim (alcoholic, ill, etc.), or evasive. His example gave you either a positive or a negative role model for blending realism and idealism; practicality and spirituality; what is and what ought to be.

If you find it hard to trust a benign Higher Power and you allow your doubting side to overwhelm your whimsical, inspired side, you might be rigidly literal, afraid to dream, expecting disappointment, reserved, shy, lonely, depressed, restrained, and vulnerable to self-doubts and illness. You might undermine yourself through guilt or irrational fears. You could be a party-pooper (especially prone to downgrading yourself), blocking your idealism or emotions, trying to deal concretely or rationally with feelings.

If you allow your fantasizing, potentially gullible side to take over, you could be uncertain about what is real, deny the physical, use imagined situations to preclude dealing with real ones, or succumb to escapism (alcoholism, drugs, fantasy, illness, etc.) rather than savoring and enjoying the facts. You might "see" (and hear and feel) only what you want to see rather than what is true, setting yourself up for more serious consequences when reality finally comes crashing in. Life requires the inspired view that there is more than the physical world along with the practicality to take sensible steps toward your dreams.

Your career ambitions are flavored with a quest for infinite love, beauty and perfection. This might manifest as an unclear view of your work or your responsibilities (where they are under- or overvalued. We can't do it all, but we should do our share). You also might idealize the work ethic and strive to do your work perfectly. A more reasonable goal involves choosing work that will make a better (or more beautiful) world. If you demand perfection from your performance on the job, you will be disappointed or frustrated. Yet you can work to ground your dreams, to inspire and uplift people through your personal efforts.

(This conjunction occurs about every 35-36 years.)

SATURN COOPERATING NEPTUNE (✶ △)

You can bring beauty, inspiration or compassion into form. This could manifest as talent in the arts, philanthropic work, medicine, psychology, film-making, advertising, architecture or other aesthetic or idealistic professions. You can help make dreams into reality. You could also work in a very practical business involving fluids (oil, chemicals, the ocean etc.).

Since you are willing to support imagination with common sense and hard work, you can accomplish a great deal. Able to visualize something better, more beautiful, or more perfect, you can also plan the essential, necessary steps to work toward the rendering of your visualization.

Your father or father figure could have nourished your gentle, intuitive, imaginative side. Perhaps he encouraged your feeling for beauty, psychic insights, compassionate impulses or urges to rescue, heal and assist. Perhaps he lived the role of artist, savior, victim, martyr, dreamer, helper or philanthropist. His example affected your faith and sense of trust (or mistrust) in the universe.

If you put your sensible and sensitive sides at odds with one another, you might give up on certain projects because they fall short of your fantasies ("If I cannot do this wonderful, ecstatic thing, I won't do anything"). Or, you might always want more than is possible—pitting your idealized images and expectations against the limits of the real world ("It should have been better, prettier, higher, more perfect, etc."). Generally, however, you have an excellent capacity to bring together the spiritual and material, sublime and practical, beauty and common sense, yearning and striving, inspiration and perspiration.

SATURN CHALLENGING NEPTUNE (□ ☍ ⊼)

You can dream the most wonderful of dreams and envision the most fantastic of vistas, but your talents can become liabilities if not handled with care and caution. You may feel torn between your practical, grounded, hardworking, sensible side and your imaginative, inspired, visionary, and compassionate side. Bringing your dreams to earth will require extra attention and effort.

Your father (or father figure) is apt to have influenced your imagination, sense of faith (or mistrust) in the universe, ideals, fantasies, compassion, and aesthetic capacities. Clashes with father are possible, especially over issues of beauty, grace, spirituality, religion or imagination. You might have felt him to be a dreamer of impossible dreams or an authoritarian figure not open to dreams. You and he might have had a savior/victim or rescuer/enabler relationship. Your interactions with authorities offer an opportunity to learn how to realistically channel your ideals and inspiration.

If you fly too high with imagination, you may want more than is possible, yearn for the unattainable, demand impossible perfection and live chronically dissatisfied because life (especially your work and physical reality) falls short of your idealized imagery. You might feel unwilling to do anything short of an incredible spiritual mission, or demand inhuman functioning (never making a mistake) from yourself.

If you overdo your focus on flaws and boundaries, you might give up and sacrifice attainable dreams. You could succumb to depression, anxiety, illness, guilt, or pessimism. You might chronically underachieve ("If I cannot find the perfect, ideal job, I won't even try.") or give up before starting, convinced failure is inevitable.

Your challenge is to balance faith and fear. You need enough faith in yourself to risk, to try, to work toward your hopes. You need enough faith in a Higher Power to not take everyone's burdens on your shoulders, to not try to play savior/rescuer/ enabler to the world. You need enough fear (or caution) to plan sensible steps toward realizing your visions, enough practicality to break large projects into incremental steps. By combining the best of both, you can become a realistic dreamer, a practical mystic and an inspired achiever.

SATURN CONJUNCT PLUTO

Control is a central issue in your life. You are apt to continually strive for a sense of mastery over yourself, your work, and the world in which you live. Endurance, tenacity, and stamina are highlighted. You may be amazingly calm and a master of the "stiff upper lip." You can survive almost anything and are willing to persevere (regardless of the cost). Once you commit to someone or something, you are intensely loyal and determined to build something and see it through.

Your relationship with your father strongly affected your balance between internal (personal) power and external power (of the world). He probably stirred intense emotional reactions on your part. His example (positive or negative) affected your handling of power issues. He might have been strong, purposeful, organized and authoritative. He could have been abusive, demanding, intimidating, dominating and authoritarian. He could have been withdrawn and denying. Your experience of authority figures molded your ambitions and your drive for power.

Your desire for self-mastery (or to avoid dominance by others) might be carried to the extreme of self-denial and asceticism. You may inhibit and hold back sensually (carrying renunciation or willpower to an extreme). You might fear poverty, rejection or deprivation (materially, sexually). Letting go of the need to control could be a challenge (emotionally and sexually). Power can be expressed through using sex or through withholding it, as well as through money, using it as a threat, bribe, or intimidation.

It is also possible to project one's own potential strength, and that can lead to others using our power against us. This can happen if we doubt our own strength and feel that the world and other people have all the power. In such cases, we are challenged to develop our own strength. The basic goal of Pluto is always to move toward shared rather than unilateral power and pleasures.

If your drive for power is channeled toward the outside world, you could be extremely effective in politics, business, the military or law enforcement. Competitive sports and games can also be good outlets. You are not likely to enjoy being "under" anyone else and are best off running your own show, or seeking an executive or leadership role in the world. Without a constructive outlet for your ambition, dominance games (Machiavellian tendencies) or power struggles are possible. Force, violence, punishment, blame or shame are less constructive alternatives. Your drive to win, to be on top, to be a force in the world can go into fighting for causes or competitive activities.

You are apt to have considerable skills in organization, handling details, precision, thoroughness and self-discipline. You may have talent for research or anything involving the systematic application of energy and focus. You have the potential of great powers of concentration. You can be strong, determined, resourceful, thrifty, excellent in crises, disciplined, and able to overcome incredible odds.

(This conjunction occurs about every 30-35 years.)

SATURN COOPERATING PLUTO (✳ △)

Organizational skills, endurance, patience and discipline are among your likely talents. You may have real business abilities, especially for working with money, resources or shared possessions. Your level of commitment is high and you naturally persevere. You may be skilled at politics, negotiation, law enforcement, military endeavors, strategy, tactics and deal-making. You can be courageous in the face of death.

You are likely to seek material security, a position in the power establishment, and are willing to work hard for monetary rewards. You are probably thrifty and strive to reduce waste. You plan for deep roots in your life, building lasting foundations (in your career, relationships, etc.). Because you tend to hang in and hang on, you may have to learn to forgive, forget, let go and release (yourself as well as others) when that is appropriate.

You may intuitively understand authority figures, and could understand how to manipulate them successfully. You are quite sensitive to the nuances revolving around the handling of power, mastery, control and dominance, and could work successfully from behind the scenes. You first developed these skills in relating to your father or father figure. His actions (positively or negatively) fed your desire to "make it," to achieve security and to be successful in conventional, material terms.

Although love and work may occasionally conflict, you are generally able to blend emotional and practical needs. You can commit to an intimate relationship and still put energy into worldly attainments. Your partner may assist your career (or support your efforts) and you are willing to work partly for the sake of a mate. You can comfortably combine feelings and pragmatism.

SATURN CHALLENGING PLUTO (□ ☍ ⚼)

Power issues are apt to surface regularly in your life. How you handle power (using, abusing or denying it) is a central learning experience for you.

Your relationship with your father was the first challenge to your mastery of power issues. (Sometimes children have to fight to defend themselves and to learn to own their power the hard way in families.) Your father may have been dominating, intimidating, manipulative, punitive, abusive, blaming or authoritarian. He could have been repressed, addicted, withholding, fearful, avoiding or rigid. Less often (with a conflict aspect), he might have used power wisely. His example, whether positive or negative, gave you an opportunity to recognize your own ambitions and need for mastery, and a chance to seek constructive outlets for it through sports, games, business, politics, the military, or other competitive activities.

If you see power as "bad" (usually because it was abused when you were young—often directed against you), you may end up inhibited, frustrated, surrounded by people who try to control, dominate, intimidate and overwhelm you. You could be repressed, self-denying and fearful, giving in or running away. If so, you need to find something you are willing to fight for, to take back some control into your own hands.

If you continually anticipate the threat of power plays from other people, you may conclude that "the best defense is a good offense" and attack first or respond to the fear of being controlled by being controlling. If you are carrying blind ambition too far you might be relentless, blaming, ruthless, insistent on your way, manipulative or power-hungry. Yet you do need a constructive and respected channel where you can be forceful, confrontive, and compelling. You can be an irresistible force. You need an arena where you have dominion, where you govern, rule or have the authority position and use your strength for results which are affirming for others as well as for yourself.

CHAPTER TEN

URANUS
INDEPENDENCE AND INNOVATION
IN YOUR HOROSCOPE

Uranus in Signs:
Revolution and Rule-Breaking

Because Uranus spends about seven years in each sign, it symbolizes issues for a rather large group of people. The house position of Uranus will help to reveal how and where each individual might deal with the issues represented by Uranus' sign. The house position of Uranus may also represent traits which are more personal, less tied to one's age peers.

URANUS IN ARIES (1928-1934)

You may be unique in self-expression and personal actions. You could challenge life directly, forcefully, courageously. You may make impulsive changes. You have a strong need for freedom and openness. When you break loose, you do so energetically, quickly, assertively.

URANUS IN TAURUS (1935-1942)

You may be unique in your approach to pleasures and possessions. You could challenge life steadily, patiently, and thoroughly. You may make deliberate changes. You seek freedom and openness within a stable context. When you break loose, you do so carefully, steadfastly and practically.

URANUS IN GEMINI (1942-1949)

You may be unique in your thinking and/or communicating. You could challenge life intermittently, logically, verbally. You may make intellectual shifts and changes. You seek freedom of thought. When you break loose, you do so in a variety of ways, mentally, cleverly, in spurts, flexibly, or adroitly.

URANUS IN CANCER (1949-1956)

You may be unique in your approach to home, family, nurturing. You could challenge life emotionally, compassionately, caringly. You may change your feelings. You seek freedom without losing emotional security and need to stay conscious of your ambivalence. When you break loose, you try to do so protectively, privately, sensitively or sympathetically.

URANUS IN LEO (1956-1962)

You may be unique in your thrill-seeking, creative acts, or love relationships. You could challenge life dramatically, enthusiastically, with showmanship and a sense of fun. You may make impressive shifts and changes. You seek freedom of expression. When you break loose, you do so with flair, with excitement, or for approval, admiration or love.

URANUS IN VIRGO (1962-1968)

You may be unique in your approach to work and/or health. You could challenge life methodically, precisely, intelligently. You may change your work routines or health regimes. You seek freedom through competence. When you break loose, you do so discreetly, efficiently, carefully and matter-of-factly.

URANUS IN LIBRA (1968-1975)

You may be unique in your relationships to others or your approach to beauty. You could challenge life gracefully, diplomatically or legally. You may change how you look for balance, how you handle partnerships. You seek freedom as well as cooperation or competition, and will have to compromise to maintain a committed partnership. When you break loose, you may do so with rituals, beauty, tact or moderation.

URANUS IN SCORPIO (1975-1981)

You may be unique in your approach to sharing the sensual/sexual world. You could challenge life intensely, compulsively, powerfully. You may change how you deal with issues of giving to and receiving from others. You seek freedom through understanding basic motives, your own and those of people who are close to you. When you break loose, you do so with resourcefulness, strength, endurance.

URANUS IN SAGITTARIUS (1981-1988)
You may be unique in your philosophy of life, beliefs or values. You could challenge life confidently, extravagantly, adventurously. You may change your faith or sense of direction in life and long-range goals. You may seek freedom through exploration, openness and high ideals. When you break loose, you do so flamboyantly, ethically, humorously, with high hopes.

URANUS IN CAPRICORN (1988-1995)
You may be unique in your approach to responsibility, power or authority. You could challenge life cautiously, purposefully, or solemnly. You might change your career or role in society. You could seek freedom through structure, stability, and a solid foundation or in defiance of traditions. When you break loose, you do so carefully, consistently, precisely.

URANUS IN AQUARIUS (1912-1919 and 1995-2003)
You may be unique in your approach to freedom, friendship, the intellect, or social causes. You could challenge life suddenly, progressively, individually. You might change your future hopes, organizational ties, or view of humanity. You need to be free, unique, different and unusual. When you break loose, you do so abruptly, defiantly or with detachment and objectivity.

URANUS IN PISCES (1919-1927 and 2003-2011)
You may be unique in your use of imagination, imagery and fantasies. You could challenge life artistically, spiritually, sensitively, sacrificially. You might change how you seek inspiration and the beautiful dream. You could seek freedom through meditation, visualization or escapism. When you break loose, you may do so serenely, romantically, compassionately.

Uranus in Houses:
Individuality and Invention

URANUS IN 1ST HOUSE

You are likely to be naturally inventive and original. You may challenge yourself constantly to go beyond the boundaries, further than you have gone before. You could be a spontaneous, instinctive rebel (and could go to the extreme of real eccentricity or flakiness). You tend to break the rules about personal expression and who you are; you refuse to be pigeonholed or stereotyped. You may occasionally do things for their shock value—to upset people's preconceptions. You want to be seen as a unique individual and detest being lumped in with others. You may periodically revolutionize your actions, appearance or personality. You change and reform yourself and your desires.

Freedom, to you, is direct, open and immediately expressed. You can be quite tolerant of honesty, enthusiasm, willfulness and impulsiveness. You are likely to energetically resist any constraints. Your friends may be active, assertive, independent, pioneering or self-centered. The collective of humanity matters to you and you may personally encourage social causes, expression of the will of the group, or tolerance and equality for all. You may be willing to fight for equal opportunity or social justice.

URANUS IN 2ND HOUSE

You are likely to challenge assumptions about finances, ownership or aesthetics. You may originate or invent sources of income, sensual gratifications or beautiful forms. You can break the rules about money matters, pleasure and sensuality. You may earn your money through an unusual route, with non-standard hours or duties, or with an individualistic flair. You could rebel in your handling of money, gratification or comfort. Your income (and outgo) could be erratic and quite varied. You may experiment with different forms of pleasures, and be open to and tolerant of many kinds of sensual gratification or tangible beauty. You can revolutionize what (and how) you earn, own and enjoy.

Freedom, for you, is tied to comfort, material security and beauty. You want financial independence. You may be willing to risk monetary safety (or break the cultural rules) in order to satisfy your desire for individuality, freedom or variety. You are attracted to possessions that are unusual or original. How you make or spend money could be tied to the greater collective (humanitarian or social causes, groups, friends, etc.).

URANUS IN 3RD HOUSE

You may rebel in your thoughts and language. You are likely to be an original thinker, with talent for inventing concepts and phrases. You change or reform ideas, information and knowledge. You probably challenge teachers, ideas, forms and styles of communication, and methods of learning. You may break the rules about knowledge, information and objectivity. You can be willfully contrary, yet have moments of genius. You may have sudden flashes of insight or understanding. Because your mind sometimes "leapfrogs" from one concept to another, other people may find your thinking erratic or hard to follow at times. You have talent for brainstorming—for seeing multiple possibilities and options. Your thinking will be unconventional; you can turn problems upside down and see solutions missed by standard approaches.

Mental freedom is imperative for you. Whether or not your behavior reflects it, you are a rebel in your head! You deal with issues of independence through relatives, people near at hand, or early schooling. You are learning to develop self-reliance without the extreme of feeling a misfit, ostracized by peers. If you deny your own uniqueness and individuality, siblings or other relatives could overdo eccentricity. They might be brilliant, strange, erratic, cool, detached or unpredictable. If these motifs are shared, you encourage each other's curiosity, desire to go beyond traditional boundaries and interest in the new, the different and the cutting edge in life.

URANUS IN 4TH HOUSE

You may challenge domestic routines and established habit patterns. You could rebel within your family system—be the maverick. You may change or reform emotional ties, avoiding standard commitments. You are likely to be inventive and original in your handling of caring, compassion and empathy. You can be detached and objective about emotional needs. You may break the rules around mothering and nurturing. You may nurture by giving people space to do their own thing. You could revolutionize your home environment and family ties.

Freedom, for you, is tied to unconditional love, and could be in conflict with conventional needs for support and nurturance. Your early family experience strongly affected your capacity to be independent and original. A parent may have been open, tolerant, like a friend and intellectually stimulating. Or, a parent may have been erratic, here and gone, cool, detached and not very supportive. Perhaps your family moved a lot, or there was a sense of unpredictability within the home. This placement suggests a parent who did not want to be tied down to the home. When you were young, that might have seemed uncaring, and thrown you more on your own inner resources. Alternately, you might have felt stifled in your early home situation and might even have run away before adulthood. As you grow older, you are apt to also manifest your own restlessness within the home. You are likely to move often, leave your home a lot, or have an unusual home, with lots of activity and changes, perhaps with other people coming and going. A few people are attracted to life in a commune. You can be more objective than most people about family issues, roots, memories and dependency/nurturance needs.

URANUS IN 5TH HOUSE

You are just naturally inventive and original; it is a form of self-expression for you. You may challenge established ideas about self-esteem, pride, shame and risk-taking. You can revolutionize life through excitement, thrills, speculation and risks. You could break the rules about love, pride and power. You may constantly change and reform your relationships to lovers and children. You need a sense of independence in your love relationships and might seek variety or play the rebel role in your expression of love, admiration, and approval. You may sometimes enjoy shocking people when you take center stage. Your charisma is connected to nonconformity. Taking chances helps you to grow.

Freedom, for you, supports self-esteem and a healthy pride in the self. If your own need for individuality is denied, your lovers or children might express it in excess. They could be strange, irresponsible, erratic, rebellious or unwilling to make commitments. If you share the tendency to resist unnecessary limits, you can encourage one another's openness, tolerance, independence, and love of variety. You may be willing to be somewhat experimental sexually as you are open to alternatives. Because you can be quite detached and objective as well as passionate, you may swing between extremes of a "heart" versus a "head" focus. The more you balance these polarities, making room for both, the more balance will exist within your love relationships.

URANUS IN 6TH HOUSE

You may change or reform work routines. You could rebel against details, analysis and focused attention—seeking variety, independence and intellectual stimulation in your job. You easily get bored vocationally, so need constant challenges lest your work be erratic or you become a job-hopper. You can satisfy your need for newness by choosing a job which is not repetitive or routine. And, your inventiveness and originality could be used to enhance efficiency and productivity. You could revolutionize your working conditions and/or health habits. You are likely to break the rules about work and health, using nonstandard approaches and avenues, or choosing unusual fields. Your work duties might be humanitarian, intellectual, free, open, unique, and allow you to be friends with your colleagues. You tend to treat everyone as equals and may hate to take orders and be willing to topple any hierarchies or upset dominance games.

Freedom, for you, rests on competence and capability. If you are able to get the job done in your own, unique fashion, you will feel best. If your freedom side is stifled, you may feel frustrated and quit or get fired. If you stay too long with a job you detest, health problems are possible. (Confinement could make you sick.) A sudden accident might also get you out of a situation in which you feel trapped. Making sure your liberty-loving side has plenty of scope when working is most advisable. You can be quite creative in what you do, and find new avenues to solve, repair, fix and improve what you do or how you do it.

URANUS IN 7TH HOUSE

You are drawn to the new, the unusual or the different in relationships. You may constantly change or reform your associations. You could rebel against joint efforts and accentuate your independence from others, or you might attract potential partners who are cool, aloof, detached and wary of commitment. You are likely to challenge assumptions about cooperation, competition and togetherness. You can break the "rules" about social interactions and may enjoy shocking people out of their little ruts. You can be a revolutionary force in partnerships. You may also invent or originate aesthetically, in a variety of fields of the graphic arts.

Freedom, for you, involves justice, fair play and even exchanges. Your relationships work best when you are friends with your partner: both open, tolerant, humanitarian and intellectually stimulating. "I give you permission to be yourself. I value your uniqueness" (You may turn friends into partners and partners into friends—still easy with one another even after a break-up.) You probably like change and variety. This does not mean you cannot make a permanent commitment, but both you and your partner need a sense of challenge and excitement. Don't let the relationship stagnate or get boring— that's the impulse for one of you to leave! You may have unusual relationships (open, experimental, long-distance, etc.) which are different from the norm. You may be attracted by people who are quite unique (in extremes, they could be strange, weird, overly eccentric or irresponsible and unpredictable) or whose background (race, religion, etc.) is quite different from your own. If you deny your own need for independence within a relationship, you may draw in potential partners who are not available (married, unwilling to attach, of a different sexual persuasion, etc.). If the electric energy of "what's next?" is shared, you and a partner can have constant (pleasant) surprises, and encourage one another's greater individuality.

URANUS IN 8TH HOUSE

You may challenge the status quo in regard to sexuality and shared resources. You could change and reform your intimate associations and the process of emotional bonding. You may invent or originate approaches for facing the Shadow (tough psychological issues), dealing with hidden depths, transforming yourself and others, and confronting issues of elimination and purification. You are likely to break the rules about giving, receiving and sharing with others and could play the rebel role in your handling of sexuality, inheritance, partner's resources and the deeper emotions. You can be driven emotionally (obsessive, compulsive, addicted), yet are also capable of great detachment and objectivity; extreme swings are possible before you integrate these very different potentials in your nature.

Freedom, for you, must confront intimacy, intensity and deep, inner drives. You are likely to feel pulled between your quest for independence and your desire to merge with another human being. You can be tolerant or even appreciate the uniqueness of others but any form of coercion or manipulation is unacceptable. Ideally, you can turn friends into lovers and lovers into friends. You may revolutionize boundaries between self and other, death and life and satisfy some of your restless curiosity by probing yourself, others, the past, and the future.

URANUS IN 9TH HOUSE

You may challenge the status quo in terms of ideas, concepts, ideals and world views. You could be a rebel in terms of beliefs, goals and values. You are likely to change and reform scientific, religious, spiritual or philosophical perspectives. You can invent and originate new ways of looking for truth and meaning in life. You may break the "rules" about religion, spirituality or faith. You could revolutionize ethics, morality, value systems or life philosophies. You have a strong streak of unconventional wit and innovative thinking. You can be a radical! You deny traditional dogma and seek your own broadly-based, open, tolerant world view.

Freedom is essential for you, and strongly connected to seeking the whatever you have chosen as your ultimate good in life. You may idealize personal liberty, friends, or humanitarian causes. You need to feel unconfined, free to explore, adventure, travel and broaden your horizons on all levels (physically, mentally, emotionally and spiritually). You may reach sudden insights through education, travel, or exposing yourself to different surroundings or theories. Learning can occur in intermittent bursts; you might lack patience for traditional higher education, preferring to find your own truth. Sudden illumination is possible. You probably trust the future and believe that the best is yet to come. You may be basically tolerant, optimistic and confident.

URANUS IN 10TH HOUSE

You are likely to challenge the status quo, the Establishment and the powers that be in life. You could change or reform the structure of society. You may rebel against predictability or rules and regulations. You are learning to blend the old and the new and could invent or originate a unique career for yourself, new power roles or new ways of confronting power people. You could break the rules of ambition, convention, and the structure of society. You are ready to revolutionize your vocation, turn authorities into peers, and generally level or break down the hierarchy. Your parent who had the authority (usually Dad) was a role model (positive or negative) for freedom and individuality. He might have been weird, eccentric, cold and aloof—or, he could have been friendly, equalitarian, tolerant or interested in anything unusual or different. His example taught you what **to** do or what **not** to do in terms of expressing your uniqueness within the context of a society with expectations, limits, rules and roles.

Freedom, for you, is tied to power, status and authority. You need a sense of openness and free flow within your professional life. You may choose a career which is unusual, unique, progressive, new age, or involves nonstandard hours or circumstances. You may be pulled between risk-taking, challenge and change, versus security and stability. You could end up job-hopping, especially if your vocation becomes routine, boring, or lacking in intellectual stimulation. You tend to question authority; their right to give orders and their claim to superior knowledge and status. Wisdom includes the knowledge of when to compromise, but to the extent that you can, you are likely to be happiest in an entrepreneurial, self-directed profession.

URANUS IN 11TH HOUSE

You may challenge assumptions about humanity, community and the future. You can invent and originate unpredictably and often. You may break the rules around associations, perspectives and exploration. You could revolutionize groups, friendships and new-age knowledge. You are likely to rebel against the old and promote the new. You may change and reform anything and everything, eager for progress. You can be tolerant of chaos, anarchy and change-in-the-making. Your friends may be individualistic, rebellious, detached, intellectual, unusual or scientifically-minded. You can relate to anyone and everyone and may have very different friends. You could get involved suddenly in groups or friendships and leave just as abruptly if you feel stifled or that your individuality is not being acknowledged.

Freedom, for you, is paramount; you fight against any strings. You seek openness and free flow of information. You are likely to resist being tied down, pinned down, hemmed in or limited in any fashion. You pursue more options, more choices and more alternatives in life. Humanitarian principles may be very important to you. Equality of opportunity appeals. You may have unusual interests and ideas. You probably have a strong streak of unconventionality and can stimulate and heighten creativity, innovation and new perspectives in others.

URANUS IN 12TH HOUSE

You may challenge the status quo in regard to ideals, hopes, and dreams. You may tune into visions which are quite strange, erratic, unusual, or miraculous. You can change and reform your faith in life and capacity for empathy. You may be a rebel in your quest for infinite love and beauty, in how you pursue Oneness with the Whole. You can invent and originate easily with intuition and creative imagination. You may break the rules around selflessness, sacrifice and martyrdom. You can revolutionize perspectives on unity and life's interconnections. You could idealize humanitarian principles, individualism, uniqueness or revolution. Astrology (or anything new-age) could be turned into a religion. Humanity (the "common man/woman") might be put on a pedestal. Groups, friends or causes could be worshipped (given too much importance) or avoided completely.

Freedom, for you, is tied to the quest for an ideal, perfect world; don't let frustrations build up because your utopian vision is unreachable. Constant change and flux might be seen as ideal—or your desire for oneness with the infinite could submerge and drown your freedom needs. Your challenge is to feed your separate, individualistic, rebellious side while still maintaining a sense of oneness with others and being able to connect emotionally. You might attract friends who are victims or saviors, idealists or doubters, romantics or skeptics, artists or con artists. You could get lost in philanthropic dreams or seduced by passive, escapist fantasies. You need to go within to find your true self—but don't shut the world out. Intuitive flashes are likely and you can increase your psychic potential by paying attention. You may be skilled at brainstorming or unusual artistic pursuits. You can be a catalyst for sudden enlightenment—in others as well as in yourself.

Uranus in Aspect: *Catalyst for Change*
(Please see section on Outer Planet Aspects on page 220.)

The nature of the planets involved in any aspect is the most important factor. For any pair of planets, please read **all three** aspect delineations: conjunction, cooperating (sextile ✶, trine △), and challenging (square □, opposition ☍, quincunx ⚻). The conjunction is the basic, most fundamental aspect and its themes carry through with other aspects. The cooperating and challenging analyses will offer additional choices regarding of constructive and nonconstructive ways of handling the basic issues.

Remember that the life issues represented by cooperating aspects (or conjunctions) may still require some attention. We might overdo certain themes, or succumb to projection, repression or displacement in trying to balance our many, different drives. It is also quite possible that you could have integrated some of the conflicts (shown by challenging aspects) which were present at birth and are now manifesting potentials more reflective of the delineations in the cooperating or conjunction sections.

Other factors will complicate the picture. The potential inherent in any given placement might be overridden by other configurations in the chart. As you read the interpretations for the various pieces of your chart, bear in mind that certain pieces will suppress others. As always, repeated themes, which recur again and again, are the most likely to manifest in your psyche and in your life.

URANUS CONJUNCT NEPTUNE
You are a potential visionary and humanitarian. Idealistic individualism is part of your core. You might idealize humanity, friends, causes, change or freedom. You may have unusual (even revolutionary) beliefs, and could be quite psychic (possibly prophetic). You might slip easily into altered states and should be cautious with drugs.

You are naturally aware of the collective, of communal efforts, teamwork and networking. You can think in systems, overviews, contexts, spirals, circles and wholistic patterns. You are likely to be concerned with equal opportunity, mass suffering, the greater good, social consciousness or ethical politics. You are driven to extend your ideals into the wider world.

If your universalist perspective is carried too far, you could lack clarity about boundaries and have trouble with close, personal relationships. Too much emphasis on the transpersonal at the expense of the face-to-face interpersonal can lead to the attitude of "I love humanity but I hate people." The saviors of spotted owls and dolphins are often ignored or attacked by the loggers whose jobs depend on cutting trees and the fishermen whose livelihood depends on catching fish. You might sacrifice to maintain your vision of equality for all life. Or if too frustrated by the greedy world, you might "tune it out" through a variety of escapisms. You can be very rational, but also need to stay grounded to address, handle and transcend earthly challenges.

You may have unique artistic talents. You could be drawn to the theatre, video, movies and media. You can be original, creative, inspired, enlightened, quixotic and imaginative.

You are learning to blend the rational and the irrational, logic and intuition, the separate intellect and the collective unconscious. Naturally attuned to the psychic side of life, it can even be a challenge to know where you end and another person begins. But with integration, you can appreciate each person's unique and irreplaceable gifts, while still understanding the underlying connections of life. You can appreciate separateness while in tune with the basic Oneness of the universe.

(This conjunction occurs about every 170 years.)

URANUS COOPERATING NEPTUNE (✶ △)

Intuitive capacities are quite possible. You may have both sudden "flashes" of insight or psychic understanding as well as simply absorbing impressions in a more receptive form. Since your rational and intuitive sides are supporting each other, you can create a valuable blend of intelligent hunches or psychically-guided reasoning. You are drawn to and can handle higher levels of consciousness.

You may be sensitive to issues of spirituality, illusions, deception, dreams, idols (including false ones) and aspirations affecting large groups of people or the world in general. (A harmony aspect existed between Uranus and Neptune during World War II when the mesmerizing powers of Hitler, Mussolini, etc. swayed the masses.) On the low side, you could misuse (abuse) your talent for emotional persuasion. On the high side, you could believe in the best in humanity, work for causes to elevate people everywhere, and extrapolate logically and wholistically from current trends into future possibilities and prophecies.

You may have a special, unique artistic or creative gift. Your originality feeds your imagination. You may be able to affect the mass mind through politics, videos, group action, media work or any form of persuasion which blends fantasies and emotions with logic and rationality. You are likely to experiment with dreams and aspirations (your own and other people's), and probably aim to extend your inspiration into the world.

You are apt to cherish individuality, while still remaining in touch with a mystical sense of life's Oneness. You can bring a unique perspective out of muddled patterns (or "cosmic mush" with everything thrown in together), and also break down separations and barriers with a compassionate, encompassing empathy.

URANUS CHALLENGING NEPTUNE (□ ♂ ⊼)

You are likely to be sensitive to issues involving humanitarian principles, spiritual ideals, justice and the greatest good for the masses. You could get constructively involved in trying to improve political or social organizations for the common good. You might sometimes succumb to the lure of a seductive group which promises attractive, easy, no-pain answers. If you get too sucked in, you might be deceived and disillusioned by social or religious movements. Or you may find yourself fighting against institutions which you feel twist the truth or take advantage of the less fortunate.

You may vacillate between a rebellious approach to life, and an ostrich-like escapism and avoidance. You might feel frustration at the world's unwillingness to work toward a higher good. You are learning to blend excitement and contemplation, rampant individualism and a mystical, merging Union. You may feel torn at times, between an intense emotional absorption in certain issues versus a detached, aloof air. Your head may vie with your heart. By combining the best from rationality and intuition, you can make them complementary rather than at odds with one another.

If you lack a viable outlet for your idealism, you might be tempted by drugs or other escapist lures. (Unwise rebellion or an ill-considered seeking of freedom from any problems could also lead to running away from reality.) An involvement with a healthy form of meditation, mysticism, political action, or fighting for causes is advisable. You may also have unique, creative, imaginative faculties which could contribute to the world through artistic, scientific, technological, or healing paths.

URANUS CONJUNCT PLUTO

You can be intensely emotionally committed to freedom yet also hungry for an emotional union. You might also want freedom for others, and pour your efforts into social causes, humanitarian principles, justice, equal opportunity, or environmental protection. (This aspect last occurred from 1963 to 1968, when people were confronting issues of inequality, abuse and pollution.) You might be involved in far-ranging collaborations or networking. You probably see strength in numbers.

If you succumb to emotional extremes, you could be attracted to rebellious (even criminal) individuals. You might be an instigator, using surprise as a weapon. You might blame society for all our ills and be deeply defiant. You might manipulate (and use) the media, groups, or friends. You could be extremist, contrary, stubborn, isolated and recalcitrant. You could also be passionately committed to equal rights. You can be an emotional caldron one instant and a detached observer the next. You might be torn between an intense desire for immersion and a total drive for autonomy.

It is important for you to maintain some freedom in your close, emotional relationships. You are likely to break out of any ties that you see as confining. (Or you might attract a potential mate who carries out your unconscious need for freedom and who pulls back from the relationship). You might find it easier to share with a group than with an individual. You could be devoted to a group, and might form passionate friendships. You can turn friends into lovers and lovers into friends. You are learning to balance moving on and hanging on.

You may be quite objective, experimental or detached about sex. Unusual sexual practices are possible, or simply tolerance of differences. You could enact the rebel role in your handling of joint resources and pleasures (money, sex, drugs, addictions, resources). You may feel torn between overt versus covert change, between secrecy versus openness.

You are capable of sudden insights and revelations. You can challenge what is hidden, and bring secrets to light. Issues of power affect you and empowerment (of yourself and others) is a goal. You can invent new ways of relating, cooperating and sharing.

(This conjunction occurs about every 110-114 years, alternating with 140-144 years.)

URANUS COOPERATING PLUTO (✳ △)

You may have an instinctive grasp of power issues. You could be shocked by injustice and sensitive to groups, organizations, governments or agencies which abuse their authority and control. You may work to empower people. You could be a reformer, with good instincts for integrating new concepts and approaches into the establishment, putting your innovative political theories to use.

With inner harmony between your deepest feelings and your rational, objective side, you can put passion into your ideas and intelligence into your emotional moves. You have the capacity to make a deep, intimate connection with a person while still preserving your unique individuality. You may, at times, feel torn between attachment and separation or closeness and independence. Mostly, though, you know how to love with openness, to commit with freedom, to share without possessiveness.

You could have psychic flashes, or sudden insights. You are capable of both a broad overview and a deep penetrating examination of issues. You may understand how to keep others guessing or off guard. You might manipulate or emotionally sway others through media, technology, groups or large, social networks (sometimes behind the scenes).

You can easily tune into psychological complexes. Your grasp of compulsions and obsessions enables you to effectively direct change. You know when to build up and when to break down, transforming negative, blocked conduits into positive free flow and tolerance. You can be a real revolutionary.

You may be deeply devoted to groups, friends or progress. You have a knack for revelations and sudden illumination. You can be a catalyst for change.

URANUS CHALLENGING PLUTO (□ ⚹ ⊼)

With an inner core of iron, you can be quite determined, deeply defiant, loyal, passionate, contrary, and extremist. People may find you hard to predict as you can be intensely emotional one moment and coolly objective the next.

You might seek power (perhaps to promote equal opportunity). You may not trust groups and may want to know the inner workings of things, particularly politics and the origins and lines of power. You could excel at collective bargaining and might want to share any power which exists.

You may focus and concentrate group energy, or consider a group more important than a partner. You might resist commitment (and even power) because you fear being trapped, controlled or hemmed in. You could seek loopholes, expose secrets and break down stereotypes.

You may feel torn between enduring, keeping on and hanging on, versus breaking loose, breaking free and breaking out. Your desire to finish up and complete projects could vie with your urge to change and take up a new challenge. Secrecy and openness may compete within your psyche until you find ways to compromise or take turns between them as appropriate.

Your rebellious, recalcitrant side might challenge or resist effective dealings with sexuality, shared finances, or issues of addiction. Alternately, your open-mindedness could be valuable. Rather than condemning, you can examine and contemplate different ways of dealing with the sensual, sexual, monetary world. You may be quite psychic and could have sudden flashes of revelation and insight, transforming your understanding of the world and perhaps the world itself.

CHAPTER ELEVEN

NEPTUNE
INSPIRATION AND ILLUSION
IN YOUR HOROSCOPE

Neptune in Signs: *Fancies and Fantasies*

Because Neptune spends about 13-14 years in each sign, its position points to issues which are relevant for a whole group of people (over half of a generation). Each person will still have his/her personal reactions to these general issues, but the underlying themes will be shared with many people. (Thanks to Marilyn Waram in *The Book of Neptune* for many historical notes which are used here.)

NEPTUNE IN ARIES

You may idealize/romanticize action, self-expression, spontaneity and courage. You can be quite imaginative and creative. You might incline toward self-sacrifice. (The opposite extreme, also possible, is identifying with the infinite and believing you have a right to anything you want.) You may seek transcendence through personal freedom and could pioneer in the arts.

Historically, Neptune in Aries (1861/62-1874/75) correlated with a tendency to glorify "masculine" pursuits, especially self-reliance, pioneering spirit and personal independence. People had an opportunity to face their illusions and reach more clarity in regard to traits such as rugged individualism. What was initially romanticized often had its glamor stripped away, with consequent disillusionment.

The Civil War highlighted the Aries issue of freedom as did the first Women's Suffrage Law (in Wyoming). The Homestead Act was also passed during this period.

NEPTUNE IN TAURUS

You may idealize/romanticize possessions, sensuality, or comfort. You probably have a strong feeling for tangible beauty. You might overvalue money, or succumb to wishful thinking around finances. Your inspiration comes best in an atmosphere of stability and ease.

Historically, this was a time (1874/75-1887/89) when people dealt with illusions around resources, wealth and acquisitions. Initially, material gratification and nature's creatures tended to be idealized and viewed through rose-colored glasses. As the period progressed, people saw the traps and dangers in a life of rampant materialism.

NEPTUNE IN GEMINI

You may idealize/romanticize communication and learning. You are working on the blend between logic and intuition; the conscious and unconscious minds. You might sacrifice for relatives or be easily influenced by the people around you. You seek inspiration by exploring many by-ways, and being open to information from any source.

Historically, this period (1887/89-1902/03) placed a high value on communication, logic and rationality. Many illusions existed around commerce in the beginning of the period, and people's veils were later stripped away, as deceptive practices were increasingly revealed in the business world.

Esperanto, the first language deliberately designed, was invented as an international tongue during this period, as were Marconi's wireless and radio signals.

NEPTUNE IN CANCER

You may idealize/romanticize home, family, motherhood or your homeland. You could sacrifice too much as a nurturer (or expect ideal support as a dependent). You are likely to be quite sensitive and could be intuitive. You may seek transcendence through gaining or giving emotional security.

Historically, this period (1901/02-1914/16) correlated with idealization of motherhood, the homeland, and family. Women were expected to be saintly and had recourse to drugs such as cocaine and heroin as "medicine" when they could not meet impossibly idealized expectations. Nationalism rose to incredible heights, culminating in World War I.

Mother's Day was established May 10, 1907.

NEPTUNE IN LEO

You may idealize/romanticize taking risks, getting thrills or being creative. You are likely to have charisma, dramatic talent or artistic flair. You may sacrifice (or expect sacrifice) in regard to lovers and children. You may seek transcendence through shining, being noticed and pouring out from your own creative center.

Historically, this was a time (1914/15-1928/29) when the world was facing idealization of extravagance, splendor, and power through success. Many kings had lost their thrones through the first world war but the "nobility," anyone with a title, could be a social lion in supposedly democratic America as wealthy parents sought them as partners for their children. Strong, charismatic personalities had great sway at the beginning of the period, but people were disillusioned with spectacle and power plays by the end of the period.

World War I ended during this period and the first sex education film was produced. The rocket was invented.

NEPTUNE IN VIRGO

You may idealize/romanticize working, being competent or being healthy. You might sacrifice on the job (doing too much) or be perfectionistic at work. You could be a talented craftsperson or a natural healer/helper. You seek to bring your dreams to earth and make them real.

Historically, this time (1928/1929-1942/43) was one when the world dealt with illusions around purity, celibacy, work, duty, service and health. The Stock Market Crash and Great Depression crushed many people's ideals about making one's way through hard work. Racial "purity" was an issue in Hitler's Germany. Many people had to confront their beliefs and dreams around service and decide what they truly owed their country while the New Deal reshaped the ethics of what the country owed its citizens.

Antibiotics and other drugs offered new hope in the health field.

NEPTUNE IN LIBRA

You may idealize/romanticize in relationships. You might sacrifice on behalf of balance and harmony, or look for a perfect partner in a perfect relationship. You are likely to have talent in the visual arts and to value justice and fair play. You want "heaven on earth" in human interactions.

Historically, this was a time (1942/43-1955/57) when psychology became widespread after the government found it useful during the second world war. Psychologists were trying to be accepted by the scientific community and many accepted the materialistic world view of science. Having given up traditional religious values, and tending to look down on the Puritan work ethic, many popular psychologists turned human relationships into their ultimate value, encouraging divorce if a partnership did not provide ultimate satisfaction. Women who had gone to work to replace the men who were drafted into the armed services were first encouraged to develop "male" skills and then encouraged to return to making marriage their ultimate value in life. Women were caught between equality versus marriage since achieving harmony in the latter often required their playing a subordinate role. We are still struggling with the fantasy about "happy ever after." A step toward equality was made by the Supreme Court's decision against segregation in schools, but the Constitutional Amendment supporting equal rights for women (ERA) was defeated. Libra can manifest as partnership or as open conflict. World War II and the Korean War did give us the opportunity to examine the fantasies about war and to strip away its glamor.

Drug use (one form of escapism and not facing reality) in the music and art world was uncovered and people's illusions were stripped away there as well.

NEPTUNE IN SCORPIO

You may idealize/romanticize intimacy, sexuality, massive wealth, or self-knowledge and self-control. You may sacrifice (or expect it of others) in sharing possessions, pleasures and finances. You may be intuitive and can pursue your dreams with incredible intensity. Depth understanding or power may inspire you.

Historically, intense emotions were idolized, with depth therapies coming into their own during this time (1955/57-1970). Illusions and refusing to face reality regarding sex, death and abuse because more and more difficult as people's veils were swept away and avoidance became almost impossible. Union corruption (involving funds and shared resources) was a news item. Anger and resentment which had been prettified and kept under cover came bursting out on campuses and other sites.

The sexual revolution began.

NEPTUNE IN SAGITTARIUS

You may idealize/romanticize philosophy, religion, education, the search for meaning or faraway, mysterious places. You may sacrifice on behalf of (or expect sacrifice for) principles, values, morality and ethics. You can be quite an idealist. You may inspire others through optimism and aiming for/expecting the best.

Historically, people initially idealized the pursuit of the truth, travel, foreign cultures, religions and spiritual quests. Many young people took a year off in Europe to "find themselves" or adopted an Eastern guru and philosophy. As the period progressed (1970-1984), the dangers of idealization were revealed in news stories of destructive cults and of the abuse of power and finances by religious figures.

Drugs in sports were another major news focus.

NEPTUNE IN CAPRICORN

You may idealize/romanticize about responsibility, authority, or conventionality. You may sacrifice (or expect it from others) in terms of your career, power, authority/authorities. You need tangible manifestation of your dreams, measurable results from your visions and aspirations.

This period (1984-1998) began by idealizing puritan virtues, executive power, conservatism and authority. Ronald Reagan was a beloved father figure for many Americans while father-centered situation comedies (such as Bill Cosby) reigned on television. Religious fundamentalism was on the rise. As the period progressed, people became disillusioned with the abuse of power in government (Reagan's scandal-ridden administration and the abuses of televangelists). Communism (Neptune promising to meet the needs of all) collapsed and

Capitalism (Capricorn with its hierarchy of power and control by the strong) ruled supreme in the world.

The drug problem (one facet of the escapism Neptune symbolizes) was seen as a threat to the very fabric of society—in the U.S. as well as Colombia.

NEPTUNE IN AQUARIUS

You may idealize/romanticize being an individual, independence or innovation. You may sacrifice on behalf of the future, the unusual, or friends (or expect them to bring perfection into your life). You seek inspiration through groups, networking, and individuality and may be quite humanitarian.

Historically, the electric telegraph and anesthesia were invented during a Neptune in Aquarius period (1834-1847/48). The next period will be 1998-2011/12. Humanity is apt to face collective idealization regarding technology (and disillusionment when we discover it cannot solve all problems), rationality and logic. Innovation and individual freedom are likely to be highly prized (perhaps to the point of anarchy), but an openness to world government is also possible.

NEPTUNE IN PISCES

You may idealize/romanticize your imagination, fantasies, mystical urges. You are likely to have artistic and/or psychic/intuitive talent. You may sacrifice for love, beauty, spirituality (or expect it of others). You seek transcendence through mysticism and experiences of union.

The last Neptune in Pisces period was 1847-1861. Brigham Young and his Mormon followers settled Utah with one form of idealism, while Marx and Engels wrote *The Communist Manifesto* also seeking utopia. The next Neptune in Pisces period will be 2011/12-2025/26. The world is likely to examine illusions, dreams and visions and seek greater clarity and insight regarding spirituality, God, nature, the arts, dreams, and Universal Oneness. It remains to be seen whether we will succumb to many savior/victim associations, run away into escapism, or reach a new height of empathy and spiritual connections.

Neptune in Houses:
Imagination and Imagery

NEPTUNE IN 1ST HOUSE

Your imagination is strong and easy to tap. You are likely to be open to the collective unconscious without even knowing it so you tune into and merge effortlessly with others, picking up their vibes (good or bad). In addition to psychic openness, you are likely to be physically sensitive and need to be more careful than the average person about drugs, medication, diet, or anything affecting your physical body. You might even unconsciously pick up other people's illnesses or bodily aches when you are feeling down or vulnerable. Some kind of meditation, psychic self-protection, artistic inspiration or a deep, abiding faith will support your physical vitality and promote good health.

You may be physically beautiful and you probably yearn to express infinite love and beauty through your own personal action. You could be graceful, drawn to beauty in motion (dancing, skating, skiing, gymnastics, Tai Chi, etc.). Miracles, magic and mysticism are a natural part of life for you. You may instinctively heal and rescue (people, plants, animals...), but you might have to guard against overdoing the savior role and ending up as a martyr. The opposite extreme is the Guru mentality, to be so identified with the Absolute that you feel you have a right to whatever you want, and that others should sacrifice to meet your needs. A safe motto is "I'll be God tomorrow. Today, it is ok to be human, hoping to be more perfect tomorrow." You may sometimes repress or deny feelings that are unpleasant or don't fit your ideals. You could delude yourself, viewing the world through rose-colored glasses and preferring to focus only on the best. If you overidealize, you'll end up disappointed and let down when life and other people prove to be fallible.

You could idealize or romanticize action, courage, freedom and self-expression and yet you can also avoid and ignore independence, openness and directness when they doesn't fit your dreams. Your challenge is to blend self-assertion and self-sacrifice, to optimally combine personal will with empathy and the urge for union. You can transcend through action, courage, assertion and being true to yourself. You find and define your personal self more clearly by connecting with your Higher Self and inner wisdom.

NEPTUNE IN 2ND HOUSE

You may idealize or romanticize comfort, financial security or pleasure. You could transcend separateness and make connections through sensuality, artistic expression, and enjoying life—or you could struggle against, avoid and ignore gratification and comfort needs which do not fit into your ideal images. You probably yearn (perhaps unconsciously) for infinite love and beauty in tangible form. Developing your artistic skills can help you to express this part of your nature. You tend to merge with others through sensual and artistic experiences. Miracles and mysticism may take physical manifestation in your life. Through the world of sensation, you can connect more fully to your Higher Self.

You have the potential of earning money through artistic or spiritual realms (and you may spend money on similar pursuits). Less ultimately satisfying is the potential of turning money into the an idol—what gives your life meaning. Your desire for the beautiful dream could lead to deluding yourself (or others) about money, possessions or pleasures. You might repress or deny feelings about ownership and finances which are unpleasant or do not fit into your ideals. Wealth may represent glamor to you, or you could become involved in savior/victim entanglements around money. You might try to heal or rescue others financially—or be too passive, trusting God to provide without effort on your part. Your imagination and visualizing capacities can enhance (or confuse) your earnings and pleasure from life. Focusing on your physical senses and material needs, but keeping them in perspective with the rest of your life and sharing what you can with others, will help you to integrate your compassion and connection to all of life.

NEPTUNE IN 3RD HOUSE

You could idealize or romanticize thinking and communication. You probably yearn for infinite love and beauty in language and could be quite poetic. You may sometimes delude yourself (or others) through elusive, confused, or "magic" thinking (such as wish fulfillment). With a wholistic approach to learning, you often "absorb" information but the phenomenon of "no boundaries" can, at times, lead to overload or "cosmic mush." Gullibility or mental laziness (expecting ideas to just flow in as gifts from "God") could displace logic and the conscious intellect. Yet, you can inspire and uplift others with your concepts or the way you convey information. You may heal or rescue through words, ideas and knowledge. You seek transcendence, reaching for higher levels, through thinking, learning and sharing information. Mysticism and miracles are natural in your perception and mental approach. Your imagination is easily accessible. You are learning to blend objectivity and subjectivity, rationality and intuition.

You may sometimes be tempted to avoid or ignore concepts, information or family members who do not fit your idealistic images. You might repress or deny feelings about siblings, relatives or neighbors which are unpleasant or do not match your dreams. Or, your quest for infinite love and beauty may be experienced through a close relative. Perhaps that person is artistic, a victim or a rescuer. Escapism could be an issue with relatives. You could idolize an early relative, or deal with one who has very high standards. You are learning to have faith, dreams and ideals within the framework of real people around you. The challenge is avoid either extreme, a permanent retreat into a dream world or a denial of your human need for visions and aspirations. You are learning to combine logic and compassion, the rational, everyday world and ineffable, otherworldly realms.

NEPTUNE IN 4TH HOUSE

You could idealize or romanticize home, family and/or mother (or mother figure). You may have yearned for infinite love and beauty in your early environment and tried to idealize home or family, repressing memories that don't match your vision. Or you might have been infinitely disappointed by your home situation. You may avoid or ignore feelings or domestic issues which do not fit into your ideal images. You could delude yourself (or others) about your emotional vulnerabilities and nurturing needs. Or you could try to make your home a refuge of love and harmony and peace, a place of emotional security even though it is not perfect. You are likely to be quite sympathetic and may see protection and support as ultimate values.

You instinctively merge and tune into others and might have to work to "shut off" psychically from the world around you.

Your faith in the universe and sense of trust was strongly influenced by your nurturing (or lack of) in your early home. Your nurturing parent may have been idealistic, artistic, escapist, absent, inspiring, religious or a victim (alcoholic, ill, etc.). Your mother (figure) provided either a positive or a negative example of how to seek infinite love and beauty, what to trust, and what aspirations are worth pursuing. Your connection to your Higher Self is stimulated in environments which involve nurturing or being nurtured. You may heal or rescue in your home (taking in the "walking wounded" of the world) though it is safer when there is an exchange of dependency and nurturing. Try to keep your feelings conscious: they are likely to run deep. You can transcend and make contact with the infinite through compassion, empathy, sensitivity and caring. Miracles/mysticism follow naturally from deep caring and strong emotional ties.

NEPTUNE IN 5TH HOUSE

You might idealize or romanticize love, fame, recognition or admiration. You can "cast a spell" or an illusion on your audience and are apt to have marked dramatic talent. You may have great abilities for emotional persuasion which could be useful in sales, advertising, films, or artistic creativity. Yet you can also delude yourself (and others) about your self-esteem or ego needs. You might raise the need for attention to the nth degree, make it an absolute value in your life, or you might repress and deny your needs for power, the limelight and attention. Your challenge is to blend the personal ego with a sense of Oneness that recognizes the unity of All. Your faith will be strengthened by letting yourself express spontaneously, pouring out from your own center in creative acts.

You are likely to yearn for perfection in your love relationships and may expect more than is humanly possible of lovers and children (or they may expect too much of you). You can easily merge with loved ones and might sacrifice yourself for them, or prefer to focus only on the positive within them. You may be "in love with love" and could ignore or avoid aspects of those you love which do not fit into your idealized images. You may look to sex to be a transcendent, inspirational, and sacred experience. Making sex an absolute value can result in actions that range from the religious celibate to the person who can only love one ideal mate to the promiscuous Cassanova who can't survive a night without sex and who always hopes that the next one will be the best yet. You are looking for ecstasy, you may want to heal and rescue through love, admiration, approval and positive feedback. You can transcend and touch infinity through taking risks, shining, being magnetic, joyful and fun-loving. Miracles and mysticism arise out of love in your life.

NEPTUNE IN 6TH HOUSE

You may yearn for the perfect job, want to do your work perfectly, or work for a more ideal world. You could idealize the work ethic and believe that doing things right matters more than anything else. The search for an ideal job only leaves one disappointed (or produces a job-hopper who keep changing, hoping for something better). Every job includes some things we would just as soon not have to do. You may heal and rescue others through your service, or create a more beautiful world through art and aesthetics. You could overdo the helper role and end as a martyr and victim. But if your ideals are also realistic, your compassion, empathy and connection to a Higher Purpose can contribute to your job and to your relationships with colleagues.

You need a sense of inspiration from your work. If your transcendent urges are not expressed through your job, ill health might offer an escape from disappointment. Mysterious, imaginary or confusing ailments are possible—or anything involving liquids (cysts, fluid retention, etc.)—if your work situation is too frustrating and security needs or guilt keep you from leaving it. You are likely to be more physically sensitive than the average person and should be extra careful with drugs (including alcohol). Any illnesses should be addressed on spiritual and metaphorical levels (what might that part of the body symbolize) as well as being treated physically. Miracles and mysticism could occur in your work and health. You might help yourself or others through spiritual healing.

Your imagination can enhance (or add confusion to) your accomplishments. You may vacillate between idealizing details and efficiency and avoiding or ignoring those duties and details which do not fit into your dreams. You may delude yourself (or others) about competence, efficiency and productivity. You are learning to blend the ideal and the real, inspiration and perspiration, imagination and effort.

NEPTUNE IN 7TH HOUSE

You are likely to idealize and romanticize partners, partnership, cooperation or beauty. You may want a dream so much that you avoid or ignore facets of your interactions with others which do not match your ideal images (of yourself, of them, or of relationships). You may expect more than is reasonable from yourself, a partner or partnership. You could delude yourself (or others) in the areas of sharing, cooperation and one-to-one interactions. You may be motivated to "marry God" (through a career in the Church), to find a Prince or Princess Charming, or you may strive to be perfect and provide ultimate meaning for another person. A positive (though never perfect) relationship can be achieved if you and your mate share basic values and goals and search together for spiritual truths, artistic inspiration or a sense of transcendent meaning.

You can merge with other people easily, often feeling their pain as your own. You are motivated to heal and rescue in interactions with others and could easily slip into savior/victim or rescuer/enabler associations. You may be highly intuitive and skilled at "psyching out" people, with marked empathy and compassion. Because you can visualize the best in others, you tend to support their Higher Selves, achieving a magical, tender, sacred bond.

Your imagination is an artistic asset and you probably have a strong feeling for aesthetics. Look for ways to satisfy your natural attraction to beauty, to further develop your creative skills, while minimizing the normal sense of human isolation through sharing with others, teamwork and aesthetic activities. Miracles and mysticism can be triggered in your life through associations with other people and through artistic endeavors.

NEPTUNE IN 8TH HOUSE

You have a deep drive to merge with a mate and seek an ecstatic peak. You could idealize or romanticize passion, power, mastery or control. You are likely to have an intuitive grasp of psychological issues, with the capacity to tune into obsessions, compulsions, and addictions as well as dreams, visions and inspirations. You yearn for intimacy on the deepest of levels, to share your most secret of selves with a soul mate (yet you may simultaneously fear revealing your "dark side"). You are seeking to transcend through depth sharing, passionate encounters and intense probing. You may heal or rescue through purification, intensity, regeneration, renovation or unflinching confrontation. The mirror of your mate helps you recognize your own Higher Self.

You might avoid or ignore facets of your inner psyche which do not fit your idealized images. You might repress or deny Shadow sides of yourself which feel unacceptable. Your imagination is drawn to explore hidden matters, death, money, passion and power. You could delude yourself (or others) around shared finances, possessions, pleasures and sexuality. You could idealize sexuality and have experiences which are magical and supremely seductive. Or, you might use sex to escape from reality (like a drug) and come crashing off your high when romantic illusions fail. Your faith will be an issue where joint resources are concerned and you must avoid the extremes of sacrificing all to a mate, or expecting everything to be given to you for your purity of spirit. You are likely to be highly intuitive and sensitive to the feelings of others. You may experience miracles or mysticism through interactions with an intimate partner, whether a personal relationship or a psychotherapist. You can discover your highest self through therapy or through self-analysis, and can use that insight to achieve self-mastery.

NEPTUNE IN 9TH HOUSE

You could idealize or romanticize the truth, "good times," religion or nature. You want to merge with Higher Truths and seek Ultimate Wisdom and Understanding. You can transcend through education, nature, religion, philosophy, travel or anything which expands your horizons. You yearn for greater knowledge, more insight, and a wider overview of the meaning of life. Your wholistic approach can sometimes lead to intellectual confusion, as you tend to take everything in and deal with very vast concepts. Your sense of wonder is alive and well. Divine mystery enthralls you. You may heal and rescue with inspiration, optimism, faith, trust and a boundless belief in the best. You can be an inspired teacher and a gifted, imaginative writer. Compassion and acceptance are important tools for you. Miracles and mysticism can be a natural part of your education and world view. Your imagination is expansive, exploring many ideas and seeking a sense of purpose and meaning in life.

You may place your faith in beauty, in healing, in mystical experiences, in God—or in any form of escapism—drugs, alcohol, fantasy, etc. You may sometimes avoid or ignore beliefs, ethics or principles which do not fit your idealistic images. You may delude yourself (or others) in terms of values, faith, morality and trust. Excessive faith can lead to gullibility, rose-colored glasses and eventual disillusionment. Excessive idealism could lead to unnecessary sacrifices. Your challenge is to blend the goals of your head with the goals of your heart—to make room for both emotional and intellectual dreams and ideals. With hearts and minds integrated, universal love can become a reality as well as a dream.

NEPTUNE IN 10TH HOUSE

You might yearn for a "calling" in life, a sense of mission to uplift and inspire you. You may want the perfect career, to function flawlessly as a professional, or to work for a utopian ideal (making the world better or more beautiful in some fashion). You are learning to ground your dreams, to bring your visions into being in the world. You could be a professional artist, savior, healer or guru. You could work with liquids, chemicals, imagery, magic, illusions or what is hidden. If rose-colored glasses are not handled properly, scandals, deception or simple confusion is possible. You may feel torn between your inner dreams and the limits of the real world. You need tangible achievements and measurable results from your imagination. Your career is supposed to make miracles happen.

Authority figures (beginning with a parent) will help you to deal with Neptunian issues. They might be idealistic, artistic, inspired, spiritual, religious, confused, escapist or victims. You might put a parent on a pedestal, believing s/he is perfect, or feel terribly disappointed and disillusioned when a parent shows his/her shortcomings. You may have had a parent who expected too much of you or of life. You could repress, deny or avoid facing certain facts about a parent, rather than giving up idealized images. This parent will influence your capacity to have faith, to trust the flow of the Universe.

You could idolize or romanticize status, success, power, authority or Daddy (authority parent). You could put your faith in the power structure and avoid or ignore those parts of reality which do not fit into your dreams. You might delude yourself (or others) in regard to effort, responsibility and willingness to work. Your challenge is to avoid the extremes of giving ultimate value to structure, order, accomplishment and security, or repressing and denying any drive for power, ambition, responsibility or control. You can blend fantasy and reality, using your creative imagination to make a difference on a basic, physical level.

NEPTUNE IN 11TH HOUSE

Your imagination is probably quite inventive, unique and future-oriented. You may yearn for brotherhood, sisterhood, progress and growth. Your ideals may be tied to humanitarian principles. You can transcend through changes, openness to the new, tolerance and acceptance of multiple options. You could idealize or romanticize individuality, freedom or the new—and you could repress or deny your individuality, need for change, and desire for stimulation. Your challenge is to maintain a clear sense of spiritual connection while feeding your authentic, individual self.

You are likely to seek a sense of merging with friends, knowledge and humanity. You might heal and rescue your friends individually, or broadly through new-age or humanitarian paths. Your rose-colored glasses might lead you into savior/victim entanglements with friends, groups or social causes. You cannot "make it **all** better" for anyone, nor can they provide a magic pill for your life. Don't let your desire to see the best in your associates blind you to what is truly there. You seek romance, kindness, faith and trust within your friends and associates in order to build your own. Shared idealism, however, can work wonders. You may be active in a quest for equal opportunity, or the urge to create a more beautiful world. Miracles and mysticism can come through friends, causes, new technology, invention or anything on the cutting edge of change.

NEPTUNE IN 12TH HOUSE

Your imagination is rich and many faceted. Your flair for fantasy can add inspiration and whimsy to your life—and can lead you down the garden path if the connection to reality becomes too tenuous. You could idealize or romanticize union, empathy, compassion, religion or beauty. You have a strong urge to merge with the universe, seeking ultimate meaning and Oneness. You can heal and rescue others in a very caring, selfless manner. You yearn for infinite love and beauty and need to transcend through uniting with the Whole, becoming one with All That Is.

You may be strongly drawn by the roles of artist, savior or victim. The artist is creating a more beautiful world, bringing a divine vision down to earth, and inspiring others with it. The savior is motivated to help, to heal, to assist, to rescue people and to make a better world (closer to utopian images). The victim also yearns for a wondrous, magical dream but feels unable or unwilling to create it, so escapes into drugs, alcohol, daydreaming, excessive TV-watching, etc. Escapism can include avoiding and ignoring anything that does not fit into your beautiful dream of how life should be. You might even repress or deny spiritual yearnings, artistic urges or assisting needs. It is possible to want so **much** perfection that it seems easier to give up than to seek something unreachably high. Or you may stop at visualizing utopia, and forget to back up your imagination with effort. You may feel that only God can handle the mess, and it is true that humans can't do it all, but they have to do their share.

Yet your faith and trust in ultimate goodness will be your bulwark in life ("everything is all right"). Involvement with beauty, spiritual paths or psychic insights can feed your spirit and strengthen your connection to your Higher Self. Your intuition can be a valuable tool (but don't rely on it to the exclusion of common sense). You can dissolve the boundaries of space and time, but don't turn escapism into a full-time job. The divine, the sacred are essential in your life. Miracles and mysticism are a natural part of life for you, triggered through art, nature, religion, spirituality or helping activities.

Neptune in Aspect: *Idealistic and Illusive*

(Please see section on Outer Planet Aspects on page 220.)

The nature of the planets involved in any aspect is the most important factor. For any pair of planets, please read **all three** aspect delineations: conjunction, cooperating (sextile ✶, trine △), and challenging (square □, opposition ✌, quincunx ⚻). The conjunction is the basic, most fundamental aspect and its themes carry through with other aspects. The cooperating and challenging analyses will offer additional choices regarding of constructive and nonconstructive ways of handling the basic issues.

Remember that the life issues represented by cooperating aspects (or conjunctions) may still require some attention. We might overdo certain themes, or succumb to projection, repression or displacement in trying to balance our many, different drives. It is also quite possible that you could have integrated some of the conflicts (shown by challenging aspects) which were present at birth and are now manifesting potentials more reflective of the delineations in the cooperating or conjunction sections.

Other factors will complicate the picture. The potential inherent in any given placement might be overridden by other configurations in the chart. As you read the interpretations for the various pieces of your chart, bear in mind that certain pieces will suppress others. As always, repeated themes, which recur again and again, are the most likely to manifest in your psyche and in your life.

NEPTUNE CONJUNCT PLUTO

You may have an affinity for the psychic or occult. You could have intuitive talent, or an attraction to magic, mysteries and the invisible, natural healing and transcendence. You are likely to work on deep, inner levels, and may make hidden transformations, dealing with subtle, psychological complexes and issues. Your emotions are apt to be intense and enduring.

If your sensitivity is carried too far, you might be subject to suspicion, obsession, lying, or misinterpreting reality due to selective attention (seeing, hearing, and feeling only what you want to). You might be persecuted or misunderstood (due to your openness to ecstatic or unfathomable realms)—or tend to scapegoat others (from an inner drive for control through assigning blame). You may take on the burdens of the world emotionally. You might be evasive, secretive, private, isolated, and illusive. Yet you are capable of an incredible level of communication with nature, tuning into the universe, and understanding the interconnections between all life forms.

You could mix together sex and spirituality, perhaps seeking a tantric path. You could seek spiritual union through sex, or try to lose yourself (totally merging) in relationships. Sex or death might represent a path of escape from overwhelming needs/feelings. You could overidealize a sexual partner, expecting him/her to be all-loving and compassionate, or seek to be unconditionally supportive of your partner, trying to provide everything s/he wants. You might succumb to savior/victim entanglements in relationships.

You are working on the tension between surrender and control, between sacrifice and sharing. You might idealize power in relationships, surrender, or control through passivity. You need periods of withdrawal to work through inner emotional tensions and to release and let go. You may, however, be tempted to use withdrawal as a punishment of others or to simply drop out in general if life seems too much.

Extremes are possible in your relationships and in your handling of the sensual/sexual/material world. You might binge periodically (with food, alcohol, sex, etc.). You could also idealize the role of the ascetic and carry it too far.

You can be highly compassionate, empathic and charismatic. You may be motivated to serve or transform humanity. You want to assure that power is wielded with compassion, that force and gentleness are blended.

This aspect last occurred 1891-1892. Neptune conjuncts Pluto every 493 years.

NEPTUNE COOPERATING PLUTO (✶ △)

You have the potential of wisely harnessing deep emotions or psychic powers. You may transform yourself through depth analysis, an intense investigation of inner issues, a willingness to confront psychological complexes and work through blocks. You may also be a catalyst for inspiring others, for offering insights or subtle perceptions about their needs. You may be open to other realms (psychic impressions, spiritual dimensions of reality, the collective, cosmic unconsciousness).

The idealism configured here could move toward concern with pollution, ecology, government waste, abuse of power or deceptive leaders (particularly those using charisma to sway people). You may be personally skilled at moving people emotionally. An alternative is the idealization of power, putting too much faith in material goods and pleasures. Appetite indulgence (around food, alcohol, drugs, possessions, etc.) is quite possible. You are working on the integration between the physical/sensual and the spiritual/sublime.

Intense emotions are highlighted and withdrawal could be a temptation. Periodic retreats to work through, release, and transform your reactions are healthy, but permanently "dropping out" won't really help you or others. Denial, avoidance, escapism, or running away might appeal, particularly if you feel helpless against the power of others. Yet you are strongest when pursuing a path that you feel is moral, compassionate, and will help and transform others.

Expectations may influence your relationship with a mate. Danger signals include seeking the ideal partner (who doesn't exist); trying to play God (save or be everything to a partner); looking for someone totally loving and accepting for yourself (who might rescue or transform you); or donning rose-colored glasses about others because you so much want a romantic, ecstatic, cosmic experience. Sharing a spiritual quest, artistic endeavors or inspirational experiences with a partner will be most effective and satisfying.

Your capacity to look beneath the surface, to understand what is invisible, to connect to all strata of life, to work with intense feelings and to seek to uplift others are your strengths and potential gifts to others.

(Neptune sextiles Pluto in most horoscopes from around 1942 til late 1993—and picks up the aspect again in the 21st century.)

NEPTUNE CHALLENGING PLUTO (□ ♂ ⚻)

Emotions are accentuated in your nature, although you may be tempted keep things inside, rather than revealing what you are feeling. You are likely to sense many layers to people and experiences, and tune into what is hidden rather than on the surface. You may be very perceptive regarding psychological complexes and the origins of drives, and you could have above average psychic ability.

Ideals might be a challenge in regard to your handling of sexuality, resources, pleasures and power. You might put too much faith in material goods, overindulging or "binge-ing" on food, alcohol, possessions, etc. You might carry self-mastery to an extreme, becoming an ascetic and inhibiting reasonable pleasures. You might idealize power and seek control of others through charisma, perpetrating or perpetuating illusions, or using emotional persuasion (blackmail). Alternately, you could try to control through weakness (or passivity), or simply withdraw from everything, giving up, running away and refusing to get involved.

Your expectations are likely to affect love relationships. You might want more than is possible from a partner, from a relationship, from material security, or from sex. You could be looking for the perfect partner who does not exist. You might fall into savior/victim associations, whether you are the one trying to "be everything" to another, or you are seeking a Prince or Princess Charming for yourself. You may entertain sexual fantasies of indulging total passivity and helplessness— or total control—over the other. Shared ideals, aesthetic projects, or spiritual quests can affirm, deepen, and strengthen your bond with another person on a positive level.

By paying attention to your inner reactions and achieving clarity regarding your motives, you can offer insight and revelations to others. By working with your deepest drives, you can turn negatives into positives, transform your life and help to transform our planet.

(Neptune squared Pluto around the beginning of the 1800s.)

CHAPTER TWELVE

PLUTO
POWER AND PERSEVERANCE
IN YOUR HOROSCOPE

Pluto in Signs: *Potent Probing*

Because Pluto's orbit is so long (248 years to circle the zodiac), it spends from 12 to 32 years in a single sign. Thus, it operates as a marker of generations, pointing to themes shared by large groups of people. Still, people's house positions for Pluto and cultural backgrounds as well as individual natures will affect how they deal with these generational Plutonian themes. (Thanks to Marion March and Joan McEvers in *The Only Way to...Learn Astrology* for many historical examples.)

PLUTO IN ARIES

You may probe deeply through crises, confrontations, anger or pioneering acts. You may bond/feel intimate through being active, assertive and self-expressive. You could focus or concentrate on doing your own thing. Control (of self or others) may be a driving need in your psyche.

Historically, Pluto was in Aries from 1823 to 1851. This period included the settling of the "Wild West" and the start of the Gold Rush to California.

PLUTO IN TAURUS
You may probe deeply in the realms of possessions, sensuality, comfort and finances. You may bond/feel intimate through sharing money, pleasures or relaxation. You could focus or concentrate on gaining stability and ease. Control of the material world and physical gratifications may be a driving need in your psyche.

Historically, Pluto was in Taurus from 1851-1883. The Civil War freed the slaves so human beings could no longer be owned as possessions in the U.S. The first transcontinental railroad was built in the U.S., facilitating an enormous expansion of the country's territory and wealth. The rise of corporations was underway and the stock ticker was invented.

PLUTO IN GEMINI
You may probe deeply in seeking information and knowledge about many areas. You may bond/feel intimate through communicating and exchanging ideas. You could focus or concentrate on relatives, learning or exposure to many possibilities. Techniques of mind control and discipline may appeal to you.

Historically, Pluto was in Gemini from 1883-1913. Intelligence tests were invented during this period. Freud's theories about the unconscious mind (psychoanalysis) were developed and popularized. The first subway was also built.

PLUTO IN CANCER
You may probe deeply in matters involving home, family, nation, women, and emotions. You may bond/feel intimate through nurturing (and/or being dependent). You could focus or concentrate on gaining emotional security. Mastery of feelings and intuitions may be a driving need in your psyche.

Historically, Pluto was in Cancer from 1913-1938. The world saw excessive patriotism lead to World War I and set the stage for World War II. Women gained political power (the vote) in the U.S.

PLUTO IN LEO
You may probe deeply in matters of love, creativity, speculation or children. You may bond/feel intimate through being onstage, seeking thrills or being passionate. You could focus on giving and receiving love, admiration, attention, or approval. You need a healthy outlet (sports, games, business) for your power drive.

Historically, Pluto was in Leo from 1938-1957. Explosive power was released with the first atomic bomb. Dictatorships (abuse of power) reigned in many parts of the world.

PLUTO IN VIRGO

You may probe deeply in your work, health or quest for competence. You may bond/feel intimate through realistic, functional relationships. You could focus or concentrate on handling details, being organized, being systematic, being effective. Mastery of your job and physical functioning is vital to you.

Historically, Pluto was in Virgo from 1957-1971. Computers began to reorganize the work place for many people. The birth control pill most effectively separated sex and conception. Women increasingly worked outside the home, putting new strains on marriage but pushing it toward more equality.

PLUTO IN LIBRA

You may probe deeply in relationships, aesthetics, or social rituals. You may bond/feel intimate through balance, harmony, or competition. You could focus or concentrate on grace, partnership, art, or fair play. An equal division of power could be an issue in your associations.

Historically, Pluto was in Libra from 1971-1983. Minorities and women sought equality of power through political movements. The U.S. ended any fixed value for our dollar which began to fluctuate against gold and other currencies. Worldwide inflation followed, exacerbated by the actions of oil-producing nations and our dependence on oil.

PLUTO IN SCORPIO

You may probe deeply and intensely into any hidden matters or subjects. You can bond/feel intimate through sharing possessions, finances and sexuality. You focus or concentrate on figuring out underlying motives and root causes. You may feel a strong drive to pursue self-insight and self-mastery.

Pluto entered Scorpio in 1983 and remained there until 1995. This period dealt with several intense emotional issues coming out of the closet: sexual harassment, child abuse and the "right to die" issue. The misuse of power (particularly in regard to sexual and economic exploitation) has been featured with governmental and religious leaders. Many countries, including the U.S., have piled up more debt than at any time in history, as the rich have become richer and the poor have become poorer. We are not learning to share the resources of the planet, but increasing numbers of people are becoming concerned about ecology, pollution, nuclear waste, etc. AIDS has received widespread publicity.

PLUTO IN SAGITTARIUS

You may probe deeply into philosophy, religion, education, the search for meaning. You may bond/feel intimate through sharing principles, values, goals, or ethics with a mate. You could focus or concentrate on optimism and aiming for/expecting the best. You may seek power through (or over) the mind, beliefs or inspiration.

Historically, Pluto was in Sagittarius from 1749 to 1762. This period included publication of the first encyclopedia and the beginning of the British Empire in India. Pluto is again in Sagittarius (1995-2008) as religious differences lead to more bloodshed in some areas and the information explosion continues via computers, cable and the Internet.

PLUTO IN CAPRICORN

You may probe deeply to figure out the laws/rules of life and the power structure. You may bond/feel intimate through learning to share power with a mate. You might seek power and authority through conventional, traditional or hardworking routes and could incline toward rigidity, trying to hang on or control for too long. You could focus or concentrate on organizational skills, on being practical, sensible and on advancing your career.

Historically, Pluto was in Capricorn from 1762 to 1778. This period included the invention of the steam engine and the American Revolution. The rigidity of power structures in many countries led to later rebellions.

PLUTO IN AQUARIUS

You may probe deeply into issues of freedom, individuality, innovation and tolerance. You may bond/feel intimate when intensely pursuing your vision of the future, the unusual, the original. You could focus or concentrate on your friends, groups, or networking abilities. You might seek power in unconventional ways or pursue equality for all.

Historically, Pluto was in Aquarius from 1778 to 1798. During this period, the U.S. won its independence, its Constitution was established, the French Revolution took place, and

Herschel discovered the planet Uranus. The first balloon and the first parachute were also tested at this time.

PLUTO IN PISCES

You may probe deeply into the imagination, fantasies, dreams and visions. You may bond/feel intimate through beauty, perfection, mysticism, meditation which connect you to a larger Whole. You could focus or concentrate on seeking union, transcendence, your Higher Self. You may seek control of everything, or hand the reins over to a Higher Power.

Historically, Pluto was in Pisces from 1798 to 1823. This was the Romantic Period in art and literature. Socialism began in Europe and Mesmer experimented with hypnosis and psychic phenomena.

Pluto in Houses: *Resolute and Resourceful*

PLUTO IN 1ST HOUSE

You seek to master yourself. You may test yourself (or others) through courage, initiative, daring, action and confrontation. At times, you may seem to "push the limits" (physically, emotionally) to see how far you can go and still survive! Self-control is an emotional issue in your life; you could swing between overcontrol (asceticism or denial) to being swept away by enthusiasm, spontaneity and instincts. You can range from total, icy control (shut down) to complete courage, energy and free self-expression. You are learning to balance your drives to hold in and to go out.

Your emotional nature is quite intense. People must realize that you are like an iceberg: nine-tenths below the surface. You may radiate a brooding, volcanic quality. If emotions are so buried that they operate solely at the unconscious level, subtle manipulations, power plays, or dominance games are possible. You can easily fall into all-or-nothing extremes. Beware of addictions, compulsions and obsessions. You have great willpower, concentration, and endurance; seek a positive channel for your competitive, forceful instincts.

You have a strong urge to probe beneath the surface— particularly your own psyche. You may play therapist to yourself, constantly questioning yourself, trying to dig out hidden motivations. You want to know and understand on the deepest levels and could be drawn to the occult, detective work, research or anything requiring thorough investigation. Much of your learning comes through the mirror of a mate, yet you can feel torn between your desire for an intimate bond with another person and your desire to maintain total personal control over your own life and actions. When you do make a commitment (to yourself, to another person, to an idea), you make a total commitment—to the death, to the end. Remember that there are times when compromise is essential, when moderation is needed. Be careful in what you want because you will probably get it. You can survive, overcome and master almost anything.

PLUTO IN 2ND HOUSE

You are seeking a sense of mastery and control within the realm of sensuality and financial resources. You may seek to sway (or intimidate or overpower) others by using money, determination, persistence or sensuality. Or you may feel controlled by others in those areas. Intense emotional reactions are likely where possessions, pleasures and resources are concerned. You are learning to give, receive and share comfortably. You may test yourself (and others) through the physical senses—in handling money, possessions, gratification and beauty.

You may experience all-or-nothing tendencies in this area and could have feast versus famine swings: over food, alcohol, sex, smoking, spending, saving, or others forms of physical indulgence. You could "binge" (on food, sex, money, etc.) and then totally restrict your involvement. Your challenge is to achieve moderation, to be comfortable while enjoying your appetites yet still maintaining mastery and self-control. You may experience obsessions, compulsions or addictions around money, possessions, pleasure, or appetite indulgence, yet you have tremendous strength, resourcefulness, concentration and skill for handling these areas.

Your desire to look beneath the surface may lead you to probe or investigate financial realms, sensual desires and what constitutes pleasure. Depth understanding of the material and financial world is important to you. You have strong feelings about possessions and may bond and feel intimate in a context of pleasure, beauty, sensuality and safety. You are likely to attract mates who are also working out the polarity between self-indulgence versus self-control (sex vs. celibacy; spending vs. saving etc.), or dealing with the other Taurus-Scorpio polarity of earning your own way vs. depending on someone else for money, possessions, etc. When other people are involved in the situation, power struggles, emotional blackmail and manipulation are possible until both of you reach both an inner and an outer compromise. You are learning to comfortably share resources, pleasures, possessions and beauty, learning to both give and receive.

PLUTO IN 3RD HOUSE

Mastery is important to you in the mental realm. You want to maintain control over your thoughts and communication style. You may swing from brooding silence to profound utterances. You may sway (or intimidate or overpower) others or they may overwhelm you through words and ideas. You tend to test yourself (and others) through mind games, concepts and language. You may be fascinated by hypnosis, research, occult studies, advertising and propaganda, or anything which involves using the mind to gain power. You can use the power of silence as well as words to influence others.

You could face issues of control and force through siblings, other relatives or the people right around you. They might be manipulative, vengeful, compulsive, addicted, emotionally paralyzed or strong, resourceful and committed. These early relatives gave you an opportunity to learn about sharing resources. If teamwork was not achieved then, you may face similar battles or retreats in a later mate relationship. The issue is learning to share power, possessions and pleasures. With confidence in your mastery over knowledge, you can communicate easily and deeply about material, sensual, sexual and/or psychological issues. You can have an intense, but equalitarian relationship. You tend to bond or feel intimate in a context of ideas, learning, communication and consciousness.

You probably find it natural to concentrate on gathering and disseminating information. You may probe or investigate anything intellectual. You could be involved in controlling communications or eliminating language, concepts and contacts you feel are superfluous. You may focus on allocating mental resources, objectivity and curiosity. You are likely to have above-average psychic ability as well as an excellent memory, though you might retain grudges and hurts as well as facts. Your mind may be exceptionally organized and thorough. You understand that knowledge is power and are driven to get to the bottom of things, to cut through superficialities to the basic layers of life.

PLUTO IN 4TH HOUSE

You are seeking a sense of mastery and control in regard to emotions, security needs, dependency and nurturance urges. You may feel controlled by your feelings, home, mother (figure) or desire for safety. You could intimidate or overpower others emotionally, in the home, or through protection and support. You are likely to have intense feelings about your home and family, but may have to dig to become fully conscious of them. Burying issues in the unconscious may be an almost automatic reaction. With time, effort and analysis, you are likely to transform your understanding of your roots. You may come to view your parents in a totally different manner.

Your nurturing parent was a role model (positive or negative) for your drive for understanding, power and self-mastery. This parent could have been psychic, intently focused, forceful and transformative—or emotionally blocked, inhibited, power-hungry, manipulative, addicted or compulsive. Shared pleasures, possessions and resources were an issue within your home. The abuse of power might have been a challenge. A strong, often unconscious bond probably existed between you and your mother (figure). This could have felt like a natural partnership—or a strangling "smother mother" association. Often, you can push each other's unconscious buttons without even knowing you are doing it. Your early nurturing (or lack of it) profoundly affected your capacity for sharing intimacy, pleasure and the material world.

You are likely to be highly intuitive and may feel driven to probe and investigate feelings, sensitivities, emotional needs and domestic issues. You may ferret out family secrets. You might fall into extremes: trying to eliminate warmth, closeness, rootedness or dependency from your life or bonding with a mate only in a context of nurturing, nourishment and protection. You grow and evolve most through experiences which stir you deeply, arousing profound reactions and survival instincts.

PLUTO IN 5TH HOUSE

You may seek a sense of mastery through speculation, lovers, children or your creative urges. You could intimidate or over-power others through a larger-than-life manner, a grandiose, exciting, overblown exaggeration. You may test yourself (or others) through thrills, the adrenaline rush, power, or risk-taking. You control (or are controlled by) your desire for excite-ment, admiration, love, power, pride and transcendence. You are likely to have strong reactions where matters of creativity are concerned and may feel torn between holding in and main-taining control, versus pouring out and taking chances with the responses of the world. You can be a catalyst for transfor-mation—in your own life and in the lives of others.

You are facing issues of control, dominance, power and transmutation in your love relationships. Giving, receiving and sharing pleasures and possessions could be an important focus. Power struggles (especially over money or sex) are pos-sible until you learn to share equally. The heat of passion may be quite important. You want to merge, to bond to another completely, but you also want to maintain control. Don't let the urge for ecstatic union turn into a dominance/submission game. Sexuality may range from an insatiable, starving hunger to a hermit-like retreat and withdrawal. All or nothing tendencies are likely. When it's good, it's very, very good (and when it's bad, it's awful). You need some constructive outlet for your competitive, forceful side. Sports, games, business, politics or fighting for causes can help channel combativeness into areas where it can be helpful. Appropriate competitive outlets also reduce the danger of fighting with team members (your chil-dren or your mate). Unless you have projected your own power into other people so you feel that they can overwhelm you, you are willing to go head-to-head with people. Confrontation comes naturally to you and it can increase mutual resourcefulness and strength. You probably have leadership skills which can be developed further as you gain self-confidence.

PLUTO IN 6TH HOUSE

You seek to master your bodily functioning and work routines. You want a sense of control in your health and on the job. You can be quite organized, focused and thorough. You might even intimidate or overpower others through a relentless pursuit of exacting details. You can get a bit compulsive about health, nutrition, physical regimes or the procedures of your career. You may control via (or be controlled by) an analytical, critical, discriminating, restrained and cautious approach. You are motivated to eliminate unproductive efforts, inefficient functioning and impractical matters.

Power over your work is important. You may fall into power struggle with co-workers, or attract manipulative, vengeful colleagues. Your challenge is to confront intense emotions through your work, but not allow them to overwhelm you. You would like your work to fascinate you, to be utterly enthralling and seductive. If your job does not satisfy your need for a kind of emotional absorption, or for control, or for reaching a sense of completeness, frustration might produce physical problems. Overcontrol, hanging on or holding in, can invite constipation, hemorrhoids, bowel or bladder problems, cysts, retention of fluids, etc. If you are out of touch with your own power needs, surgery is an extreme option (aggression from the outside to remove "dead" or dysfunctional parts). By staying conscious of your emotions, choosing work which you can control or which gives you a competitive outlet, and channeling your will and concentration into healthy habits, you can keep optimal physical functioning. Healing requires open flow. Don't block expression of emotions until they turn toxic. Do let go, release, transmute and transform negatives into positives.

You may bond or feel intimate within a context of realism, efficiency, competence and restraint. You may meet a mate through your work, work with a partner, or have a job that involves sharing resources or efforts with others. You are likely to test yourself (and others) through duties, work, health issues and service. You can be intensely committed to doing things well, to taking care of business.

PLUTO IN 7TH HOUSE

You are facing power issues in your close partnerships. Your challenge is to neither overpower and intimidate others, nor to allow them to overwhelm you. Your associates should act like mirrors to your own, inner issues. A mate reflects to you conflicts and concerns which you need to recognize and handle. Avoid projecting all the strengths (or all the difficulties) onto your intimate other. Your partner is **not** the source of all problems nor the solution. This relationship is a two-way street of reflecting each other's challenges and assets. Together, you are learning about sharing the sensual, sexual, and financial world. Either of you may feel, at times, tempted to try to control the other, possibly with jealousy, manipulation, emotional blackmail or other game-playing techniques.

Manipulation is a sign of weakness. As you both attain confidence as well as full consciousness of yourselves and of each other and are able to communicate feelings openly, you can attain a beautiful and enduring partnership. Compromise is an essential part of any team effort, whether you are dealing with business, personal or counseling relationships. Any face-to-face confrontations or joint efforts may bring up issues of control and dominance. If some battles do occur, remember that you are both building your own strength and resourcefulness through these interpersonal exchanges. But try to keep most of the battles for competition against an opposing team and strive toward teamwork with partners. Shared aesthetic interests and artistic talents may both strengthen and "lighten" your relationships.

You are likely to deal with issues of emotional retention in relationships. It is easy for you to hang on to feelings (be it guilt, resentment, anger, fear, avoidance, etc.). The only lesson of some relationships is knowing when to say "Good bye." Don't stick around for endless punishment. Justice and balance matter to you. You can be fascinated by the "dark side" of life and your relationships are apt to bring up obsessions, compulsions and addictions on both sides. The challenge is to transform and transcend without destroying one another or your shared bond.

You need passion, intensity and depth in your relationships. You are inclined to probe beneath the surface of any interactions, to seek other levels, to get at underlying motivations. Superficialities cannot hold your interest. You need a partner who will go to the wall, to the end, to the death, to face the fears, anxieties and Shadows, to join with you in a full and complete commitment.

PLUTO IN 8TH HOUSE

Self-mastery and self-control are strong drives within your nature. You wish to master your appetites. You may control (or be controlled by) sexual urges, physical resources, intense emotions or the urge for deep insight. You could swing from an intense, voracious sensual focus to a total withdrawal and acetic self-denial. Try to avoid the extremes of total financial dependency or providing completely for someone else. You may deal with issues of addiction, compulsion or obsession. You can concentrate on insight, removing waste, sharing power and purifying your psyche. Your challenge is to eliminate whatever is no longer useful or valid in your life and to transmute negatives into positives (on emotional and financial levels).

You are likely to learn how to share and allocate resources, possessions and pleasures within an intimate relationship. Your mate will reflect back to you issues within your own psyche which you need to face and handle. You may test yourself (and others) through intensity, passion, purification, penetration, confrontation and an unflinching investigation of anything to the very end. An all-or-nothing quality could pervade your associations. At times, your challenge might involve knowing "when is enough and how to let go." But, once you have decided that something is "dead" for you, you may not only bury it, you may act as if it never existed. You can be thoroughly enthralled, by a person, a desired possession, a power goal, and you can turn icy cold! You are likely to bond and feel intimate within a context of depth, regeneration and transformation; you may be deeply changed by some relationships. You can cut to the heart of experiences, to the essence of issues.

You are probably drawn to probe hidden matters, death and anything arousing strong feelings. You may be fascinated by the "dark side" of life. Sometimes you could push the limits (physically, mentally, emotionally and/or spiritually) to see how far you can go and still survive. Your motto might be "no surrender." You have tremendous strength of will and perseverance.

PLUTO IN 9TH HOUSE

You are seeking a sense of mastery through religion, philosophy, travel, education or other expansive activities. You may control (or be controlled by) principles, faith, trust, optimism and beliefs. You are naturally drawn to probe and investigate world views, belief systems, concepts and ethics, or you may focus all your attention on your own ultimate values and goals.

You may sometimes overpower or intimidate others (or they overwhelm you) through grandiosity, big dreams, spirituality or philosophizing. You tend to have intense feelings about faith issues and may sometimes slip into fanaticism or seek principles to rationalize and justify your emotional drives. You naturally concentrate on questions of morality, ethics, right and wrong. You may want to eliminate outmoded beliefs, values, ideas and understanding or you may hold on to them against all odds. Be careful what you destroy during spiritual purges. Neither extreme—hanging onto everything or rejecting everything—is healthy. You may project (facets of yourself you would rather not face) onto religious figures, nature, or philosophical systems of thought. Recognize the messages for you within gurus and educational experiences. You have a deep, relentless urge to seek understanding; both depth and breadth of focus are suggested.

You are likely to bond and feel intimate in a context of optimism, humor, trust, generosity and expansiveness. Or, you might avoid a committed relationship in order to remain free to seek other values, such as financial or political power. If emotional sharing is made into an ultimate value, you may expect more than is possible of yourself, a mate or a committed relationship. Sex, power, control or dominance could be given too much importance. Shared power (teamwork) and a joint focus on spiritual issues can work well. You and a mate may seek the truth together—without expecting perfection from one another. You can share, evaluate, and allocate ideas, concepts, religions and philosophies with one another and help each other reach your mutual goals.

PLUTO IN 10TH HOUSE
Issues of power, authority, dominance and control will be significant in your life. You probably had intense feelings about your authority parent. That parent might have been dictatorial, manipulative, intrusive, demanding (or, in extremes—abusive). The opposite extreme is a parent who was emotionally paralyzed, repressed, inhibited, addicted or compulsive. Still another possibility is a parent who allowed you to be a partner, sharing the power and responsibility. Your rulemaker parent was a role model (positive or negative) for handling shared resources, sexuality, power and intensity. If your parent pro-

vided a good example, s/he could have been resourceful, strong and intuitive and you may have had a deep, nonverbal bond. Your parent could have provided a positive mirror of healthy self-control.

You are likely to have picked up unconscious imprinting from your authority parent which affects your capacity for intimacy, particularly your ability to share pleasures, possessions and money with another person. Sex and money could be battlegrounds until you can share openly—without manipulation or power plays—naturally tuning into one another's needs, drives and inner, emotional issues. You are likely to bond and feel intimate in a context of caution, responsibility, safety and structure.

You need a sense of mastery in your career. You may be ambitious concerning your place in society. You could intimidate or overpower (or just stay ahead of) others through competence, hard work, realism and an innate sense of authority. You can be quite organized, thorough and dedicated. If you carry this to an extreme, you may end up controlled by your duties, vocational demands, ambitions, and status needs. You naturally focus and concentrate on success, achievement and the rules of life (but might overdo to the point of paralysis at times). A desire for more than is possible or a tendency to overrate the power of the world can both lead to giving up. But you are far more likely to be successful. You may have skill for business, management, anything involving joint resources (insurance, taxes, government funds), or any kind of depth work (psychotherapy, archaeology, investigative work, history, research, etc.).

You might feel driven to probe and investigate the limits of power, responsibility, structure and societal institutions. You could sometimes push the limits (testing yourself or others) in regard to authority (your own or that of others), your profession or your place in the world. You are learning when to eliminate responsibilities, guilts and demands which are outmoded and when to share duties, practical demands, pressures and necessary limits. You could have phenomenal endurance.

PLUTO IN 11TH HOUSE

You seek a sense of mastery in regard to the new, the unusual, the avant garde and the progressive. You may feel driven to probe and investigate new ideas, changes, unusual perspectives and technological innovations. You could control (or be controlled by) rebellious urges, humanitarian instincts and ideas on the cutting edge. You may test yourself (or others) through confrontations involving issues of tolerance, openmindedness, and free flow of information. You can go to extremes in regard to friends, groups, new age knowledge, and the future. You may totally eliminate friendships, associations, ideas and inventions which you feel are no longer productive. You could intimidate and overpower friends or groups (or find them overwhelming and feel paralyzed emotionally). You are likely to meet some deep, buried issues from your own psyche (obsessions, compulsions, emotional needs and drives) through friends, causes or your community. They can act as mirrors to further your understanding and growth.

You are likely to bond and feel intimate in a context of freedom, individuality, openness, tolerance and equality. You tend to concentrate on the unusual, the different, the unique and the new. You may feel willing to share with all of humanity, seeking connections. You could turn friends into mates and mates into friends (even after a break up). Your friendships are deeper than the average and may sometimes be close to therapy. You could experience intense emotional exchanges, unconscious bonds or psychic rapport with friends. You need space and individuality in your intimate connections. You are working on the balance between freedom and closeness, passion and detachment, security and risk, sexuality and the intellect. You might polarize on these issues with friends or mates until you achieve integration. You are learning to love intensely, passionately, completely, to be absorbed and consumed by love, and yet to retain your own unique individuality and an appreciation of your beloved's special essence.

PLUTO IN 12TH HOUSE

You are likely to seek a sense of mastery with your dreams, visions and ideals. You could be highly intuitive, perhaps even prophetic on occasion. You may be driven to examine unconscious compulsions and obsessions, to probe and investigate fantasies, ideas and escapist urges. You could control (or be controlled by) your imagination and pipeline to the Infinite. You naturally concentrate on beauty, union, spirituality and absolutes. You can be ruthless in your visualizations and may inhibit or repress uncomfortable emotional issues—or eliminate dreams and imagination. Going inward is an instinctive focus. Retreat might be carried to an extreme as the ultimate in self-control. Your urge for insight is intense; your Higher Self will stimulate transformation, transcendence and radical reworking of your psyche.

Depth sharing, fusion and nonverbal communication may be idolized. If faith in a Higher Power is lacking, you might put power on a pedestal (power over people, possessions, personal sensuality, etc.). Fantasies of omnipotence may seem more appealing than dealing with the outside world. Jealousy, possessiveness or manipulation may be presented in alluring disguises as ways to produce the results you consider right for others. Savior/victim games may be played around money, possessions, sensuality or sexuality. You might sometimes intimidate (or feel intimidated) and have to deal with issues of passivity, weakness, escapism or avoidance. Yet you always have a deep inner well of strength and power. You can slay dragons!

You will probably bond or feel intimate in a context of sensitivity, empathy, merging, selflessness, compassion and beauty. You are likely to be highly intuitive, open to the feelings of others. Visions, aesthetic urges, spiritual drives and inspirational needs feed your urge to unite with another person. You may test yourself (or others) against an ideal image and standard for infinite love and beauty. You could seek the "perfect" love and be chronically dissatisfied with a mate or be seduced by rose-colored glasses into believing a mate is ideal—only to be disappointed later. You could hesitate to commit to one person, thinking that someone more ideal will eventually appear. (The worship of sex can lead to promiscuity). A lasting and mutually satisfying relationship can be attained if you share the quest for utopia with your beloved—without either of you trying to be everything or provide ultimate meaning for the other. You can easily slip into viewing the world (and people) as polarized extremes: absolute good and absolute evil. Your challenge is to transmute perceived negatives and positives into a constructive, human whole.

Pluto in Aspect: *Intense and Intimate*

There are no Pluto aspects listed here because Pluto is the last planet (currently known) and thus its aspects have already been discussed in earlier material. See, for example, Sun conjunct Pluto, Moon challenging Pluto, etc., in earlier sections.

EPILOGUE

Each horoscope is a complex, interconnected, many-layered depiction of a human psyche (soul). Like the human being it represents, an astrological chart can be expressed on many different levels. The value of astrology lies in helping us to identify and enhance our strengths and talents while minimizing, compensating for, and overcoming our weaknesses and challenges.

Every piece of a horoscope has a positive (and a negative) potential, just as every drive within our personalities can be directed for good or ill. The more fully and deeply we understand our needs, our desires and our yearnings, the more successfully we can create a life which satisfies our basic nature and brings fulfillment to ourselves and others. It is my hope that this book will prove a useful tool in your quest for understanding, illumination, and gratification, that some of the passages within will provide insight into your depths and the inner recesses of those closest to you.

Astrology is much deeper and richer than just the natal (or birth) horoscope. In the appendix you will find some descriptions of other astrological tools and resources which you may find helpful.

Although astrology surpasses other psychological tools in its richness, depth and complexity, "the map is not the territory." You are much more than everything in your chart. Like any tool, astrology is helpful only when put to constructive use. Allow it to bring added dimensions, choices, options and opportunities into your life—not to restrict or limit your view of yourself! You are a unique, irreplaceable human being. You are special in the world and I wish you much joy, love, laughter, excitement and intellectual stimulation in your path to The Light.

GLOSSARY

Air: One of the metaphorical elements of astrology. Air is associated with the signs of Gemini, Libra, Aquarius; the houses 3rd, 7th and 11th; the planets Mercury, Venus and Uranus. Air represents our objective capacity, our perception, the world of the mind and communication, theories, abstractions and detachment.

Ascendant: The degree of the zodiac which was rising at the birthplace when that individual was born. Or, the intersection of the horizon and the ecliptic in the east. On the horoscope, the horizontal line to the left designates the Ascendant and is the beginning of the 1st house.

Aspects: The angular distances between two factors (e.g., planets) in the horoscope, in celestial longitude. The most commonly used aspects are the **conjunction 0°, opposition 180°, square 90°, trine 120°, sextile 60°, and quincunx 150°.** Other aspects also exist. Aspects between planets (and other points in the chart) are assumed to indicate certain themes of cooperation, challenge, pulling apart, etc., in terms of personality, events, and relationships with others.

Asteroids (also called minor planets): Thousands of small bodies, found mostly between the orbits of Mars and Jupiter. The four major ones utilized are Ceres, Pallas, Juno and Vesta (three of which are the largest and all among the first discovered). Some astrologers put asteroids as well as planets in their horoscopes.

Birth information: The basic information needed to erect a horoscope is — date (day, month, year), time (hour and minute) and place (latitude and longitude) of birth.

Cardinal: one of the three qualities of astrology. Cardinal signs are Aries, Cancer, Libra and Capricorn. Cardinal (also called angular) houses are 1st, 4th, 7th and 10th. Cardinal planets are Mars, Moon, Venus and Saturn. The cardinal quality is associated with changes in one's life structure (identity, home, partnership, career), breaks, action and overt events.

Challenging Aspects: Square, Quincunx and Opposition are the major challenging aspects.

Chiron: A small body (planetoid) between the orbits of Saturn and Uranus. Discovered by Charles Kowal on November 1, 1977. Named after the mythical centaur who tutored many heroes and was noted for healing.

Conjunction 0°: See **Aspects**. Assumed to indicate the combining or blending of the themes symbolized by conjuncting planets.

Contra-parallel: An aspect in declination when two planets are within one degree of each other, but one is north and the other is south declination. Its meaning is similar to a mini-opposition.

Cooperating Aspects: Sextile and Trine are the major cooperating aspects.

Cusp: (1) The degree of the ecliptic where the end of one sign is separated from the beginning of the next sign; (2) the point (a zodiacal position) which marks the boundary of one house from the next.

Declination: A coordinate system measuring positions north or south of the celestial equator.

Descendant: The 7th house cusp of a chart, assumed to indicate attributes we seek and attract in others (particularly partners). Astronomically, the intersection of the horizon and the ecliptic in the west.

Directions: A system of examining the current patterns in a person's life. Generally, the "directed" planets are compared to the natal planets. Planets can be directed forward or backward, with a number of different systems. All forms of directions involve moving everything in the chart a uniform amount. This amount could be based on the Sun's progressed motion in one year (solar arc directions), the movement of the progressed Ascendant in a year (Ascendant arc directions) or general integers, e.g., 1°, 5°, etc., per year.

Earth: (1) the planet on which we live, the third out from our Sun, (2) an astrological element associated with the signs Taurus, Virgo and Capricorn; the 2nd, 6th and 10th houses and the planets Venus, Mercury and Saturn. Earth symbolizes the need for tangible results, practicality, realism, competence, effort, thoroughness, responsibility, and skill with details.

Ecliptic: The Earth's path around the Sun. This path, extended into space, is divided into 12 sections to form the zodiac.

Elements: An astrological metaphor which divides life into four basic components—fire, earth, air and water. Each sign is assigned to a particular element (see fire, earth, air and water). In addition, the houses of the natural zodiac and the planets which rule them can be assigned to an element. Some astrologers refer to the elements as quadruplicities.

Ephemeris: A book which supplies the positions of the Sun, Moon and planets, usually daily. Positions are generally given in celestial longitude, latitude and declination. Other information (i.e., sidereal time, the nodes of the Moon, ingresses) may also be supplied. Positions are usually given at either noon or midnight, for Greenwich, England.

Fire: a metaphorical quality associated with the signs Aries, Leo and Sagittarius; the 1st, 5th and 9th houses and the planets Mars, Jupiter and the Sun. Fire represents the initiation of action, confidence, outreach, spontaneity, creativity, eagerness, zest, excitement and the need to do something new.

Fixed: one of the qualities of astrology. Fixed signs are Taurus, Leo, Scorpio, and Aquarius. Fixed (also called succeedent) houses are the 2nd, 5th, 8th and 11th. Fixed planets are Venus, Sun, Pluto and Uranus. The fixed quality is associated with enduring self-will, dogged determination, perseverence, appetite control issues, and the balance between security and risk.

Gauquelin Sector: division of zodiac circle into 18 or 36 sections. Research by Michel and Francoise Gauquelin found certain planets in particular sectors for various professions and for character trait descriptions in biographies with odds tens of thousands to one against chance. The significant Gauquelin sectors or "zones of power" are roughly equivalent to the Placidian 9th and 12th houses.

Geocentric: Refers to a system of Earth-centered astrology, where the positions of other planets and the Sun and Moon are in reference to our perspective here on Earth. Most astrologers work with geocentric horoscopes, but a few are experimenting with the heliocentric perspective (looking from the point of view of the Sun).

Heliocentric: Charts using the perspective of the Sun as the center. Earth appears in these charts, instead of the Sun. The further a planet is from the Sun, the less its geocentric position varies from its heliocentric one. The inner planets (Mercury and Venus) can vary by as much as 180°.

Horary: The art of answering questions through astrology. A chart is erected for the time a question is asked and the answer is sought by interpreting the horoscope using the rules of horary astrology.

Horoscope: Symbolic map of the heavens based on a specific birth time, place and date.

Houses: A system of dividing up the space within which the Earth rotates. The ecliptic is divided into twelve sections, generally of unequal size. Systems of house division include Placidus, Alcabitius, Campanus, Equal, Koch, Meridian, Porphyry, Regiomontanus and Topocentric. Houses are assumed to symbolize certain psychological drives and indicate various life areas. Placidus is the house system used by the vast majority of astrologers.

IC: see **Imum Coeli**.

Imum Coeli: Also called the I.C. or 4th house cusp. Signifies home, family, domestic base and nurturing parent as well as one's own tendencies in regard to dependency and caretaking instincts.

Ingress: The exact moment at which a planet enters a sign (reaches a position of 0° 0′ in that sign).

Interception: Because most house divisions are unequal, it is quite common—at some latitudes on Earth—to have a horoscope where two opposite signs are entirely contained within the houses. No degree of either sign appears on the cusp. In such a case, two other opposing signs (either just after or just before the two "intercepted") will appear on two houses cusps. Planets occupying signs which are intercepted are also called intercepted. Some astrologers interpret intercepted planets as being blocked in expression; others see them as being emphasized and highlighted; and some astrologers give no significance to interceptions.

Latitude, Celestial: Angular distance, measured in degrees, minutes and seconds, north or south of the ecliptic.

Latitude, Terrestrial: Angular distance, north or south of the Equator, measured in degrees, minutes and seconds.

Local Sidereal Time: The time of birth at the birthplace converted to sidereal (star) time. This is the figure from which the house cusps of a horoscope are derived.

Longitude, Celestial: Distances along the ecliptic, measured in degrees, minutes and seconds, going east from the vernal point (which is defined as 0° Aries), which is determined by the Sun crossing the celestial equator going from south to north.

Longitude, Terrestrial: Distances measured east and west, in degrees, minutes and seconds. The 0° point is the Prime Meridian through Greenwich, England.

Midheaven: The point at which the Meridian (of the birthplace) intersects the ecliptic (above the horizon). This point is also defined as the beginning of the 10th house in most house systems. The intersection of the Meridian and ecliptic below the horizon forms the IC (*Imum Coeli*) or 4th house cusp. The Midheaven is represented by a straight, vertical line at the top of most horoscopes.

Midnight: Can be defined as 00:00 hours, the beginning of the day or as 24:00 hours, the end of the preceding day. Where not specified the standard convention is that "midnight" means 24:00 hours.

Midpoints: Sensitive points halfway between two factors in the chart. One can consider, for example, that the point exactly midway between the Sun and Moon in a horoscope represents qualities of both the Sun and Moon.

Mutable: One of the qualities of astrology. Mutable signs are Gemini, Virgo, Sagittarius and Pisces. Mutability can also be assigned to Mercury, Jupiter and Neptune and to the 3rd, 6th, 9th and 12th houses. Mutability is associated with a mental focus, the ability to learn vicariously, flexibility, multiple talents, the danger of scattering and a tendency toward high expectations. Mutable signs are also called common; mutable houses are also called cadent.

Natal Horoscope: A symbolic map of the state of the heavens at the moment an individual was born. The positions of the Sun, Moon, planets and sensitive points are given in celestial longitude. The planet's longitudes depend only upon the Universal Time (UT) of birth. The planet's placements in the houses of the horoscope depend upon sidereal time as well as the UT of birth.

Nodes of the Moon: Points derived from the intersection of the Moon's orbit with the orbit of the Earth. When the Moon is moving into north declination, this intersection of orbits marks the North Node. When the Moon moves into south declineation, the intersection marks the South Node. Even if an individual has no other oppositions in the chart, the Nodes are always opposite each other and so point to relevant polarities for that person, by their house and sign placements.

Opposition 180°: An aspect (angular distance) between two planets, signifying a tendency to polarize, to swing between extremes, to identify with one side and attract other people who live out the opposite. The easiest of challenging aspects to integrate as opposite signs (and houses) are natural partners—each supplying themes the other lacks.

Orb: The amount allowed on either side of an aspect for that aspect to still be considered valid, (e.g., a square is an aspect of 90°). If an orb of 5° is allowed, any two planets which are 85° to 95° from one another would be considered square each other. If an orb of 8° is allowed, planets from 82° to 98° distant from each other would be square.

Parallel: An aspect in declination where two planets are in the same degree (with an orb of 1°), both north or both south of the celestial equator. Its meaning is considered similar to a mini-conjunction—a focus or concentration, blending, combination.

Placidus: The most common method of house division. See also **Houses**.

Planets: The traditional "planets" used in a horoscope are the Sun, Moon, Mercury, Venus, Mars, Jupiter, Saturn, Uranus, Neptune and Pluto. The Sun is actually a star and the Moon a satellite of Earth. The Sun and Moon are sometimes called "the Lights" to distinguish them from the planets, but generally all are lumped together for convenience. Earth is not included in most horoscopes because they are geocentric— viewing everything from the perspective of Earth. One could visualize Earth as occupying the exact center of the horoscope.

Progressions: A system of examining current and future trends in a horoscope. One unit of time is equated with another (longer) unit of time, for symbolic purposes. The most common form, **Secondary Progressions**, equates one day with one year. Thus, if a person is now 30 years old, the positions thirty **days** after birth are considered symbolic of that thirtieth year. Other systems of progressions equate a lunar month with a year, a day with a lunar month and so on.

Qualities: A way of grouping signs (and planets and houses) which share certain themes. Astrology theorizes three qualities: cardinal, fixed and mutable. Qualities are also called **triplicities**.

Quincunx 150°: An aspect which is thought to indicate two very different drives in the nature which feel incompatible. One may make a "forced choice" and real effort and adjustment is necessary to find a compromise positions which allows expression of both drives.

Retrograde: Apparent backward motion, which occurs when Earth passes a slower-moving, outer planet or when Earth is passed by a faster-moving inner planet. Designated by the symbol ℞ in the horoscope. The outer planets are retrograde over 40% of the time.

Sextile 60°: An aspect assumed to symbolize mild harmony, opportunities or compatibility.

Signs: Twelve 30° segments of the ecliptic which can be defined tropically or sidereally. (See Zodiac, below.)

Solar Return: A horoscope cast for the moment when the Sun returns to the exact degree/minute/second of celestial longitude which it occupied at birth. This moment will be within a day or two of one's birthday. The horoscope is considered symbolic of the coming year.

Square 90°: An aspect assumed to indicate challenges. May be a sense of confrontation, blocking or frustration. Points to areas where the individual needs to integrate different drives, making a place for each in the life, without denying any.

Station: The point at which a planet appears motionless from the perspective of the Earth, about to change from retrograde to direct (forward) or direct to retrograde.

Transits: (1) The actual positions of the planets on any given date. (2) The passage of a planet through a sign or house (e.g., the Sun transits Aries from about March 20 to April 20). (3) The passage of a planet over any degree which forms significant aspects to any planet or important point in a (natal, progressed, horary) chart.

Water: represents one of the elements of astrology. Water signs are Cancer, Scorpio and Pisces. Water houses are the 4th, 8th and 12th. Water planets are the Moon, Pluto and Neptune. Water represents sensitivity (to one's own needs as well as those of others), the unconscious mind, automatic processing, habits, sleep, union, absorption, assimilation and psychic openness.

Trine 120°: An aspect assumed to symbolize talents, abilities, and drives which reinforce and amplify one another. Can show strengths, but also excesses. Usually feels like an easy flow.

Zodiac, Astronomical: The groupings of certain constellations into a rough circle. The signs of the astronomical zodiac are of unequal lengths, based on the physical characteristics of the constellations.

Zodiac, Sidereal: The division of the ecliptic into twelve 30° segments, originally based on a Babylonian system using the fixed stars Aldebaran and Antares as the markers for the center of their signs (Taurus and Scorpio).

Zodiac, Tropical: The division of the ecliptic into twelve 30° segments, based on the Earth's seasons. The location of the Sun at the vernal equinox (when day and night are equal in the spring) defines 0° Aries. The vast majority of American astrologers use the tropical zodiac.

zones of power: see Gauquelin sector.

APPENDIX

There are a variety of forms for looking at current and future (as well as past) trends in the horoscope. Four major systems for looking ahead (or behind) exist.

Transits

Transits simply refer to the current positions of the planets and asteroids. Since planetary motions are (relatively) regular, humans can create listings which note not only where the planets are right now, but also where they will be in the future. A book which lists the degree, sign and minute in the zodiac occupied by each of the planets on various dates is called an ephemeris (plural—ephemerides).

The best book to begin working with transits is *Future Signs: Quck Astrological Prediction* by Maria Kay Simms (1996 ACS Publications, code BFS, $14.95*) Maria provides an easy-to-follow system for loking ahead and gives interpretations for each transiting aspect and each transiting planet through each house.

As an example, if you were married on June 15, 1980, you would look in an ephemeris at the date of June 15, 1980, and note where each of the planets was in the zodiac. (The transiting Sun was 24 Gemini; transiting Venus was also 24 Gemini—an appropriate conjunction for a wedding.) Those planetary positions are the **transits** for June 15, 1980. Similarly, if you wish to look ahead, you simply turn to the correct page in an ephemeris and note the transits for any date you wish.

Generally, one looks at aspects between transiting planets and natal planets, as well as considering the houses of the horoscope through which each transiting planet is traveling. If you look **only** at the transits themselves, you are considering the astrological "weather" which everyone in the world is facing. That is, on June 15, 1980, everyone has the opportunity to experience Sun/Venus issues (such as love, artistic creativity, extravagance, sensual indulgence, pleasure, etc.). However, people whose **natal** charts are strongly aspected by that tran-

*Postage/handling charges will apply. Call 1-800-888-9983

siting Sun/Venus conjunction (and the other transits of that period) are much more likely to have a significant, noteworthy experience than people whose charts do not "tie into" the transiting positions. If 24 degrees of Gemini does not strongly aspect your natal chart, that Sun/Venus transit is not likely to be significant for you.

Some astrologers limit aspects from transits to a one-degree orb. Others use a three- or even five-degree orb.

Astro Communications offers the following popular transit reports:

(1) **A Concise Planetary Guide to Your Future** – Text is a condensed version of *Future Signs*. This bound, laser printed personalized report gives only your most significant transits, the conjunctions and the challenging. Outer planet transits are given at the beginning of each month. Sun, Mercury, Venus and Mars aspects are given on the day they are exact. New Moon/Full Moon/Eclipse interpretations appear on the day they occur. CODE: AB4 6 MOS - $15.95*, 1 YEAR - $29.95*

(2) **A Planetary Guide to Your Future** – This deluxe personalized report essentially looks up all the text in *Future Signs* for you. All major and minor aspect interpretations are given, conjunction, challenging and cooperating, with the specific aspect named. House transits are included, too. Outer planets appear at the beginning of each month. Sun, Mercury, Venus and Mars aspects appear on the day exact, as do the New Moon/Full Moon/Eclipse interpretations. It's a BIG laser printed and bound book. CODE: DTIX 6 MOS - $29.95*, 1 YEAR - $45.95*

If you want to do your own interpreting, Astro can provide lists of transits for any dates (4000 B.C. - 2500 A.D.) which interest you.

(1) **Calendar Transits** (listing aspects made by transiting planets to your Natal Chart) presented as one page per month, with boxes of aspects for each day. CODE: CAT 1 YEAR - $20.00*

(2) **Outer Planet Transits** list each aspect from a transiting outer planet—Jupiter, Saturn, Uranus, Neptune and Pluto—to your Natal Chart. CODE: OPTL $5.00/YR*

(3) **9-Planet Transits** each aspect from a transiting planet [the Moon is **ex**cluded] to your Natal Chart. CODE: T $14.00/YR*
*Postage/handling charges will apply. Call 1-800-888-9983

Progressions

Progressions are a symbolic form of current patterns. In each system of progressions, a certain unit of time is considered **symbolically equivalent** to a different unit of time. For example, the most popular system of progressions is variously called Major Progressions, Secondary Progressions or Day-For-A-Year Progressions. All of these different names refer to the same system which symbolically equates one day of planetary motion with one year in the life of the individual.

As an example, if you were married on June 15, 1980, you would calculate how old you were at that time. If you were **25 years old**, you would look to the patterns in an ephemeris **25 days** after you were born. Those patterns (25 days after your birth) are considered symbolic of your 25th year of life.

This rough approximation (of "one day equals one year") will not give you **absolutely accurate** positions in secondary progressions, but it will give you a good general idea. Ephemerides provide planetary positions once a day (either at noon [12:00] or at midnight [0:00] for Greenwich, England). Unless you were born in Greenwich at exactly noon or exactly midnight, counting one day in the ephemeris for each year of life will give you only your **approximate** secondary progressions. Instructions for calculating exact secondary progressions are supplied in *The Changing Sky* by Steven Forrest (B122X, $14.95*), *Progressions, Directions and Rectification* by Zipporah Dobyns (B232X, $7.00*) and *The Only Way to ... Learn about Tomorrow* by Marion March and Joan McEvers (B136X, $14.95*). You can also order several forms of secondary progressions through Astro Communications Services. Call for details.

Directions

Directions involve positions which did not ever occur in the sky. In directions, the entire chart is rotated (as if on a wheel) a certain amount. The amount depends on the form of directions which are used. For example, solar arc directions move everything in the natal chart the same distance as was travelled by

*Postage/handling charges will apply. Call 1-800-888-9983

the Sun in secondary progressions. (The Sun moves approximately one degree per day. That is, the transiting Sun is about one degree later each day than the day before. Since a day is equivalent to a year in secondary progressions, the secondary progressed Sun moved about one degree per year in the life.)

Returns

Return charts involve erecting an entire horoscope for the instant in time when a planet returns to its exact natal position (the same degree, sign, minute and second in the zodiac). A Solar Return is erected for the instant when the (transiting) Sun reaches the exact position of your natal Sun. Solar Returns occur once a year as the Sun goes around the zodiac in one year. The longitude and latitude used to erect any return chart can be either the longitude and latitude of birth or the longitude and latitude of the place of residence when the return occurs. March and McEvers strongly recommend calculating Return Charts for where you are actually living at the time. Astro can interpret your Solar Return for the next year. CODE: YYA 1 YEAR - $21.95*

Lunar Returns can be erected as well. They occur about once a month. Astro can interpret your Lunar Return for the next month. (CODE: YMA 1 YEAR - $21.95*) **Venus Returns** occur about once a year. Saturn Returns occur about once every 28-30 years, etc. Each return chart is considered symbolic of the period of time until the next return chart. Thus, Solar Return charts are considered symbolic of one year in the life, while Mars Returns hold for about 22 months, etc. It is not advisable to attempt returns for the three outermost planets as they move too slowly to pin the time down to a particular minute. Furthermore, current lifespans would not include a Neptune or Pluto Return.

While Solar Returns are considered applicable to the life in general for the year which is involved, most astrologers feel that other return charts are symbolic of matters pertaining to the planet whose return it is. Thus, for example, we would look to a **Venus Return** as indicating trends concerning money, comfort, art and love relationships. We would look to a **Mars**

Return for physical energy, assertion, self-expression and spontaneity. We would look to a **Mercury Return** for studies, mental development, learning and teaching, speaking and writing, etc.

What Do You Do Next?

Future Signs is the easiest introduction to using astrology to look ahead. There are also a number of excellent books on astrological compatibility, prediction, personal growth and more. The recommended reading list which follows offers descriptions and suggestions. You might also wish to request a FREE catalog from your ONE-Stop astrological service:

Astro Communications Services, Inc
5521 Ruffin Road
San Diego, CA 92123
(619) 492-9919
1-800-888-9983 orders only
(619) 492-9919 for information
(619) 654-2817 Astro OnLine BBS
http://www.astrocom.com

For Further Reading

The following books are possibilities for readers who wish to venture further into the fascinating field of astrology. Those marked with an asterisk (*) can be ordered through Astro Communications Services, Inc. at 1-800-888-9983.

Astro-Alchemy Joan Negus.
A good, basic text on making the most of your transits, looking for positive as well as negative options.　　　　B115X, $9.95*

Astrological Games People Play Bernie Ashman.
An excellent introduction to some of the syndromes, obsessions and "games" played by people with emphasis on various signs, planets and houses. Shows positive options as well.
B117X, $12.95*

Astrology, Psychology and the Four Elements Stephen Arroyo.
A classic. Awarded British Astrological Association's Astrology Prize.

The Book of Jupiter Marilyn Waram.
A complete look at our largest planet in signs, houses and aspects with a case study of Herman Hesse.　　B150X, $14.95*

The Book of Neptune Marilyn Waram.
A sensitive, insightful look at Neptune in signs, houses and aspects. Captures the richness, whimsy, compassion and pitfalls of this elusive planet.　　　　　　　　　　　B121X, $14.95*

The Changing Sky Steven Forrest.
A good overview of secondary progressions and transits (two forms of current patterns) by a writer whose words flow beautifully.　　　　　　　　　　　　　　　　B122X, $14.95*

Chart Interpretation Handbook Stephen Arroyo.
Interpretation through combining keywords. Focus on synthesis. One of humanistic astrology's leading lights.

Complete Horoscope Interpretation Maritha Pottenger.
Excellent follow-up to *Astro Essentials*. Teaches you to find repeated themes in the horoscope. Identifies basic life areas (relationships, career, parents, mind, money, etc.) and offers tips on delineating each life area. Focus is on synthesis.
B123X, $24.95*

*Postage/handling charges will apply. Call 1-800-888-9983

Dynamics of Aspect Analysis Bil Tierney
Analyzes relationships between planets. Good rounded approach.

*Encounter Astrology by Maritha Pottenger.
Experiential approach to learning & teaching astrology. Exercises to facilitate awareness of astrological archetypes.
B229X, $7.50*

*Expanding Astrology's Universe Dr. Zipporah Dobyns.
A fabulous collection of wisdom from astrology's leader in psychological understanding. Covers topics as diverse as the 12th house, power issues, psychokinesis and relocation issues in the horoscope.
B127X, $9.95*

*Future Signs: Quick Astrological Prediction Maria Kay Simms
An easy introduction to looking ahead with astrology. Teaches meanings of all the aspects (conjunct, cooperating, challenging) from transiting planets to your birth chart. Looks at transits through the houses.
BFS, $14.95*

*Healing with the Horoscope by Maritha Pottenger.
An introduction to psychological research on what works in counseling relationships. Exercises as well as intellectual insights for the counseling astrologer.
B129X, $12.95*

*Node Book Dr. Zipporah Dobyns.
A good summary of the meaning of the Moon's Nodes in a horoscope. Covers all the sign and house polarities with case examples. Understand the emotional impact shown by these two sensitive points.
B231X, $7.00*

*The Only Way to Learn About Tomorrow
Marion D. March and Joan McEvers.
Covers progressions, directions, returns and transits in their usual clear style with lots of examples. A gifted teaching team.
B136X, $14.95*

*Planets in Transit Rob Hand.
The "Bible" on the subject. Need I say more?
B225X, $24.95*

*Progressions, Directions and Rectification
by Dr. Zipporah Dobyns.
A good, basic introduction to current patterns. Major focus is, however, rectification—figuring out unknown birth times.
B232X, $7.00*

*Postage/handling charges will apply. Call 1-800-888-9983

Psychology of the Planets Francoise Gauquelin.
One of the few books in astrology based on solid research. See what keywords (personality traits) registered as significant in biographies of famous people with various planets prominent astrologically. B141X, $8.95*

Roadmap to Your Future Bernie Ashman
A thorough discussion of transits and progressions—two forms of looking ahead. Bernie covers all the major aspects (conjunction, sextile, square, trine, quincunx, opposition) with progressed and transiting planets. He also discusses aspects to the Midheaven and Ascendant. Throughout, he gives the up ("light") and the down ("shadow") potentials of each combination. Very comprehensive!! B152X, $21.95*

Your Magical Child Maria Kay Simms
Written to help parents use astrology to understand the unique and special magic with which each child is born, and to support and assist the child to be happy and fulfilled within his or her own magical style. It has easy instruction and look-up interpretations for planets in signs, houses, and aspects. Can also be used to work with your own inner child. B154X, $16.00*

Your Starway to Love Maritha Pottenger
An introductory book on the topic of astrological compatibility. An easy worksheet allows you to get a "LoveLine" score for your relationship—and compare it to famous couples. Full discussion of each partner's self-esteem issues, emotional needs, communication skills, styles of affection, and sexual drive. Both challenges and strengths are covered, with suggestions for making the most of your relationship. B153X, $14.95*

Basic References

To work with transits, you need an ephemeris. The most accurate (and reasonably priced) is *The American Ephemeris for the 20th Century, 1900-2000*. I recommend midnight, but noon is also available. B104X, $21.95*

To erect horoscopes without a computer (or computing service), you would need an atlas of latitudes, longitudes and time change information. The best choices are *The American Atlas*

*Postage/handling charges will apply. Call 1-800-888-9983

by Thomas Shanks (B110X, $39.95*) and *The International Atlas* by Thomas Shanks (B112X, $39.95*). The former has 150,000 towns (anything big enough to have a post office) in the United States. The latter volume covers the rest of the world.

You would also need a table of houses to erect horoscopes. The most popular house system is Placidus and you can get that from *The American Book of Tables* complied and programmed by Neil F. Michelsen (B111X, $12.95*). (*The Koch Book of Tables* (B113X, $12.95*) is also available for people who prefer the Koch house system.)

Enjoy your explorations and discoveries!

Software

The Electronic Astrologer Reveals Your Horoscope

This is a very easy, but very high quality Windows program to calculate and interpret natal charts. It is designed for people who are new to astrology, so it assumes no previous knowledge. The data entry is very easy, and once you have the chart up on the screen, all you have to do is point to a planet, click your mouse, and the interpretation pops up on the screen. An extensive help section has a huge amount of information on astrology in general. A personalized report printed from this program would run about 40 pages, in total.   IBMWEA, $59.95*

The Electronic Astrologer Reveals Your Future

This second module in the *Electronic Astrologer* series is, essentially, an electronic version of *Future Signs*, plus another entire interpretive text on progressions, which is another predictive technique. The easy data entry system results in a triple wheel chart, so that you can look at your natal chart in the center with the transits and progressions wrapped around it. As in the natal module, you point and click to bring up the interpretations. Also includes an extensive help section, and prints a huge amount of personalized interpretive text.   IBMWEAF, $59.95*

Your Horoscope
FREE!
an $8 Value

Also by ACS Publications

All About Astrology Series of booklets
The American Atlas, Expanded Fifth Edition (Shanks)
The American Book of Tables (Michelsen)
The American Ephemeris for the 20th Century [Noon or Midnight] 1900 to 2000, Rev. 5th Ed.
The American Ephemeris for the 21st Century [Noon or Midnight] 2001-2050, Rev. 2nd Ed.
The American Heliocentric Ephemeris 1901-2000
The American Heliocentric Ephemeris 2001-2025
The American Midpoint Ephemeris 1996-2000
The American Sidereal Ephemeris 1976-2000, 2nd Edition
The American Sidereal Ephemeris 2001-2025
Asteroid Goddesses (George & Bloch)
Astro-Alchemy (Negus)
Astrological Insights into Personality (Lundsted)
Astrology for the Light Side of the Brain (Rogers-Gallagher)
Basic Astrology: A Guide for Teachers & Students (Negus)
Basic Astrology: A Workbook for Students (Negus)
The Book of Jupiter (Waram)
The Book of Neptune (Waram)
The Book of Pluto (Forrest)
The Book of Uranus (Negus)
The Changing Sky (Forrest)
Complete Horoscope Interpretation (Pottenger)
Cosmic Combinations (Negus)
Dial Detective (Simms)
Easy Tarot Guide (Masino)
Expanding Astrology's Universe (Dobyns)
Finding our Way Through the Dark (George)
Hands That Heal (Burns)
Healing with the Horoscope (Pottenger)
The Inner Sky (Forrest)
The International Atlas, Revised Fourth Edition (Shanks)
The Koch Book of Tables (Michelsen)
Midpoints (Munkasey)
New Insights into Astrology (Press)
The Night Speaks (Forrest)
The Only Way to... Learn Astrology, Vols. I-VI (March & McEvers)
    Volume I - Basic Principles
    Volume II - Math & Interpretation Techniques
    Volume III - Horoscope Analysis
    Volume IV- Learn About Tomorrow: Current Patterns
    Volume V - Learn About Relationships: Synastry Techniques
    Volume VI - Learn About Horary and Electional Astrology
Planetary Heredity (M. Gauquelin)
Planets in Solar Returns (Shea)
Planets on the Move (Dobyns/Pottenger)
Psychology of the Planets (F. Gauquelin)
Roadmap to your Future (Ashman)
Skymates (S. & J. Forrest)
Spirit Guides: We Are Not Alone (Belhayes)
Tables of Planetary Phenomena (Michelsen)
Twelve Wings of the Eagle (Simms)
Your Magical Child (Simms)
Your Starway to Love, 2nd Edition (Pottenger)

List of Sign and Planet Glyphs

♈	Aries
♉	Taurus
♊	Gemini
♋	Cancer
♌	Leo
♍	Virgo
♎	Libra
♏	Scorpio
♐	Sagittarius
♑	Capricorn
♒	Aquarius
♓	Pisces
☉	Sun
☽	Moon
☿	Mercury
♀	Venus
♂	Mars
♃	Jupiter
♄	Saturn
♅	Uranus
♆	Neptune
♇ or ♀̣	Pluto

Notes

Notes

Notes

Maritha Pottenger (M.A. in Clinical Psychology), a professional astrologer for over 16 years, has lectured all over the U.S., Canada, Mexico, Western Europe, and Russia. Her other books include *Encounter Astrology, Healing with the Horoscope, Complete Horoscope Interpretation, Your Starway to Love*, and *Planets on the Move*. She is active as an astrological writer, editor, and consultant. Some of her columns appear on the Internet through Home Office Computing, Parent Soup (*America Online*), and Astro Communications (*http://www.astrocom.com*).